Le

BOOKS BY DR. STEVE WARNER FOR COLLEGE BOUND STUDENTS

28 New SAT Math Lessons to Improve Your Score in One Month
      Beginner Course
      Intermediate Course
      Advanced Course
New SAT Math Problems arranged by Topic and Difficulty Level
New SAT Verbal Prep Book for Reading and Writing Mastery
320 SAT Math Subject Test Problems
      Level 1 Test
      Level 2 Test
The 32 Most Effective SAT Math Strategies
SAT Prep Official Study Guide Math Companion
Vocabulary Builder
320 ACT Math Problems arranged by Topic and Difficulty Level
320 GRE Math Problems arranged by Topic and Difficulty Level
320 SAT Math Problems arranged by Topic and Difficulty Level
320 AP Calculus AB Problems
320 AP Calculus BC Problems
555 Math IQ Questions for Middle School Students
555 Advanced Math Problems for Middle School Students
555 Geometry Problems for High School Students
Algebra Handbook for Gifted Middle School Students
SHSAT Verbal Prep Book to Improve Your Score in Two Months

CONNECT WITH DR. STEVE WARNER

www.facebook.com/SATPrepGet800

www.youtube.com/TheSATMathPrep

www.twitter.com/SATPrepGet800

www.linkedin.com/in/DrSteveWarner

www.pinterest.com/SATPrepGet800

plus.google.com/+SteveWarnerPhD

320 AP CALCULUS AB
Problems arranged
by Topic and Difficulty Level

320 Level 1, 2, 3, 4, and 5 AP
Calculus Problems

Dr. Steve Warner

iii

Table of Contents

ACTIONS TO COMPLETE BEFORE YOU READ THIS BOOK

1. Sign up for free updates

Visit the following webpage and enter your email address to receive updates and supplementary materials for free when they become available.

www.thesatmathprep.com/APcalcABtx.html

2. Like my Facebook page

This page is updated regularly with AP Calculus advice, tips, tricks, strategies, and practice problems. Visit the following webpage and click the 'like' button.

www.facebook.com/Get800

THE PROPER WAY TO PREPARE

*T*here are many ways that a student can prepare for the AP Calculus AB exam. But not all preparation is created equal. I always teach my students the methods that will give them the maximum result with the minimum amount of effort.

The book you are now reading is self-contained. Each problem was carefully created to ensure that you are making the most effective use of your time while preparing for the AP Calculus exam. By grouping the problems given here by level and topic I have ensured that you can focus on the types of problems that will be most effective to improving your score.

1. Using this book effectively
- Begin studying at least three months before the AP Calculus exam
- Practice AP Calculus problems twenty to thirty minutes each day
- Choose a consistent study time and location

You will retain much more of what you study if you study in short bursts rather than if you try to tackle everything at once. So try to choose about a thirty-minute block of time that you will dedicate to AP Calculus each day. Make it a habit. The results are well worth this small time commitment.

- Every time you get a question wrong, **mark it off, no matter what your mistake**.
- Begin each study session by first redoing problems from previous study sessions that you have marked off.
- If you get a problem wrong again, **keep it marked off**.

2. Overview of the AP Calculus exam
There are four types of questions that you will encounter on the AP Calculus exam:

7

- Multiple choice questions where calculators are not allowed (Section 1, Part A, 30 Questions, 60 Minutes).
- Multiple choice questions where calculators are allowed (Section 1, Part B, 15 Questions, 45 Minutes).
- Free response questions where calculators are allowed (Section 2, Part A, 2 Questions, 30 Minutes).
- Free response questions where calculators are not allowed (Section 2, Part B, 4 Questions, 60 Minutes).

This book will prepare you for all of these question types. In this book, questions that require a calculator are marked with an asterisk (*).

If a question is not marked with an asterisk, then it could show up on a part where a calculator is or is not allowed. I therefore recommend always trying to solve each of these questions both with and without a calculator. It is especially important that you can solve these without a calculator.

The AP Calculus exam is graded on a scale of 1 through 5, with a score of 3 or above interpreted as "qualified." To get a 3 on the exam you will need to get about 50% of the questions correct.

3. Structure of this book

This book has been organized in such a way to produce maximum results with the least amount of effort. Every question that is in this book is similar to a question that has appeared on an actual AP Calculus exam. Furthermore, just about every question type that you can expect to encounter is covered in this book.

The organization of this book is by Level and Topic. At first you want to practice each of the four general math topics given on the AP Calculus exam and improve in each independently. The four topics are **Precalculus**, **Differentiation**, **Integration**, and **Limits and Continuity**. The first 3 Levels are broken into these four topics. Level 4 is broken into just two of these topics, differentiation and integration. And Level 5 mixes all the topics together in the form of free response questions just like the ones you will encounter in Section 2 of the exam.

Speaking of Level, you will want to progress through the 5 Levels of difficulty at your own pace. Stay at each Level as long as you need to. Keep redoing each problem you get wrong over and over again until you can get each one right on your own.

I strongly recommend that for each topic you *do not* move on to the next level until you are getting most of the questions from the previous level correct. This will reduce your frustration and keep you from burning out.

There are two parts to this book. The first part contains 160 problems, and the solution to each problem appears right after the problem is given. The second part contains 160 supplemental problems with an answer key at the very end. Full solutions to the supplemental problems are not given in this book. Most of these additional problems are similar to problems from the first section, but the limits, derivatives and integrals tend to be a bit more challenging.

Any student that can successfully answer all 160 questions from *either* part of this book should be able to get a 5 on the exam.

4. Practice in small amounts over a long period of time

Ideally you want to practice doing AP Calculus problems twenty to thirty minutes each day beginning at least three months before the exam. You will retain much more of what you study if you study in short bursts than if you try to tackle everything at once.

So try to choose about a thirty-minute block of time that you will dedicate to AP Calculus every night. Make it a habit. The results are well worth this small time commitment.

5. Redo the problems you get wrong over and over and over until you get them right

If you get a problem wrong, and never attempt the problem again, then it is extremely unlikely that you will get a similar problem correct if it appears on the AP exam.

Most students will read an explanation of the solution, or have someone explain it to them, and then never look at the problem again. This is *not* how you optimize your score on a standardized test. To be sure that you will get a similar problem correct on the actual exam, you must get the problem correct before the exam—and without actually remembering the problem. This means that after getting a problem incorrect, you should go over and understand why you got it wrong, wait at least a few days, then attempt the same problem again. If you get it right, you can cross it off your list of problems to review. If you get it wrong, keep revisiting it every few days until you get it right. Your score *does not* improve by getting problems correct.

Your score improves when you learn from your mistakes.

6. Check your answers properly

When you are taking the exam and you go back to check your earlier answers for careless errors *do not* simply look over your work to try to catch a mistake. This is usually a waste of time. Always redo the problem without looking at any of your previous work. If possible, use a different method than you used the first time.

7. Take a guess whenever you cannot solve a problem

There is no guessing penalty on the AP Calculus AB exam. Whenever you do not know how to solve a problem take a guess. Ideally you should eliminate as many answer choices as possible before taking your guess, but if you have no idea whatsoever do not waste time overthinking. Simply put down an answer and move on. You should certainly mark it off and come back to it later if you have time.

Try not to leave free response questions completely blank. Begin writing anything you can related to the problem. The act of writing can often spark some insight into how to solve the problem, and even if it does not, you may still get some partial credit.

8. Pace yourself

Do not waste your time on a question that is too hard or will take too long. After you've been working on a question for about a minute you need to make a decision. If you understand the question and think that you can get the answer in a reasonable amount of time, continue to work on the problem. If you still do not know how to do the problem or you are using a technique that is going to take a very long time, mark it off and come back to it later.

If you do not know the correct answer to a multiple choice question, eliminate as many answer choices as you can and take a guess. But you still want to leave open the possibility of coming back to it later. Remember that every multiple choice question is worth the same amount. Do not sacrifice problems that you may be able to do by getting hung up on a problem that is too hard for you.

PROBLEMS BY LEVEL AND TOPIC WITH FULLY EXPLAINED SOLUTIONS

LEVEL 1: PRECALCULUS

1. Let $f(x) = 3$ and $g(x) = x^4 - 2x^3 + x^2 - 5x + 1$. Then $(f \circ g)(x) =$

   (A) 3
   (B) 22
   (C) 10,648
   (D) $3x^4 - 6x^3 + 3x^2 - 15x + 3$

Solution: $(f \circ g)(x) = f(g(x)) = 3$, choice (A).

Notes: (1) $f(x) = 3$ can be read as "f of *anything* is 3." So, in particular, "f of $g(x)$ is 3," i.e. $f(g(x)) = 3$.

(2) For completeness we have

$$(f \circ g)(x) = f(g(x)) = f(x^4 - 2x^3 + x^2 - 5x + 1) = 3.$$

(3) $(f \circ g)(x) = f(g(x))$ is called the **composition** of the functions f and g. We literally plug the function g in for x inside the function f. As an additional simple example, if $f(x) = x^2$ and $g(x) = x + 1$, then

$$f(g(x)) = f(x + 1) = (x + 1)^2 \quad \text{and} \quad g(f(x)) = g(x^2) = x^2 + 1$$

Notice how, for example, $f(\boxed{\text{something}}) = (\boxed{\text{something}})^2$.

The "something" here is $x + 1$. Note how we keep it in parentheses.

2. What is the domain of $k(x) = \sqrt[3]{8 - 12x^2 + 6x - x^3}$?

   (A) All real numbers
   (B) $x < -2$
   (C) $-2 < x < 2$
   (D) $x > 2$

Solution: The domain of $f(x) = 8 - 12x^2 + 6x - x^3$ is all real numbers since $f(x)$ is a polynomial. The domain of $g(x) = \sqrt[3]{x}$ is also all real numbers. The function $k(x)$ is the composition of these two functions and therefore also has domain all real numbers. So the answer is choice (A).

11

Notes: (1) Polynomials and cube roots do not cause any problems. In other words, you can evaluate a polynomial at any real number and you can take the cube root of any real number.

(2) Square roots on the other hand do have some problems. We cannot take the square root of negative real numbers (in the reals). We have the same problem for any even root, and there are no problems for odd roots.

For example $\sqrt{-8}$ is undefined, whereas $\sqrt[3]{-8} = -2$ because

$$(-2)^3 = (-2)(-2)(-2) = -8.$$

(3) See problem 5 for more information about polynomials.

3. If $K(x) = \log_5 x$ for $x > 0$, then $K^{-1}(x) =$

   (A) $\log_x 5$
   (B) 5^x
   (C) $\frac{x}{5}$
   (D) $\frac{5}{x}$

Solution: The inverse of the logarithmic function $K(x) = \log_5 x$ is the exponential function $K^{-1}(x) = 5^x$, choice (B).

Notes: (1) The word "logarithm" just means "exponent."

(2) The equation $y = \log_b x$ can be read as "y is the exponent when we rewrite x with a base of b." In other words we are raising b to the power y. So the equation can be written in exponential form as $x = b^y$.

In this problem $b = 5$, and so the logarithmic equation $y = \log_5 x$ can be written in exponential form as $x = 5^y$.

(3) In general, the functions $y = b^x$ and $y = \log_b x$ are inverses of each other. In fact, that is precisely the definition of a logarithm.

(4) The usual procedure to find the inverse of a function $y = f(x)$ is to interchange the roles of x and y and solve for y. In this example, the inverse of $y = \log_5 x$ is $x = \log_5 y$. To solve this equation for y we can simply change the equation to its exponential form $y = 5^x$.

4.   If $g(x) = e^{x+1}$, which of the following lines is an asymptote to the graph of $g(x)$?

      (A) $x = 0$
      (B) $y = 0$
      (C) $x = -1$
      (D) $y = -1$

Solution: The graph of $y = e^x$ has a horizontal asymptote of $y = 0$. To get the graph of $y = e^{x+1}$ we shift the graph of $y = e^x$ to the left one unit. A horizontal shift does not have any effect on a horizontal asymptote. So the answer is $y = 0$, choice (B).

Notes: (1) It is worth reviewing the following basic transformations:

Let $y = f(x)$, and $k > 0$. We can move the graph of f around by applying the following basic transformations.

      $y = f(x) + k$ shift up k units
      $y = f(x) - k$ shift down k units
      $y = f(x - k)$ shift right k units
      $y = f(x + k)$ shift left k units
      $y = -f(x)$ reflect in x-axis
      $y = f(-x)$ reflect in y-axis.

For the function $g(x) = e^{x+1}$, we are replacing x by $x + 1$ in $f(x) = e^x$. In other words, $g(x) = f(x + 1)$. So we get the graph of g by shifting the graph of f 1 unit to the left.

(2) The horizontal line with equation $y = b$ is a **horizontal asymptote** for the graph of the function $y = f(x)$ if y approaches b as x gets larger and larger, or smaller and smaller (as in very large in the negative direction).

(3) We can also find a horizontal asymptote by plugging into our calculator a really large negative value for x such as $-999,999,999$ (if a calculator is allowed for the problem). We get $e^{-999,999,999+1} = 0$.

(Note that the answer is not really zero, but the calculator gives an answer of 0 because the actual answer is so close to 0 that the calculator cannot tell the difference.)

(4) It is worth memorizing that $y = e^x$ **has a horizontal asymptote of** $y = 0$, **and** $y = \ln x$ **has a vertical asymptote of** $x = 0$.

13

As an even better alternative, you should be able to visualize the graphs of both of these functions. Here is a picture.

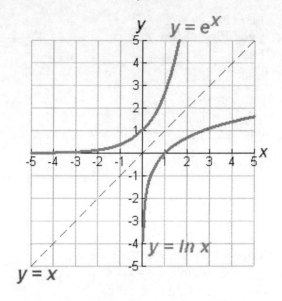

5. Which of the following equations has a graph that is symmetric with respect to the y-axis?

$$(A)\ y = (x + 1)^3 - x$$
$$(B)\ y = (x + 1)^2 - 1$$
$$(C)\ y = 2x^6 - 3x^2 + 5$$
$$(D)\ y = \frac{x-1}{2x}$$

Solution: The equation $y = 2x^6 - 3x^2 + 5$ is a polynomial equation with only even exponents. It is therefore an even function, and so its graph is symmetric with respect to the y-axis. So the answer is (C).

Notes: (1) A function f with the property that $f(-x) = f(x)$ for all x is called an **even** function. Even functions have graphs which are **symmetric with respect to the y-axis**.

(2) A function f with the property that $f(-x) = -f(x)$ for all x is called an **odd** function. Odd functions have graphs which are **symmetric with respect to the origin**.

(3) A **polynomial** has the form $a_n x^n + a_{n-1} x^{n-1} + \cdots + a_1 x + a_0$ where $a_0, a_1,...,a_n$ are real numbers. For example, $2x^6 - 3x^2 + 5$ is a polynomial.

(4) Polynomial functions with only even powers of x are even functions (and therefore are symmetric with respect to the y-axis). Keep in mind that a constant c is the same as cx^0 , and so c is an even power of x. For example 5 is an even power of x. From this observation we can see that the polynomial in answer choice (C) is an even function.

(5) Polynomial functions with only odd powers of x are odd functions (and therefore are symmetric with respect to the origin). Keep in mind that x is the same as x^1, and so x is an odd power of x. An example of an odd function is the polynomial $y = -4x^3 + 2x$.

(6) Note that the functions given in answer choices (A) and (B) are also polynomials. This can be seen by expanding the given expressions. For example, let's look at the function given in choice (B).

$$(x + 1)^2 - 1 = (x + 1)(x + 1) - 1 = x^2 + x + x + 1 - 1 = x^2 + 2x.$$

Since this expression has both an even and an odd power of x, the polynomial given in choice (B) is neither even nor odd.

I leave it as an exercise to expand $(x + 1)^3 - x$ and observe that it has both even and odd powers of x.

(7) A **rational function** is a quotient of polynomials. The function given in choice (D) is a rational function. To determine if this function is even we need to use the definition of being even:

$$\frac{(-x)-1}{2(-x)} = \frac{-x-1}{-2x} = \frac{x+1}{2x} \neq \frac{x-1}{2x}$$

It follows that the function is not even, and therefore its graph is not symmetric with respect to the y-axis.

(8) The graph of an even function is **symmetric with respect to the y-axis**. This means that the y-axis acts like a "mirror," and the graph "reflects" across this mirror. If you put choice (C) into your graphing calculator, you will see that this graph has this property.

Similarly, the graph of an odd function is **symmetric with respect to the origin**. This means that if you rotate the graph 180 degrees (or equivalently, turn it upside down) it will look the same as it did right side up. If you put the polynomial $y = -4x^3 + 2x$ into your graphing calculator, you will see that this graph has this property.

Put the other three answer choices in your graphing calculator and observe that they have neither of these symmetries.

(9) If we were allowed to use a calculator, we could solve this problem by graphing each equation, and checking to see if the y-axis acts like a mirror.

6. If $f(x) = x^3 + Ax^2 + Bx + C$, and if $f(0) = -2$, $f(-1) = 7$, and $f(1) = 4$, then $AB + \dfrac{3}{4} =$

    (A) 36
    (B)   18
    (C) -18
    (D) It cannot be determined from the information given

Solution: Since $f(0) = -2$, we have

$$-2 = 0^3 + A(0)^2 + B(0) + C = C.$$

Since $f(-1) = 7$, we have

$$7 = (-1)^3 + A(-1)^2 + B(-1) + C = -1 + A - B + C.$$

We already found that $C = -2$, so we have

$$7 = -1 + A - B - 2 = A - B - 3.$$

So $A - B = 10$.

Since $f(1) = 4$, we have

$$4 = 1^3 + A(1)^2 + B(1) + C = 1 + A + B - 2 = A + B - 1.$$

So $A + B = 5$.

Let's add these last two equations.

$$
\begin{aligned}
A - B &= 10 \\
\underline{A + B} &= \underline{5} \\
2A \phantom{{}- B} &= 15
\end{aligned}
$$

It follows that $A = \frac{15}{2}$, and so $B = 5 - A = 5 - \frac{15}{2} = -\frac{5}{2}$.

Finally, $AB + \frac{3}{4} = \left(\frac{15}{2}\right)\left(-\frac{5}{2}\right) + \frac{3}{4} = -\frac{75}{4} + \frac{3}{4} = -\frac{72}{4} = -18$, choice (C).

7. If the solutions of $g(x) = 0$ are $-3, \frac{1}{2}$ and 5, then the solutions of $g(3x) = 0$ are

   (A) $-1,\quad \frac{1}{6}\quad$ and $\quad\frac{5}{3}$

   (B) $-9,\quad \frac{3}{2}\quad$ and $\quad 15$

   (C) $-6, -\frac{5}{2}\quad$ and $\quad 2$

   (D) $\ 0,\quad \frac{7}{2}\quad$ and $\quad 8$

Solution: We simply set $3x$ equal to $-3, \frac{1}{2}$, and 5, and then solve each of these equations for x. We get $-1, \frac{1}{6}$, and $\frac{5}{3}$. So the answer is choice (A).

Notes: (1) Since -3 is a solution of $g(x) = 0$, it follows that $g(-3) = 0$. So we have $g(3(-1)) = 0$. So -1 is a solution of $g(3x) = 0$.

(2) To get that -1 is a solution of $g(3x) = 0$ formally, we simply divide -3 by 3, or equivalently, we solve the equation $3x = -3$ for x.

(3) Similarly, we have $g\left(3\left(\frac{1}{6}\right)\right) = 0$ and $g\left(3\left(\frac{5}{3}\right)\right) = 0$, and we can formally find that $\frac{1}{6}$ and $\frac{5}{3}$ are solutions of $g(3x) = 0$ by solving the equations $3x = \frac{1}{2}$ and $3x = 5$.

8. If $k(x) = \frac{x^2-1}{x+2}$ and $h(x) = \ln x^2$, then $k\big(h(e)\big) =$

   (A) 0.12
   (B) 0.50
   (C) 0.51
   (D) 0.75

Solution: $h(e) = \ln e^2 = 2$. So $k(h(e)) = k(2) = \frac{2^2-1}{2+2} = 0.75$, choice (D).

Notes: (1) We first substituted e into the function h to get 2. We then substituted 2 into the function k to get 0.75.

17

(2) See the notes at the end of problem 3 for more information on logarithms.

(3) There are several ways to compute $\ln e^2$.

<u>Method 1</u>: Simply use your calculator (if allowed).

<u>Method 2</u>: Recall that the functions e^x and $\ln x$ are inverses of each other. This means that $e^{\ln x} = x$ and $\ln e^x = x$. Substituting $x = 2$ into the second equation gives the desired result.

<u>Method 3</u>: Remember that $\ln x = \log_e x$. So we can rewrite the equation $y = \ln e^2$ in exponential form as $e^y = e^2$. So $y = 2$.

<u>Method 4</u>: Recall that $\ln e = 1$. We have $\ln e^2 = 2 \ln e = 2(1) = 2$. Here we have used the last law in the following table:

Laws of Logarithms: Here is a review of the basic laws of logarithms.

Law	Example
$\log_b 1 = 0$	$\log_2 1 = 0$
$\log_b b = 1$	$\log_6 6 = 1$
$\log_b x + \log_b y = \log_b(xy)$	$\log_5 7 + \log_5 2 = \log_5 14$
$\log_b x - \log_b y = \log_b(\frac{x}{y})$	$\log_3 21 - \log_3 7 = \log_3 3 = 1$
$\log_b x^n = n\log_b x$	$\log_8 3^5 = 5\log_8 3$

LEVEL 1: DIFFERENTIATION

9. If $f(x) = x^2 + x - \cos x$, then $f'(x) =$

   (A) $2x + 1 - \sin x$
   (B) $2x + 1 + \sin x$
   (C) $2x - \sin x$
   (D) $\frac{1}{3}x^3 + \frac{1}{2}x^2 - \sin x$

Solution: $f'(x) = 2x + 1 + \sin x$. This is choice (B).

Notes: (1) If n is any real number, then the derivative of x^n is nx^{n-1}.

Symbolically, $\frac{d}{dx}[x^n] = nx^{n-1}$.

For example, $\frac{d}{dx}[x^2] = 2x^1 = 2x$.

As another example, $\frac{d}{dx}[x] = \frac{d}{dx}[x^1] = 1x^0 = 1(1) = 1$.

(2) Of course it is worth just remembering that $\frac{d}{dx}[x] = 1$.

(3) You should know the derivatives of the six basic trig functions:

$$\frac{d}{dx}[\sin x] = \cos x \qquad\qquad \frac{d}{dx}[\csc x] = -\csc x \cot x$$

$$\frac{d}{dx}[\cos x] = -\sin x \qquad\qquad \frac{d}{dx}[\sec x] = \sec x \tan x$$

$$\frac{d}{dx}[\tan x] = \sec^2 x \qquad\qquad \frac{d}{dx}[\cot x] = -\csc^2 x$$

(4) If g and h are functions, then $(g + h)'(x) = g'(x) + h'(x)$.

In other words, when differentiating a sum, we can simply differentiate term by term.

Similarly, $(g - h)'(x) = g'(x) - h'(x)$.

(5) In the given problem we differentiate each of x^2, x, and $\cos x$ separately and then use note (4) to write the final answer.

10. If $g(x) = \frac{x+2}{x-2}$, then $g'(-2) =$

(A) $-\frac{1}{4}$

(B) -1

(C) 1

(D) $\frac{1}{4}$

Solution: $g'(x) = \frac{(x-2)(1)-(x+2)(1)}{(x-2)^2} = \frac{x-2-x-2}{(x-2)^2} = \frac{-4}{(x-2)^2}$. So we have $g'(-2) = \frac{-4}{(-2-2)^2} = \frac{-4}{(-4)^2} = \frac{-4}{16} = -\frac{1}{4}$, choice (A).

Notes: (1) We used the **quotient rule** which says the following:

If $f(x) = \frac{N(x)}{D(x)}$, then

$$f'(x) = \frac{D(x)N'(x) - N(x)D'(x)}{[D(x)]^2}$$

I like to use the letters N for "numerator" and D for "denominator."

19

(2) The derivative of $x + 2$ is 1 because the derivative of x is 1, and the derivative of any constant is 0.

Similarly, the derivative of $x - 2$ is also 1.

(3) If we could use a calculator for this problem, we can compute $g'(-2)$ using our TI-84 calculator by first selecting nDeriv((or pressing 8) under the MATH menu, then typing the following: (X + 2)/(X − 2), X, −2), and pressing ENTER. The display will show approximately −.25.

11. If $h(x) = \frac{1}{12}x^3 - 2\ln x + \sqrt{x}$, then $h'(x) =$

(A) $\frac{1}{3}x^2 - \frac{2}{x} + \frac{1}{2\sqrt{x}}$

(B) $\frac{1}{4}x^2 - \frac{2}{\ln x} + \frac{2}{3}x^{\frac{3}{2}}$

(C) $\frac{1}{4}x^2 - \frac{2}{x} + \frac{1}{2\sqrt{x}}$

(D) $\frac{1}{4}x^2 - \frac{2}{\ln x} + \frac{1}{2\sqrt{x}}$

Solution: $h'(x) = \frac{1}{12} \cdot 3x^2 - 2\left(\frac{1}{x}\right) + \frac{1}{2}x^{-\frac{1}{2}} = \frac{1}{4}x^2 - \frac{2}{x} + \frac{1}{2\sqrt{x}}$, choice (C).

Notes: (1) The derivative of a constant times a function is the constant times the derivative of the function.

Symbolically, $\frac{d}{dx}[cg(x)] = c\frac{d}{dx}[g(x)]$.

For example, $\frac{d}{dx}\left[\frac{1}{12}x^3\right] = \frac{1}{12}\frac{d}{dx}[x^3] = \frac{1}{12}(3x^2) = \frac{1}{4}x^2$.

(2) The derivative of $\ln x$ is $\frac{1}{x}$.

Symbolically, $\frac{d}{dx}[\ln x] = \frac{1}{x}$.

(3) Combining (1) and (2), we have $\frac{d}{dx}[2\ln x] = 2\frac{d}{dx}[\ln x] = 2\left(\frac{1}{x}\right) = \frac{2}{x}$.

(4) $\sqrt{x}$ can be written as $x^{\frac{1}{2}}$. So the derivative of $\sqrt{x}$ is $\frac{1}{2}x^{-\frac{1}{2}}$.

(5) $x^{-\frac{1}{2}} = \frac{1}{x^{\frac{1}{2}}} = \frac{1}{\sqrt{x}}$.

(6) Combining (4) and (5) we have $\frac{d}{dx}[\sqrt{x}] = \frac{d}{dx}[x^{\frac{1}{2}}] = \frac{1}{2}x^{-\frac{1}{2}} = \frac{1}{2\sqrt{x}}$.

(7) Here is a review of the laws of exponents:

Law	Example
$x^0 = 1$	$3^0 = 1$
$x^1 = x$	$9^1 = 9$
$x^a x^b = x^{a+b}$	$x^3 x^5 = x^8$
$x^a / x^b = x^{a-b}$	$x^{11}/x^4 = x^7$
$(x^a)^b = x^{ab}$	$(x^5)^3 = x^{15}$
$(xy)^a = x^a y^a$	$(xy)^4 = x^4 y^4$
$(x/y)^a = x^a/y^a$	$(x/y)^6 = x^6/y^6$
$x^{-1} = 1/x$	$3^{-1} = 1/3$
$x^{-a} = 1/x^a$	$9^{-2} = 1/81$
$x^{1/n} = \sqrt[n]{x}$	$x^{1/3} = \sqrt[3]{x}$
$x^{m/n} = \sqrt[n]{x^m} = \left(\sqrt[n]{x}\right)^m$	$x^{9/2} = \sqrt{x^9} = \left(\sqrt{x}\right)^9$

12. The slope of the tangent line to the graph of $y = e^{3x}$ at $x = \ln 2$ is

    (A) $8 \ln 2$
    (B) 8
    (C) $24 \ln 2$
    (D) 24

Solution: $y' = e^{3x}(3) = 3e^{3x}$. When $x = \ln 2$, we have that the slope of the tangent line is

$$y'|_{x=\ln 2} = 3e^{3\ln 2} = 3e^{\ln 2^3} = 3e^{\ln 8} = 3(8) = 24.$$

This is choice (D).

Notes: (1) To find the slope of a tangent line to the graph of a function, we simply take the derivative of that function. If we want the slope of the tangent line at a specified x-value, we substitute that x-value into the derivative of the function.

(2) The derivative of $f(x) = e^x$ is $f'(x) = e^x$

(3) In this problem we used the **chain rule** which says the following:

If $f(x) = (g \circ h)(x) = g(h(x))$, then

$$f'(x) = g'(h(x)) \cdot h'(x)$$

Here we have $h(x) = 3x$ and $g(x) = e^x$. So $h'(x) = 3$, and

21

$$g'(h(x)) = e^{h(x)} = e^{3x}.$$

(4) See the notes at the end of problem 3 for information on logarithms.

(5) $\ln x$ is an abbreviation for $\log_e x$.

(6) The functions e^x and $\ln x$ are inverses of each other. This means that $e^{\ln x} = x$ and $\ln e^x = x$.

(7) $n \ln x = \ln x^n$

(8) Using notes (6) and (7) together we get $e^{3 \ln 2} = e^{\ln 2^3} = e^{\ln 8} = 8$.

(9) See the notes at the end of problem 8 for a review of the laws of logarithms.

(10) If we could use a calculator for this problem, we can compute y' at $x = \ln 2$ using our TI-84 calculator by first selecting nDeriv((or pressing 8) under the MATH menu, then typing the following: e^(3X), X, ln 2), and pressing ENTER. The display will show approximately 24.

13. The instantaneous rate of change at $x = 3$ of the function $f(x) = x\sqrt{x + 1}$ is

(A) $\dfrac{1}{4}$

(B) $\dfrac{3}{4}$

(C) $\dfrac{5}{4}$

(D) $\dfrac{11}{4}$

Solution: $f'(x) = x \cdot \dfrac{1}{2}(x + 1)^{-\frac{1}{2}} + \sqrt{x + 1}(1) = \dfrac{x}{2\sqrt{x+1}} + \sqrt{x + 1}.$

So $f'(3) = \dfrac{3}{2\sqrt{3+1}} + \sqrt{3 + 1} = \dfrac{3}{2\sqrt{4}} + \sqrt{4} = \dfrac{3}{2 \cdot 2} + 2 = \dfrac{3}{4} + \dfrac{8}{4} = \dfrac{11}{4},$ choice (D).

Notes: (1) We used the **product rule** which says the following:

If $f(x) = u(x)v(x)$, then

$$f'(x) = u(x)v'(x) + v(x)u'(x)$$

(2) The derivative of x is 1.

(3) $\sqrt{x+1}$ can be written as $(x+1)^{\frac{1}{2}}$. So the derivative of $\sqrt{x+1}$ is $\frac{1}{2}(x+1)^{-\frac{1}{2}}$ (technically we need to use the chain rule here and also take the derivative of $x+1$, but $\frac{d}{dx}[x+1]$ is just 1).

(4) $(x+1)^{-\frac{1}{2}} = \frac{1}{(x+1)^{\frac{1}{2}}} = \frac{1}{\sqrt{x+1}}$.

(5) Combining (3) and (4) we have

$$\frac{d}{dx}\left[\sqrt{x+1}\right] = \frac{d}{dx}\left[(x+1)^{\frac{1}{2}}\right] = \frac{1}{2}(x+1)^{-\frac{1}{2}} = \frac{1}{2\sqrt{x+1}}.$$

(6) See problem 11 for a review of all of the laws of exponents you should know.

(7) If we can use a calculator for this problem, we can compute $f'(3)$ using our TI-84 calculator by first selecting nDeriv((or pressing 8) under the MATH menu, then typing the following: X√(X+1), X, 3), and pressing ENTER. The display will show approximately 2.75. Type 2.75, then press MATH ENTER ENTER to change this decimal to $\frac{11}{4}$.

14. $\frac{d}{dx}\left[e^5 + \frac{1}{\sqrt[3]{x^2}} + 11^x\right] =$

Solution:

$$\frac{d}{dx}\left[e^5 + \frac{1}{\sqrt[3]{x^2}} + 11^x\right] = 0 - \frac{2}{3}x^{-\frac{5}{3}} + 11^x(\ln 11) = -\frac{2}{3\sqrt[3]{x^5}} + (\ln 11)11^x.$$

Notes: (1) e^5 is a constant. Therefore $\frac{d}{dx}[e^5] = 0$.

(2) $\frac{1}{\sqrt[3]{x^2}} = \frac{1}{x^{\frac{2}{3}}} = x^{-\frac{2}{3}}$. So $\frac{d}{dx}\left[\frac{1}{\sqrt[3]{x^2}}\right] = \frac{d}{dx}\left[x^{-\frac{2}{3}}\right] = -\frac{2}{3}x^{-\frac{2}{3}-1} = -\frac{2}{3}x^{-\frac{5}{3}}$.

(3) $-\frac{2}{3}x^{-\frac{5}{3}} = -\frac{2}{3x^{\frac{5}{3}}} = -\frac{2}{3\sqrt[3]{x^5}}$.

(4) If $b > 0$, then $\frac{d}{dx}[b^x] = b^x(\ln b)$.

In particular, $\frac{d}{dx}[11^x] = 11^x(\ln 11)$.

(5) For $b > 0$, $b^x = e^{x\ln b}$.

23

To see this, first observe that $e^{x \ln b} = e^{\ln b^x}$ by the power rule for logarithms (see problem 8 for the laws of logarithms).

Second, recall that the functions e^x and $\ln x$ are inverses of each other. This means that $e^{\ln x} = x$ and $\ln e^x = x$. Replacing x by b^x in the first formula yields $e^{\ln b^x} = b^x$.

(6) The formula in note (5) gives an alternate method for differentiating 11^x. We can rewrite 11^x as $e^{x \ln 11}$ and use the chain rule. Here are the details:

$$\frac{d}{dx}[11^x] = \frac{d}{dx}\left[e^{x \ln 11}\right] = e^{x \ln 11}(\ln 11) = 11^x(\ln 11).$$

Note that in the last step we rewrote $e^{x \ln 11}$ as 11^x.

(7) There is one more method we can use to differentiate 11^x. We can use **logarithmic differentiation**.

We start by writing $y = 11^x$.

We then take the natural log of each side of this equation: $\ln y = \ln 11^x$.

We now use the power rule for logarithms to bring the x out of the exponent: $\ln y = x \ln 11$.

Now we differentiate implicitly to get $\frac{1}{y} \cdot \frac{dy}{dx} = \ln 11$.

Solve for $\frac{dy}{dx}$ by multiplying each side of the last equation by y to get $\frac{dy}{dx} = y \ln 11$.

Finally, replacing y by 11^x gives us $\frac{dy}{dx} = 11^x(\ln 11)$.

(8) **Logarithmic differentiation** is a general method that can often be used to handle expressions that have exponents with variables.

(9) See problem 45 for more information on implicit differentiation.

15. If $y = x^{\cos x}$, then $y' =$

Solution: We take the natural logarithm of each side of the given equation to get $\ln y = \ln x^{\cos x} = (\cos x)(\ln x)$.

We now differentiate implicitly to get

$$\frac{1}{y}y' = (\cos x)\left(\frac{1}{x}\right) + (\ln x)(-\sin x) = \frac{\cos x - x\,(\ln x)(\sin x)}{x}$$

Multiplying each side of this last equation by y yields

$$y' = y\left[\frac{\cos x - x\,(\ln x)(\sin x)}{x}\right] = x^{\cos x}\left[\frac{\cos x - x\,(\ln x)(\sin x)}{x}\right]$$

Notes: (1) Since the exponent of the expression $x^{\cos x}$ contains the variable x, we used logarithmic differentiation (see problem 14 for more details).

(2) $(\cos x)\left(\frac{1}{x}\right) + (\ln x)(-\sin x) = (\cos x)\left(\frac{1}{x}\right) + \left(\frac{x}{x}\right)[(\ln x)(-\sin x)]$

$$= \frac{\cos x}{x} + \frac{x(\ln x)(-\sin x)}{x} = \frac{\cos x - x(\ln x)(\sin x)}{x}.$$

(3) Remember to replace y by $x^{\cos x}$ at the end.

(4) See problem 45 for more information on implicit differentiation.

16. Differentiate $f(x) = \dfrac{e^{\cot 3x}}{\sqrt{x}}$ and express your answer as a simple fraction.

Solution:

$$f'(x) = \frac{\sqrt{x}(e^{\cot 3x})(-\csc^2 3x)(3) - e^{\cot 3x}\left(\frac{1}{2\sqrt{x}}\right)}{x} = \frac{-6x(\csc^2 3x)e^{\cot 3x} - e^{\cot 3x}}{2x\sqrt{x}}.$$

Notes: (1) $\dfrac{d}{dx}[e^x] = e^x$

$\dfrac{d}{dx}[\cot x] = -\csc^2 x$

$\dfrac{d}{dx}[3x] = 3$

$\dfrac{d}{dx}\left[\sqrt{x}\right] = \dfrac{d}{dx}\left[x^{\frac{1}{2}}\right] = \dfrac{1}{2}x^{-\frac{1}{2}} = \dfrac{1}{2}\cdot\dfrac{1}{x^{\frac{1}{2}}} = \dfrac{1}{2}\cdot\dfrac{1}{\sqrt{x}} = \dfrac{1}{2\sqrt{x}}$

(2) We start off using the quotient rule (see problem 10 for a detailed explanation of the quotient rule). Here we get

$$\frac{\sqrt{x}\cdot\frac{d}{dx}[e^{\cot 3x}] - e^{\cot 3x}\cdot\frac{d}{dx}[\sqrt{x}]}{(\sqrt{x})^2}$$

25

(3) $\frac{d}{dx}[e^{\cot 3x}]$ requires two applications of the chain rule. See problem 12 for a detailed explanation of the chain rule. Here we get

$$\frac{d}{dx}[e^{\cot 3x}] = e^{\cot 3x}(-\csc^2 3x)(3).$$

(4) After differentiating we wind up with a complex fraction:

$$\frac{\sqrt{x}(e^{\cot 3x})(-\csc^2 3x)(3) - e^{\cot 3x}(\frac{1}{2\sqrt{x}})}{x}$$

We simplify this complex fraction by multiplying the numerator and denominator by $2\sqrt{x}$.

Note the following:

$x(2\sqrt{x}) = 2x\sqrt{x}$ (this is where the final denominator comes from).

$\sqrt{x}(e^{\cot 3x})(-\csc^2 3x)(3)(2\sqrt{x}) = -6\sqrt{x}\sqrt{x}(\csc^2 3x)e^{\cot 3x} = -6x(\csc^2 3x)e^{\cot 3x}$

$e^{\cot 3x}\left(\frac{1}{2\sqrt{x}}\right)(2\sqrt{x}) = e^{\cot 3x}$

The last two results together with the distributive property give the final numerator.

LEVEL 1: INTEGRATION

17. $\int(x^4 - 6x^2 + 3)\, dx =$

    (A) $5x^5 - 18x^3 + 3x + C$

    (B) $4x^3 - 12x + 3x + C$

    (C) $\frac{x^5}{4} - 3x^2 + 3x + C$

    (D) $\frac{x^5}{5} - 2x^3 + 3x + C$

Solution:

$$\int(x^4 - 6x^2 + 3)\, dx = \frac{x^5}{5} - \frac{6x^3}{3} + 3x + C = \frac{x^5}{5} - 2x^3 + 3x + C.$$

This is choice (D).

Notes: (1) If n is any real number, then an antiderivative of x^n is $\frac{x^{n+1}}{n+1}$.

26

Symbolically, $\int x^n dx = \frac{x^{n+1}}{n+1} + C$, where C is an arbitrary constant.

For example, $\int x^4 dx = \frac{x^5}{5} + C$.

As another example, $\int 3dx = \int 3x^0 dx = \frac{3x^1}{1} + C = 3x + C$.

(2) Of course it is worth just remembering that $\int kdx = kx$ for any constant k.

(3) If g and h are functions, then

$$\int [g(x) + h(x)]dx = \int g(x)dx + \int h(x)dx.$$

In other words, when integrating a sum we can simply integrate term by term.

Similarly, $\int [g(x) - h(x)]dx = \int g(x)dx - \int h(x)dx$.

(4) If g is a function and k is a constant, then

$$\int kg(x)dx = k \int g(x)dx$$

For example, $\int 6x^2 dx = 6 \int x^2 dx = 6\left(\frac{x^3}{3}\right) + C = 2x^3 + C$.

(5) In the given problem we integrate each of x^4, x^2, and 3 separately and then use notes (3) and (4) to write the final answer.

(6) We do not need to include a constant C for each individual integration since if we add or subtract two or more constants we simply get a new constant. This is why we simply add one constant C at the end of the integration.

(7) It is also possible to solve this problem by differentiating the answer choices. For example, if we start with choice (C), then we have that $\frac{d}{dx}\left(\frac{x^5}{4}\right) = \frac{5x^4}{4}$. So we can immediately see that choice (C) is incorrect.

When we differentiate choice (D) however, we get

$$\frac{d}{dx}[\frac{x^5}{5} - 2x^3 + 3x + C] = \frac{5x^4}{5} - 3(2x^2) + 3 + 0 = x^4 - 6x^2 + 3.$$

This is the **integrand** (the expression between the integral symbol and dx) that we started with. So the answer is choice (D).

(8) Note that the derivative of any constant is always 0, ie. $\frac{d}{dx}[C] = 0$.

18. $\int_{-1}^{2}(3x^2 - 2x)\, dx =$

      (A) 2
      (B) 4
      (C) 6
      (D) 14

Solution: $\int_{-1}^{2}(3x^2 - 2x)\, dx = (\frac{3x^3}{3} - \frac{2x^2}{2})\Big|_{-1}^{2} = (x^3 - x^2)\Big|_{-1}^{2} =$
$(2^3 - 2^2) - ((-1)^3 - (-1)^2) = (8 - 4) - (-1 - 1) = 4 - (-2) = 6.$

This is choice (C).

Notes: (1) $\int_{a}^{b} f(x)dx = F(b) - F(a)$ where F is any antiderivative of f.

In this example, $F(x) = x^3 - x^2$ is an antiderivative of the function $f(x) = 3x^2 - 2x$. So $\int_{-1}^{2} f(x)dx = F(2) - F(-1)$

(2) We sometimes write $F(b) - F(a)$ as $F(x)\Big|_{a}^{b}$.

This is just a convenient way of focusing on finding an antiderivative before worrying about plugging in the **upper** and **lower limits of integration** (these are the numbers b and a, respectively).

(3) For details on how to find an antiderivative here, see the notes at the end of the solution to problem 17.

19. $3 \int e^{3x}\, dx =$

      (A) $e^{-3x} + C$
      (B) $e^{-x} + C$
      (C) $e^{x} + C$
      (D) $e^{3x} + C$

Solution: $3 \int e^{3x}dx = \int e^{3x}(3dx) = e^{3x} + C$, choice (D).

Notes: (1) We can formally make the substitution $u = 3x$. It then follows that $du = 3dx$. So we have

$$\int e^{3x}(3dx) = \int e^{u}du = e^{u} + C = e^{3x} + C.$$

We get the leftmost equality by replacing $3x$ by u, and $3dx$ by du.

We get the second equality by the basic integration formula

$$\int e^u du = e^u + C.$$

And we get the rightmost equality by replacing u with $3x$.

(2) Note that the function $f(x) = e^{3x}$ can be written as the composition $f(x) = g(h(x))$ where $g(x) = e^x$ and $h(x) = 3x$.

Since $h(x) = 3x$ is the inner part of the composition, it is natural to try the substitution $u = 3x$.

Note that the derivative of $3x$ is 3, so that $du = 3dx$.

(3) With a little practice, we can evaluate an integral like this very quickly with the following reasoning: The derivative of $3x$ is 3. So to integrate $3e^{3x}$ we simply pretend we are integrating e^x but as we do it we leave the $3x$ where it is. This is essentially what was done in the above solution.

Note that the 3 "goes away" because it is the derivative of $3x$. We need it there for everything to work.

(4) We can also solve this problem by differentiating the answer choices. In fact, we have $\frac{d}{dx}[e^{3x} + C] = e^{3x}(3) + 0 = 3e^{3x}$. So the answer is choice (D).

20. $\int (x^2 + 2)\sqrt{x}\, dx =$

(A) $x^2 + 4x^{\frac{3}{2}} + x + C$

(B) $\frac{2}{7}x^{\frac{7}{2}} + \frac{4}{3}x^{\frac{3}{2}} + C$

(C) $\frac{2}{5}x^{\frac{5}{2}} + 2x^{\frac{1}{2}} + C$

(D) $\frac{5}{2}\sqrt{x} + \frac{2}{\sqrt{x}} + c$

Solution:

$$\int (x^2 + 2)\sqrt{x}\, dx = \int (x^2\sqrt{x} + 2\sqrt{x})dx = \int x^2 x^{\frac{1}{2}}dx + \int 2x^{\frac{1}{2}}\, dx$$

$$= \int x^{\frac{5}{2}}dx + \int 2x^{\frac{1}{2}}\, dx = \frac{2}{7}x^{\frac{7}{2}} + \frac{4}{3}x^{\frac{3}{2}} + C$$

29

This is choice (B).

Notes: (1) $\sqrt{x} = x^{\frac{1}{2}}$. So $2\sqrt{x} = 2x^{\frac{1}{2}}$.

(2) $x^2 x^{\frac{1}{2}} = x^{2+\frac{1}{2}} = x^{\frac{4}{2}+\frac{1}{2}} = x^{\frac{5}{2}}$.

(3) See problem 11 for more information on the laws of exponents used here.

(4) To integrate we used the power rule twice: $\int x^n dx = \dfrac{x^{n+1}}{n+1} + C$.

$$\int x^{\frac{1}{2}}dx = \frac{x^{\frac{3}{2}}}{\frac{3}{2}} + C = x^{\frac{3}{2}} \div \frac{3}{2} + C = x^{\frac{3}{2}} \cdot \frac{2}{3} + C = \frac{2}{3}x^{\frac{3}{2}} + C.$$

It follows that $\int 2x^{\frac{1}{2}}dx = 2\int x^{\frac{1}{2}}dx = 2 \cdot \frac{2}{3}x^{\frac{3}{2}} + C = \frac{4}{3}x^{\frac{3}{2}} + C.$

$$\int x^{\frac{5}{2}}dx = \frac{x^{\frac{7}{2}}}{\frac{7}{2}} + C = x^{\frac{7}{2}} \div \frac{7}{2} + C = x^{\frac{7}{2}} \cdot \frac{2}{7} + C = \frac{2}{7}x^{\frac{7}{2}} + C.$$

21. $\int_0^2 (x^2 - 4x)e^{6x^2-x^3} dx =$

    (A) $-\dfrac{e^{16}}{3}$

    (B)   0

    (C) $\dfrac{e^{16}}{3}$

    (D) $\dfrac{1-e^{16}}{3}$

Solution:

$$\int_0^2 (x^2 - 4x)e^{6x^2-x^3} dx = -\frac{1}{3}e^{6x^2-x^3} \Big|_0^2 = -\frac{1}{3}e^{16} - \left(-\frac{1}{3}e^0\right) = \frac{-e^{16}+1}{3}$$

This is equivalent to choice (D).

Notes: (1) To evaluate $\int(x^2 - 4x)e^{6x^2-x^3} dx$, we can formally make the substitution $u = 6x^2 - x^3$. It then follows that

$$du = (12x - 3x^2)dx = 3(4x - x^2)dx = -3(x^2 - 4x)dx$$

Uh oh! There is no factor of -3 inside the integral.

But constants never pose a problem. We simply multiply by -3 and $-\frac{1}{3}$ at the same time. We place the -3 inside the integral where it is needed, and we leave the $-\frac{1}{3}$ outside of the integral sign as follows:

$$\int (x^2 - 4x)e^{6x^2 - x^3}\,dx = -\frac{1}{3}\int (-3)(x^2 - 4x)e^{6x^2 - x^3}\,dx$$

We have this flexibility to place the -3 and $-\frac{1}{3}$ where we like because multiplication is commutative, and constants can be pulled outside of the integral sign freely.

We now have

$$\int (x^2 - 4x)e^{6x^2 - x^3}\,dx = -\frac{1}{3}\int (-3)(x^2 - 4x)e^{6x^2 - x^3}\,dx$$

$$= -\frac{1}{3}\int e^u\,du = -\frac{1}{3}e^u + C = -\frac{1}{3}e^{6x^2 - x^3} + C$$

(2) If we are doing the substitution formally, we can save some time by changing the limits of integration. We do this as follows:

$$\int_0^2 (x^2 - 4x)e^{6x^2 - x^3}\,dx = -\frac{1}{3}\int_0^2 (-3)(x^2 - 4x)e^{6x^2 - x^3}\,dx$$

$$= -\frac{1}{3}\int_0^{16} e^u\,du = -\frac{1}{3}e^u\,\Big|_0^{16} = -\frac{1}{3}(e^{16} - e^0) = \frac{-e^{16}+1}{3}$$

Notice that the limits 0 and 2 were changed to the limits 0 and 16, respectively. We made this change using the formula that we chose for the substitution: $u = 6x^2 - x^3$. When $x = 0$, we have $u = 0$ and when $x = 2$, we have $u = 6(2)^2 - 2^3 = 6 \cdot 4 - 8 = 24 - 8 = 16$.

22. $\int (\frac{2}{x^2} + \frac{1}{x} - 5\sqrt{x} + \frac{7}{\sqrt[3]{x^5}})\,dx =$

Solution: $\int (\frac{2}{x^2} + \frac{1}{x} - 5\sqrt{x} + \frac{7}{\sqrt[3]{x^5}})\,dx = \int (2x^{-2} + \frac{1}{x} - 5x^{\frac{1}{2}} + 7x^{-\frac{5}{3}}\,dx$

$$= \frac{2x^{-1}}{-1} + \ln|x| - \frac{5x^{\frac{3}{2}}}{\frac{3}{2}} + \frac{7x^{-\frac{2}{3}}}{-\frac{2}{3}} + C = -\frac{2}{x} + \ln|x| - \frac{10}{3}\sqrt{x^3} - \frac{21}{2\sqrt[3]{x^2}} + C.$$

Notes: (1) Recall from problem 11 that $\frac{d}{dx}[\ln x] = \frac{1}{x}$. It therefore seems like it should follow that $\int \frac{1}{x}\,dx = \ln x + C$. But this is *not* completely accurate.

31

Observe that we also have $\frac{d}{dx}[\ln(-x)] = \frac{1}{-x}(-1) = \frac{1}{x}$ (the chain rule was used here). So it appears that we also have $\int \frac{1}{x} dx = \ln(-x) + C$.

How can the same integral lead to two different answers? Well it doesn't. Note that $\ln x$ is only defined for $x > 0$, and $\ln(-x)$ is only defined for $x < 0$.

Furthermore, observe that $\ln|x| = \begin{cases} \ln x & \text{if } x > 0 \\ \ln(-x) & \text{if } x < 0 \end{cases}$.

It follows that

$$\int \frac{1}{x} dx = \ln|x| + C.$$

(2) $\frac{2}{x^2} = 2\left(\frac{1}{x^2}\right) = 2x^{-2}$. It follows that $\int \frac{2}{x^2} dx = \int 2x^{-2} dx = \frac{2x^{-1}}{-1} + C$.

Also, $\frac{2x^{-1}}{-1} = -2x^{-1} = -2\left(\frac{1}{x}\right) = -\frac{2}{x}$.

(3) $\sqrt{x} = x^{\frac{1}{2}}$. It follows that $\int \sqrt{x}\, dx = \int x^{\frac{1}{2}} dx = \frac{x^{\frac{3}{2}}}{\frac{3}{2}} + C$.

Also, $\frac{x^{\frac{3}{2}}}{\frac{3}{2}} = x^{\frac{3}{2}} \div \frac{3}{2} = x^{\frac{3}{2}} \cdot \frac{2}{3} = \frac{2x^{\frac{3}{2}}}{3} = \frac{2\sqrt{x^3}}{3}$.

(4) $\frac{7}{\sqrt[3]{x^5}} = \frac{7}{x^{\frac{5}{3}}} = 7\left(\frac{1}{x^{\frac{5}{3}}}\right) = 7x^{-\frac{5}{3}}$. It follows that

$$\int \frac{7}{\sqrt[3]{x^5}} dx = \int 7x^{-\frac{5}{3}} dx = 7\left(\frac{x^{-\frac{2}{3}}}{-\frac{2}{3}}\right) + C.$$

Also, $\frac{x^{-\frac{2}{3}}}{-\frac{2}{3}} = x^{-\frac{2}{3}} \div \left(-\frac{2}{3}\right) = x^{-\frac{2}{3}} \cdot \left(-\frac{3}{2}\right) = \frac{1}{x^{\frac{2}{3}}} \cdot \left(-\frac{3}{2}\right) = -\frac{3}{2x^{\frac{2}{3}}} = -\frac{3}{2\sqrt[3]{x^2}}$.

(5) See problem 11 for more information on the laws of exponents used here.

23. $\int \frac{1}{x \ln x} dx =$

Solution: $\int \frac{1}{x \ln x} dx = \ln|\ln x| + C$.

Note: To evaluate $\int \frac{1}{x \ln x} dx$, we can formally make the substitution $u = \ln x$. It then follows that $du = \frac{1}{x} dx$. So we have

$$\int \frac{1}{x \ln x} dx = \int \frac{1}{\ln x} \cdot \frac{1}{x} dx = \int \frac{1}{u} du = \ln|u| + C = \ln|\ln x| + C.$$

To get the first equality we simply rewrote $\frac{1}{x \ln x}$ as $\frac{1}{x} \cdot \frac{1}{\ln x} = \frac{1}{\ln x} \cdot \frac{1}{x}$. This way it is easier to see exactly where u and du are.

To get the second equality we simply replaced $\ln x$ by u, and $\frac{1}{x} dx$ by du.

To get the third equality we used the basic integration formula

$$\int \frac{1}{x} du = \ln|x| + C \text{ (see problem 22 for details).}$$

To get the last equality we replaced u by $\ln x$ (since we set $u = \ln x$ in the beginning).

24. $\int 5^{\cot x} \csc^2 x \, dx =$

Solution: $\int 5^{\cot x} \csc^2 x \, dx = -\frac{5^{\cot x}}{\ln 5} + C$

Notes: (1) Recall from problem 14 that $\frac{d}{dx}[5^x] = 5^x (\ln 5)$. It follows that $\int 5^x \, dx = \frac{5^x}{\ln 5} + C$.

To verify this, note that

$$\frac{d}{dx}\left[\frac{5^x}{\ln 5} + C\right] = \frac{1}{\ln 5} \frac{d}{dx}[5^x] + \frac{d}{dx}[C] = \frac{1}{\ln 5} \cdot 5^x (\ln 5) + 0 = 5^x.$$

More generally, we have that for any $b > 0$, $b \neq 1$, $\int b^x \, dx = \frac{b^x}{\ln b}$

(2) As an alternative way to evaluate $\int 5^x \, dx$, we can rewrite 5^x as $e^{x \ln 5}$ and perform the substitution $u = x \ln 5$, so that $du = (\ln 5) \, dx$. So we have

$$\int 5^x \, dx = \int e^{x \ln 5} \, dx = \frac{1}{\ln 5} \int e^{x \ln 5} (\ln 5) \, dx = \frac{1}{\ln 5} \int e^u \, du$$

$$= \frac{1}{\ln 5} e^u + C = \frac{1}{\ln 5} e^{x \ln 5} + C = \frac{1}{\ln 5} 5^x + C = \frac{5^x}{\ln 5} + C.$$

(3) To evaluate $\int 5^{\cot x} \csc^2 x \, dx$, we can formally make the substitution $u = \cot x$. It then follows that $du = -\csc^2 x \, dx$. So we have

$$\int 5^{\cot x} \csc^2 x \, dx = -\int 5^{\cot x} (-\csc^2 x) dx = -\int 5^u \, du = -\frac{5^u}{\ln 5} + C$$

$$= -\frac{5^{\cot x}}{\ln 5} + C.$$

(4) As an alternative, we can combine notes (2) and (3) to evaluate the integral in a single step by rewriting $5^{\cot x} \csc^2 x$ as $e^{(\cot x)(\ln 5)} \csc^2 x$, and then letting $u = (\cot x)(\ln 5)$, so that $du = (-\csc^2 x)(\ln 5)dx$. I leave the details of this solution to the reader.

LEVEL 1: LIMITS AND CONTINUITY

25. $\lim\limits_{x \to 7} \dfrac{2x^2 - 13x - 7}{x - 7} =$

    (A) ∞
    (B) 0
    (C) 2
    (D) 15

Solution 1: $\lim\limits_{x \to 7} \dfrac{2x^2 - 13x - 7}{x - 7} = \lim\limits_{x \to 7} \dfrac{(x-7)(2x+1)}{x - 7} = \lim\limits_{x \to 7} (2x + 1)$

$$= 2(7) + 1 = 15.$$

This is choice (D).

Notes: (1) When we try to substitute 7 in for x we get the **indeterminate form** $\frac{0}{0}$. Here is the computation:

$$\frac{2(7)^2 - 13(7) - 7}{7 - 7} = \frac{98 - 91 - 7}{7 - 7} = \frac{0}{0}.$$

This means that we cannot use the method of "plugging in the number" to get the answer. So we have to use some other method.

(2) One algebraic "trick" that works in this case is to factor the numerator as $2x^2 - 13x - 7 = (x - 7)(2x + 1)$. Note that one of the factors is $(x - 7)$ which is identical to the factor in the denominator. This will *always* happen when using this "trick." This makes factoring pretty easy in these problems.

(3) **Most important limit theorem:** If $f(x) = g(x)$ for all x in some interval containing $x = c$ *except* possibly at c itself, then we have $\lim_{x \to c} f(x) = \lim_{x \to c} g(x)$.

In this problem, our two functions are

$$f(x) = \frac{2x^2 - 13x - 7}{x - 7} \text{ and } g(x) = 2x + 1.$$

Note that f and g agree everywhere *except* at $x = 7$. Also note that $f(7)$ is undefined, whereas $g(7) = 15$.

(4) To compute a limit, first try to simply plug in the number. This will only fail when the result is an indeterminate form. The two **basic** indeterminate forms are $\frac{0}{0}$ and $\frac{\infty}{\infty}$ (the more **advanced** ones are $0 \cdot \infty$, $\infty - \infty$, 0^0, 1^∞, and ∞^0, but these can always be manipulated into one of the two basic forms).

If an indeterminate form results from plugging in the number, then there are two possible options:

Option 1: Use some algebraic manipulations to create a new function that agrees with the original except at the value that is being approached, and then use the limit theorem mentioned in note (3).

This is how we solved the problem above.

Option 2: Try L'Hôpital's rule (see solution 2 below).

Solution 2: We use L'Hôpital's rule to get

$$\lim_{x \to 7} \frac{2x^2 - 13x - 7}{x - 7} = \lim_{x \to 7} \frac{4x - 13}{1} = 4(7) - 13 = 15, \text{ choice (D)}.$$

Notes: (1) L'Hôpital's rule says the following: Suppose that

(i) g and k are differentiable on some interval containing c (except possibly at c itself).

(ii) $\lim_{x \to c} g(x) = \lim_{x \to c} k(x) = 0$ or $\lim_{x \to c} g(x) = \lim_{x \to c} k(x) = \pm\infty$

(iii) $\lim_{x \to c} \frac{g'(x)}{k'(x)}$ exists, and

(iv) $k'(x) \neq 0$ for all x in the interval (except possibly at c itself).

Then $\lim\limits_{x \to c} \frac{g(x)}{k(x)} = \lim\limits_{x \to c} \frac{g'(x)}{k'(x)}$.

In this problem $g(x) = 2x^2 - 13x - 7$ and $k(x) = x - 7$.

(2) It is very important that we first check that the expression has the correct form before applying L'Hôpital's rule.

In this problem, note that when we substitute 7 in for x in the given expression we get $\frac{0}{0}$ (see note 1 above). So in this case L'Hôpital's rule can be applied.

26. If $h(x) = \frac{5x^2 - 3x + 2}{3x^2 - 2x}$, then $\lim\limits_{x \to 1} h(x) =$

   (A) 4

   (B) $\frac{7}{4}$

   (C) $\frac{5}{3}$

   (D) 0

Solution: $\lim\limits_{x \to 1} h(x) = \lim\limits_{x \to 1} \frac{5x^2 - 3x + 2}{3x^2 - 2x} = \frac{5(1)^2 - 3(1) + 2}{3(1)^2 - 2(1)} = \frac{5 - 3 + 2}{3 - 2} = \frac{4}{1} = 4$.

This is choice (A).

Notes: (1) We simply substituted 1 in for x. Since we did *not* get an indeterminate form, we see that the answer is 4.

(2) It would be incorrect to try to apply L'Hôpital's rule here! Let's see what happens if we try:

$$\lim\limits_{x \to 1} \frac{5x^2 - 3x + 2}{3x^2 - 2x} = \lim\limits_{x \to 1} \frac{10x - 3}{6x - 2} = \frac{10(1) - 3}{6(1) - 2} = \frac{7}{4}.$$

So we get choice (D) which is **wrong!**

If we tried to apply L'Hôpital's rule twice we would get

$$\lim\limits_{x \to 1} \frac{5x^2 - 3x + 2}{3x^2 - 2x} = \lim\limits_{x \to 1} \frac{10x - 3}{6x - 2} = \lim\limits_{x \to 1} \frac{10}{6} = \frac{5}{3}.$$

So we get choice (C), also **wrong!**

27. $\displaystyle\lim_{x\to\infty} \frac{3x^2-2x+1}{7x^2+5x-3}$

(A) $-\frac{1}{3}$

(B) $\frac{3}{7}$

(C) $\frac{7}{3}$

(D) ∞

Solution: $\displaystyle\lim_{x\to\infty} \frac{3x^2-2x+1}{7x^2+5x-3} = \lim_{x\to\infty} \frac{3x^2}{7x^2} = \frac{3}{7}$, choice (B).

Notes: (1) If p and q are polynomials, then $\displaystyle\lim_{x\to\infty} \frac{p(x)}{q(x)} = \lim_{x\to\infty} \frac{a_n x^n}{b_m x^m}$ where

$$p(x) = a_n x^n + a_{n-1}x^{n-1} + \cdots + a_1 x + a_0 \text{ and}$$

$$q(x) = a_m x^m + a_{m-1}x^{m-1} + \cdots + a_1 x + a_0.$$

(2) If $n = m$, then $\displaystyle\lim_{x\to\infty} \frac{a_n x^n}{b_m x^m} = \frac{a_n}{b_m}$.

(3) Combining notes (1) and (2), we could have gotten the answer to this problem immediately by simply taking the coefficients of x^2 in the numerator and denominator and dividing.

The coefficient of x^2 in the numerator is 3, and the coefficient of x^2 in the denominator is 7. So the final answer is $\frac{3}{7}$.

(4) If $n > 0$, then $\displaystyle\lim_{x\to\infty} \frac{1}{x^n} = 0$.

(5) For a more rigorous solution, we can multiply both the numerator and denominator of the fraction by $\frac{1}{x^2}$ to get

$$\frac{3x^2-2x+1}{7x^2+5x-3} = \frac{\left(\frac{1}{x^2}\right)}{\left(\frac{1}{x^2}\right)} \cdot \frac{(3x^2-2x+1)}{(7x^2+5x-3)} = \frac{3-\frac{2}{x}+\frac{1}{x^2}}{7+\frac{5}{x}-\frac{3}{x^2}}.$$

It follows that $\displaystyle\lim_{x\to\infty}\frac{3x^2-2x+1}{7x^2+5x-3} = \frac{\lim\limits_{x\to\infty} 3 - 2\lim\limits_{x\to\infty}\left(\frac{1}{x}\right) + \lim\limits_{x\to\infty}\frac{1}{x^2}}{\lim\limits_{x\to\infty} 7 + 5\lim\limits_{x\to\infty}\left(\frac{1}{x}\right) - 3\lim\limits_{x\to\infty}\left(\frac{1}{x^2}\right)} = \frac{3-2(0)+(0)}{7+5(0)-3(0)} = \frac{3}{7}$.

(6) L'Hôpital's rule can also be used to solve this problem since the limit has the form $\frac{\infty}{\infty}$:

$$\lim_{x\to\infty} \frac{3x^2-2x+1}{7x^2+5x-3} = \lim_{x\to\infty} \frac{6x-2}{14x+5} = \lim_{x\to\infty} \frac{6}{14} = \frac{3}{7}.$$

37

Observe that we applied L'Hôpital's rule twice. The first time we differentiated the numerator and denominator with respect to x to get another expression of the form $\frac{\infty}{\infty}$.

28. If the function g is continuous for all real numbers and if $g(x) = \frac{x^2-x-6}{x-3}$ for all $x \neq 3$, then $g(3) =$

    (A) 0
    (B) 1
    (C) 2
    (D) 5

Solution 1: $g(3) = \lim\limits_{x \to 3} \frac{x^2-x-6}{x-3} = \lim\limits_{x \to 3} \frac{(x-3)(x+2)}{x-3} = \lim\limits_{x \to 3}(x+2)$

$$= 3 + 2 = 5.$$

This is choice (D).

Notes: (1) A function f is continuous at $x = a$ if $\lim\limits_{x \to a} f(x) = f(a)$.

In this problem we want the function g to be continuous for all real numbers. In particular, we need g to be continuous at $x = 3$. So we must have $g(3) = \lim\limits_{x \to 3} g(x) = \lim\limits_{x \to 3} \frac{x^2-x-6}{x-3}$.

(2) When we try to substitute 3 in for x we get the **indeterminate form** $\frac{0}{0}$. Here is the computation:

$$\frac{3^2-3-6}{3-3} = \frac{9-9}{3-3} = \frac{0}{0}.$$

This means that we cannot use the method of "plugging in the number" to compute the limit. We used the same method from the first solution in problem 25.

(3) As an alternative we could have used L'Hôpital's rule (just like we did for the second solution in problem 25). Here are the details:

$g(3) = \lim\limits_{x \to 3} \frac{x^2-x-6}{x-3} = \lim\limits_{x \to 3} \frac{2x-1}{1} = 2(3) - 1 = 5$, choice (D).

See problem 25 for more information about L'Hôpital's rule.

29. $\lim\limits_{x\to 0}\dfrac{\sin^3 5x}{x^3}$

    (A) -125

    (B) 5

    (C) 125

    (D) The limit does not exist

Solution: $\lim\limits_{x\to 0}\dfrac{\sin^3 5x}{x^3} = \lim\limits_{5x\to 0} 5^3\dfrac{\sin^3 5x}{5^3 x^3} = 125\lim\limits_{5x\to 0}\dfrac{(\sin 5x)^3}{(5x)^3}$

$$= 125\lim\limits_{u\to 0}\left(\dfrac{\sin u}{u}\right)^3 = 125(\lim\limits_{u\to 0}\dfrac{\sin u}{u})^3 = 125(1)^3 = 125.$$

This is choice (C).

Notes: (1) A basic limit worth memorizing is

$$\lim\limits_{x\to 0}\dfrac{\sin x}{x} = 1.$$

(2) The limit in note (1) is actually very easy to compute using L'Hôpital's rule:

$$\lim\limits_{x\to 0}\dfrac{\sin x}{x} = \lim\limits_{x\to 0}\dfrac{\cos x}{1} = \cos 0 = 1$$

(3) It is not hard to see that $x \to 0$ if and only if $5x \to 0$. This is why we can replace x by $5x$ in the subscript of the limit above.

(4) $\sin^n x$ is an abbreviation for $(\sin x)^n$.

In particular, $\sin^3 x = (\sin x)^3$, and so $\sin^3 5x = (\sin 5x)^3$.

(5) $\dfrac{\sin 5x}{x}$ can be rewritten as $5\dfrac{\sin 5x}{5x}$.

It follows that we can rewrite $\dfrac{\sin^3 5x}{x^3}$ as $5^3\dfrac{\sin^3 5x}{5^3 x^3}$.

(6) $5^3 x^3 = (5x)^3$ by a basic law of exponents, and $\dfrac{(\sin 5x)^3}{(5x)^3} = \left(\dfrac{\sin 5x}{5x}\right)^3$ by another basic law of exponents.

(7) Using the substitution $u = 5x$, we have

$$\lim\limits_{5x\to 0}\left(\dfrac{\sin 5x}{5x}\right)^3 = \lim\limits_{u\to 0}\left(\dfrac{\sin u}{u}\right)^3.$$

(8) If $\lim\limits_{x \to c} f(x)$ and $\lim\limits_{x \to c} g(x)$ both exist, then

$$\lim_{x \to c} [f(x)\, g(x)] = \lim_{x \to c} f(x) \cdot \lim_{x \to c} g(x)$$

In particular,

$$\lim_{x \to c} [f(x)]^2 = \lim_{x \to c} [f(x)\, f(x)] = \lim_{x \to c} f(x) \cdot \lim_{x \to c} f(x) = [\lim_{x \to c} f(x)]^2$$

More generally, $\lim\limits_{x \to c} [f(x)]^n = [\lim\limits_{x \to c} f(x)]^n$

This is why we have $\lim\limits_{u \to 0} \left(\dfrac{\sin u}{u}\right)^3 = (\lim\limits_{u \to 0} \dfrac{\sin u}{u})^3$.

30. $\lim\limits_{x \to 0} \dfrac{3 \tan x - 3 \cos^2 x \tan x}{x^3}$

     (A) 0

     (B) $\dfrac{1}{3}$

     (C) 3

     (D) ∞

Solution: $\lim\limits_{x \to 0} \dfrac{3 \tan x - 3 \cos^2 x \tan x}{x^3} = \lim\limits_{x \to 0} \dfrac{3 \tan x (1 - \cos^2 x)}{x^3}$

$= \lim\limits_{x \to 0} \dfrac{3 \tan x \sin^2 x}{x^3} = 3 \left(\lim\limits_{x \to 0} \dfrac{\tan x}{x}\right) \cdot (\lim\limits_{x \to 0} \dfrac{\sin x}{x})^2 = 3(1)(1) = 3.$

This is choice (C).

Notes: (1) We get the first equality by factoring $3 \tan x$.

(2) To get the second equality we used the most basic Pythagorean identity

$$\cos^2 x + \sin^2 x = 1$$

Subtracting $\cos^2 x$ from each side of this equation gives us

$$\sin^2 x = 1 - \cos^2 x$$

(3) For the third equality we use a basic limit rule concerning products. See problem 29 for details.

(4) As noted in problem 29, $\lim\limits_{x \to 0} \dfrac{\sin x}{x} = 1.$

We also have $\lim\limits_{x \to 0} \dfrac{\tan x}{x} = 1$.

Both of these results can easily be seen by using L'Hôpital's rule.

For the second one, we have

$$\lim_{x \to 0} \frac{\tan x}{x} = \lim_{x \to 0} \frac{\sec^2 x}{1} = \sec^2 0 = (\sec 0)^2 = \left(\frac{1}{\cos 0}\right)^2 = 1.$$

31. If the function f is continuous for all x in the interval $[a, b]$, then at any point c in the interval (a, b), which of the following must be true?

    (A) $\lim\limits_{x \to c} f(x) = f(c)$

    (B) $f'(c)$ exists

    (C) $f(c) = 0$

    (D) $f(c) = f(b) - f(a)$

Solution: f is continuous at $x = c$ if and only if $\lim\limits_{x \to c} f(x) = f(c)$, choice (A).

Notes: (1) This question is simply asking us to pick out the definition of continuity at a value $x = c$.

(2) The function $f(x) = |x|$ on the interval $[-1,1]$ is a counterexample to choices (B), (C), and (D).

Note that $f(x) = |x|$ is continuous for all x. In particular, f is continuous for all x in $[-1,1]$.

$f'(0)$ does not exist, since the graph of f has a "sharp edge" there. This allows us to eliminate choice (B).

$$f\left(\tfrac{1}{2}\right) = \tfrac{1}{2} \neq 0 \text{ and } f(-1) - f(1) = 1 - 1 = 0.$$

This allows us to eliminate choices (C) and (D).

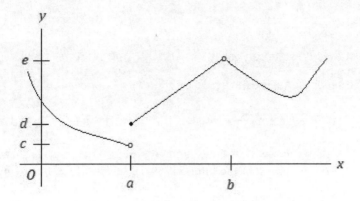

32. The graph of the function h is shown in the figure above. Which of the following statements about h is true?

    (A) $\lim\limits_{x \to a} h(x) = c$

    (B) $\lim\limits_{x \to a} h(x) = d$

    (C) $\lim\limits_{x \to b} h(x) = e$

    (D) $\lim\limits_{x \to b} h(x) = h(b)$

Solution: From the graph we see that $\lim\limits_{x \to b} h(x) = e$, choice (C).

Notes: (1) The open circles on the graph at a and b indicate that there is *no* point at that location. The darkened circle at a indicates $h(a) = d$.

(2) $\lim\limits_{x \to a^-} h(x) = c$ and $\lim\limits_{x \to a^+} h(x) = d$. Therefore $\lim\limits_{x \to a} h(x)$ does not exist.

(3) h is not defined at $x = b$, ie. $h(b)$ does not exist. In particular, h is not continuous at b. So $\lim\limits_{x \to b} h(x) \neq h(b)$.

LEVEL 2: PRECALCULUS

33. If $g(f(x)) = \dfrac{5\ln(2^x+1)-2}{\ln(2^x+1)+3}$ and $g(x) = \dfrac{5x-2}{x+3}$, then $f(x) =$

    (A) $\ln x$
    (B) $\ln 2^x$
    (C) $\ln(2^x + 1)$
    (D) $\ln x^2$

Quick solution by observation: What do we replace x by in $g(x)$ to get $g(f(x))$? By observation the answer is $\ln(2^x + 1)$, choice (C).

Notes: (1) $g(f(x))$ is the **composition** of the function g with the function $f(x)$.

(2) We compute $g(f(x))$ by replacing x in the function $g(x)$ with $f(x)$. Since we do not know what $f(x)$ is in this problem, we must answer the question "what should I replace x by in the function $g(x)$?

(3) If you do not immediately see what to replace x with in the function $g(x)$, use the answer choices as a guide. If you have no idea which one will work, then, as usual, you should begin by checking choice (C) first.

(4) If we are "guessing" that choice (C) is the answer, then we have that $g(f(x)) = g(\ln(2^x + 1)) = \frac{5\ln(2^x+1)-2}{\ln(2^x+1)+3}$. So choice (C) is correct.

34. Suppose that g is a function that is defined on $(-\infty, \infty)$. Which of the following conditions guarantees that g^{-1} exists?

(A) g is symmetric with respect to the origin.
(B) g is continuous at all real numbers.
(C) g has no points of inflection.
(D) g is a strictly decreasing function.

Solution: A strictly decreasing function is always **one-to-one**, and therefore invertible. So the answer is choice (D).

Notes: (1) A function f is **one-to-one** if different x-values always lead to different y-values.

Symbolically this can be written as $a \neq b \rightarrow f(a) \neq f(b)$.

An equivalent way to write this is by using the contrapositive:

$$f(a) = f(b) \rightarrow a = b.$$

Below is a picture showing the graph of a function which is one-to-one. Notice how $f(a)$ and $f(b)$ are different.

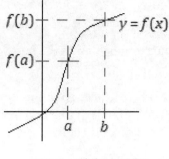

$$a \neq b \rightarrow f(a) \neq f(b).$$

(2) A one-to-one function has a graph that passes the **horizontal line test**. This means that *every* horizontal line hits the graph of the function *at most* once.

(3) Using the horizontal line test, it is easy to see that every strictly increasing or strictly decreasing function is one-to-one (see the figure above for an example of a strictly increasing function).

It is worth committing to memory the fact that every strictly increasing or decreasing function is one-to-one.

(4) There are examples of functions that are one-to-one whose graphs are neither strictly increasing nor strictly decreasing. Such a function could not be continuous however.

Below is a picture showing the graph of a one-to-one function that is neither strictly increasing nor strictly decreasing.

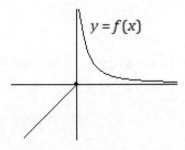

(5) If f is one-to-one, then f is invertible. The **inverse** of f is written f^{-1}, and is defined by $f^{-1}(x) = y$ if and only if $f(y) = x$.

Graphically, the function f^{-1} is the reflection of the function f in the line $y = x$.

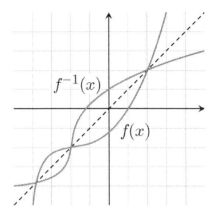

(6) Below is the graph of a noninvertible function g that is symmetric with respect to the origin and continuous at all real numbers. This eliminates choices (A) and (B).

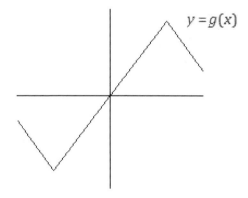

(7) The function $g(x) = x^2$ is an example of a noninvertible function with no points of inflection. This eliminates choice (C).

35. Let $g(x) = \sin(\arctan x)$. The range of g is

(A) $\{x| -1 \leq x \leq 1\}$
(B) $\{x| -1 < x < 1\}$
(C) $\{x| 0 \leq x \leq 1\}$
(D) $\{x| 0 \leq x < 1\}$

Solution: For all x, $-\frac{\pi}{2} < \arctan x < \frac{\pi}{2}$. It follows that

$$-1 < \sin(\arctan x) < 1.$$

So the answer is choice (B).

Notes: (1) Let's take a look at the graph of the function $f(x) = \tan x$.

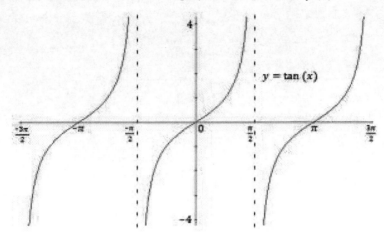

Note that the graph of $\tan x$ shown above has consecutive vertical asymptotes of $x = -\frac{\pi}{2}$ and $\frac{\pi}{2}$. If we restrict the domain of $\tan x$ to $-\frac{\pi}{2} < x < \frac{\pi}{2}$, we have a one-to-one function.

So although $f(x) = \tan x$ is not invertible (it fails the horizontal line test), the *restricted* function $f(x) = \tan x$, $-\frac{\pi}{2} < x < \frac{\pi}{2}$ is invertible, and we call its inverse $f^{-1}(x) = \arctan x$. Note that $f^{-1}(x) = \arctan x$ has domain all real numbers, and range $-\frac{\pi}{2} < x < \frac{\pi}{2}$ as we can see in the following figure.

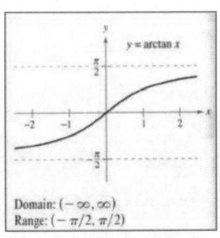

Domain: $(-\infty, \infty)$
Range: $(-\pi/2, \pi/2)$

46

(2) Let's take a look at the graph of $f(x) = \sin x$.

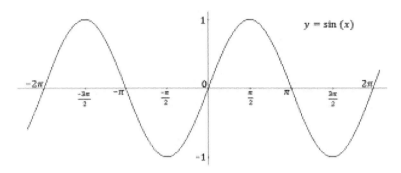

Note that for $-\frac{\pi}{2} < x < \frac{\pi}{2}$, $-1 < \sin x < 1$ (in particular -1 and 1 do not "get hit" by $\sin x$ for any of these x-values).

(3) Putting notes (1) and (2) together, we have $-1 < \sin(\arctan x) < 1$.

(4) See problem 34 for more general information on one-to-one functions and inverses.

36. If $\log_b(5^b) = \frac{b}{3}$, then $b =$

    (A) 125
    (B) 25
    (C) 5
    (D) 3

Solution: Changing to exponential form, we have $5^b = b^{\frac{b}{3}}$. We raise each side of this equation to the power of $\frac{3}{b}$ to get

$$\left(5^b\right)^{\frac{3}{b}} = \left(b^{\frac{b}{3}}\right)^{\frac{3}{b}}$$
$$5^3 = b$$
$$125 = b$$

So the answer is $b = 125$, choice (A).

Notes: (1) See the notes at the end of problem 3 for more information on logarithms.

(2) $(x^{\frac{j}{k}})^{\frac{k}{j}} = x^{\frac{j}{k} \cdot \frac{k}{j}} = x^1 = x$.

(3) It follows from note (2) that we can eliminate an exponent on one side of an equation by raising each side of the equation to the reciprocal of that exponent.

(4) In note (2) we used the law of exponents $(x^c)^d = x^{cd}$.

(5) See problem 11 for more information on the laws of exponents used here.

37. What is the range of the following function?

$$T(x) = 2\cos(3x - 2\pi) - 5$$

(A) $3 \le y \le 7$
(B) $-3 \le y \le 7$
(C) $-3 \le y \le 2$
(D) $-7 \le y \le -3$

Solution: The amplitude of $T(x)$ is 2 and there is a vertical shift of -5. So the minimum and maximum values of $T(x)$ are $-2 - 5 = -7$ and $2 - 5 = -3$. So the range is $-7 \le y \le -3$, choice (D).

Notes: (1) The **amplitude** of a function of the form $a\cos(bx + c) + d$ is $|a|$.

(2) The **vertical shift** of such a function is d.

(3) The **range** of such a function is $-|a| + d \le y \le |a| + d$.

(4) In this problem we do not need to worry about the **phase shift** $bx + c$.

(5) This problem can also be solved using the graphing functions on your TI-84 calculator (if a calculator is allowed for the problem). Make sure the calculator is in radian mode (Press MODE and select Radian), enter the function under Y=, find a viewing window that captures the lowest and highest points of the function (you can start by pressing ZOOM 7 to get a standard trig window, and then change Ymin and Ymax under WINDOW to -10 and 0, respectively, for example), then use the minimum and maximum features under CALC to find the smallest and largest values in the range.

48

38. * If $a(x) = \sqrt[5]{x^3 - 2}$, what is $a^{-1}(2.2)$?

(A) 3.77
(B) 4.23
(C) 4.87
(D) 5.01

Solution by starting with choice (C): We are looking for a value of x so that $a(x) = 2.2$. Let's start with choice (C) and guess that $x = 4.87$. We have $a(4.87) = \sqrt[5]{4.87^3 - 2} \approx 2.6$. This is too big so we can eliminate choices (C) and (D).

Let's try choice (A) next and guess that $x = 3.77$. We have that $a(3.77) = \sqrt[5]{3.77^3 - 2} \approx 2.2$. So the answer is choice (A).

Solution by finding the inverse function: We interchange the roles of x and y and solve for y.

$$a(x) = \sqrt[5]{x^3 - 2}$$
$$y = \sqrt[5]{x^3 - 2}$$
$$x = \sqrt[5]{y^3 - 2}$$
$$x^5 = y^3 - 2$$
$$x^5 + 2 = y^3$$
$$\sqrt[3]{x^5 + 2} = y$$
$$a^{-1}(x) = \sqrt[3]{x^5 + 2}$$

So $a^{-1}(2.2) = \sqrt[3]{2.2^5 + 2} \approx 3.77$, choice (A).

39. What is the period of the graph of $y = \frac{2}{3}\tan(\frac{5}{2}\pi\theta - 2)$?

(A) $\frac{4}{15}$

(B) $\frac{2}{5}$

(C) $\frac{2}{3}$

(D) $\frac{4\pi}{15}$

Solution: The period of the graph of $y = a\tan(bx - c)$ is $\frac{\pi}{b}$. So the period of the graph of the given function is $\frac{\pi}{\frac{5\pi}{2}} = \pi \div \frac{5\pi}{2} = \pi \cdot \frac{2}{5\pi} = \frac{2}{5}$, choice (B).

40. If $\arcsin(\sin x) = \frac{\pi}{4}$ and $0 \le x \le 2\pi$, then x could equal

    (A) 0

    (B) $\frac{\pi}{6}$

    (C) $\frac{\pi}{3}$

    (D) $\frac{3\pi}{4}$

Solution: x could certainly equal $\frac{\pi}{4}$, but $\frac{\pi}{4}$ is not an answer choice. So we need to find $x \ne \frac{\pi}{4}$ so that $\sin x = \sin\frac{\pi}{4}$.

Since $\sin x > 0$ in quadrant II, we find the corresponding second quadrant angle. This is $\pi - \frac{\pi}{4} = \frac{4\pi - \pi}{4} = \frac{3\pi}{4}$, choice (D).

LEVEL 2: DIFFERENTIATION

41. If $y = \sin^2 5x$, then $\frac{dy}{dx} =$

    (A) $2 \sin 5x$
    (B) $10 \sin 5x$
    (C) $2 \sin 5x \cos 5x$
    (D) $10 \sin 5x \cos 5x$

Solution: $\frac{dy}{dx} = 2 (\sin 5x)(\cos 5x)(5) = 10 \sin 5x \cos 5x$, choice (D).

Notes: (1) $\sin^2 x$ is an abbreviation for $(\sin x)^2$.

Therefore $\sin^2 5x$ is really $(\sin 5x)^2$.

(2) The derivative of $f(x) = \sin x$ is $f'(x) = \cos x$.

(3) We used two applications of the chain rule here. Letting $y = f(x)$, we have

$$f(x) = (g \circ h \circ k)(x) = g(h(k(x))),$$

where $k(x) = 5x$, $h(x) = \sin x$, and $g(x) = x^2$. So we have that

$k'(x) = 5$, $h'(x) = \cos x$, and $g'(x) = 2x$

$$f'(x) = g'(h(k(x))) \cdot h'(k(x)) \cdot k'(x) = 2 (\sin 5x)(\cos 5x)(5)$$

42. If $T(x) = \tan^2(5 - x)$, then $T'(0)$ is equal to which of the following?

(A) $-2 \tan 5 \sec 5$

(B) $-2 \tan 5 \sec^2 5$

(C) $-2 \tan^2 5 \sec 5$

(D) $-2 \tan^2 5 \sec^2 5$

Solution:

$T'(x) = 2\tan(5 - x)\sec^2(5 - x)(-1) = -2\tan(5 - x)\sec^2(5 - x)$.

So $T'(0) = -2\tan 5 \sec^2 5$, choice (B).

Notes: (1) $\tan^2 x$ is an abbreviation for $(\tan x)^2$.

Therefore $\tan^2(5 - x)$ is really $(\tan(5 - x))^2$.

(2) The derivative of $f(x) = \tan x$ is $f'(x) = \sec^2 x$.

(3) We used two applications of the chain rule here.

We have $T(x) = (g \circ h \circ k)(x) = g(h(k(x)))$, where

$k(x) = 5 - x$, $h(x) = \tan x$, and $g(x) = x^2$. So we have that

$k'(x) = -1$, $h'(x) = \sec^2 x$, and $g'(x) = 2x$

$g'(h(k(x))) \cdot h'(k(x)) \cdot k'(x) = 2\tan(5 - x)\sec^2(5 - x)(-1)$

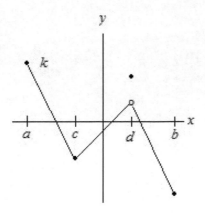

43. The function k, whose graph consists of three line segments, is shown above. Which of the following are true for k on the open interval (a, b) ?

    I. $\lim\limits_{x \to c} k(x)$ exists.

    II. The domain of the derivative of k is the open interval (c, d).

    III. The derivative of k is negative on the interval (d, b).

    (A) I only
    (B) II only
    (C) III only
    (D) I and III only

Solution: Since $\lim\limits_{x \to c^-} k(x) = \lim\limits_{x \to c^+} k(x)$, $\lim\limits_{x \to c} k(x)$ exists. So I is true.

On (a, b), the function k fails to be differentiable at $x = c$ and $x = d$ only. So the domain of the derivative of k contains points that are not in (c, d). So II is false.

The function k is decreasing on (d, b). Therefore the derivative of k is negative on (d, b). So III is true.

It follows that the answer is choice (D).

Notes: (1) $\lim\limits_{x \to c} k(x)$ exists because as we approach c from both the left and the right, we are heading toward the same point.

In this case it is actually true that the function k is continuous at $x = c$ because the value that we are approaching is actually attained.

Note however that k is *not* differentiable at $x = c$ because there is a "sharp edge" there. More specifically, the slope of the tangent line from the left is negative because the function is decreasing to the left of c, and the slope of the tangent line from the right is positive because the function is increasing to the right of c.

Let's compare this to the situation at $x = d$. $\lim_{x \to d} k(x)$ exists because as we approach d from both the left and the right, we are heading toward the same point.

In this case however the function k is *not* continuous at $x = d$ because the value that we are approaching is *not* the same as $k(d)$ which is a larger number (because it is *higher* on the graph).

Of course k is not differentiable at $x = d$ since continuity is required for differentiability.

(2) The domain of the derivative of k is $(a, c) \cup (c, d) \cup (d, b)$. In other words, the derivative of k exists at all x values between a and b *except* for $x = c$ and $x = d$.

The derivative of k does not exist at $x = c$ because there is a "sharp edge" there, and the derivative of k does not exist at $x = d$ because k is discontinuous at $x = d$.

(3) If f is differentiable, then the derivative of f is positive if and only if f is increasing, and the derivative of f is negative if and only if f is decreasing.

In this problem, the function k is differentiable and increasing on (c, d). Therefore $k'(x) > 0$ for all x in (c, d).

The function k is decreasing on the intervals (a, c) and (d, b). Therefore $k'(x) < 0$ for all x in (a, c) and for all x in (d, b).

44. If $f(x) = x\sqrt{3x + 5}$, then $f'(x) =$

(A) $\dfrac{9x+10}{2\sqrt{3x+5}}$

(B) $\dfrac{9x}{2\sqrt{3x+5}}$

(C) $\dfrac{9x}{\sqrt{3x+5}}$

(D) $\dfrac{9}{2\sqrt{3x+5}}$

Solution:

$$f'(x) = x \cdot \frac{1}{2}(3x+5)^{-\frac{1}{2}}(3) + (\sqrt{3x+5})(1) =$$

$$\frac{3x}{2\sqrt{3x+5}} + \frac{(\sqrt{3x+5})}{1}\frac{(2\sqrt{3x+5})}{(2\sqrt{3x+5})} = \frac{3x}{2\sqrt{3x+5}} + \frac{2(3x+5)}{2\sqrt{3x+5}} = \frac{3x+6x+10}{2\sqrt{3x+5}} = \frac{9x+10}{2\sqrt{3x+5}}.$$

This is choice (A).

Notes: (1) We begin with the product rule.

$f(x) = u(x)v(x)$, where $u(x) = x$, and $v(x) = \sqrt{3x+5}$.

$$f'(x) = u(x)v'(x) + v(x)u'(x)$$

(2) $u'(x) = \frac{d}{dx}[x] = 1$

(3) $v(x) = \sqrt{3x+5}$ can be written as $v(x) = (3x+5)^{\frac{1}{2}}$. To take the derivative of v requires the chain rule. We have

$$v'(x) = \frac{1}{2}(3x+5)^{-\frac{1}{2}}(3)$$

Note that $v(x) = g(h(x))$, where $g(x) = \sqrt{x}$ and $h(x) = 3x+5$.

By the chain rule, $v'(x) = g'(h(x)) \cdot h'(x)$.

(4) $(3x+5)^{-\frac{1}{2}} = \frac{1}{(3x+5)^{\frac{1}{2}}} = \frac{1}{\sqrt{3x+5}}$.

(5) Combining (3) and (4) we have

$$\frac{d}{dx}\left[\sqrt{3x+5}\right] = \frac{d}{dx}\left[(3x+5)^{\frac{1}{2}}\right] = \frac{1}{2}(3x+5)^{-\frac{1}{2}}(3) = \frac{3}{2\sqrt{3x+5}}.$$

(6) See problem 11 for a review of all of the laws of exponents you should know.

(7) We would like to express $\frac{3x}{2\sqrt{3x+5}} + \frac{(\sqrt{3x+5})}{1}$ as a single fraction. To do this we multiply the numerator and denominator of the second term by $2\sqrt{3x+5}$.

(8) By the definition of the positive square root, $\sqrt{x} \cdot \sqrt{x} = x$. So we have $\sqrt{3x+5} \cdot \sqrt{3x+5} = 3x+5$.

45. The slope of the tangent line to the curve $xy^5 - x^3y^4 = 10$ at $(-2, -1)$ is

(A) 0

(B) $-\frac{2}{7}$

(C) $-\frac{13}{42}$

(D) $-\frac{1}{3}$

Solution: We have

$$x\left(5y^4 \cdot \frac{dy}{dx}\right) + y^5(1) - x^3\left(4y^3 \cdot \frac{dy}{dx}\right) + y^4(-3x^2) = 0.$$

We now substitute -2 for x and -1 for y to get

$$(-2)\left(5(-1)^4 \cdot \frac{dy}{dx}\right) + (-1)^5(1) - (-2)^3\left(4(-1)^3 \cdot \frac{dy}{dx}\right) + (-1)^4(-3(-2)^2) = 0$$

$$(-2)\left(5 \cdot 1 \cdot \frac{dy}{dx}\right) + (-1)(1) - (-8)\left(4(-1) \cdot \frac{dy}{dx}\right) + (1)(-3 \cdot 4) = 0$$

$$-10\frac{dy}{dx} - 1 - 32\frac{dy}{dx} - 12 = 0$$

$$-42\frac{dy}{dx} - 13 = 0$$

So we have $-42\frac{dy}{dx} = 13$, and therefore $\frac{dy}{dx} = -\frac{13}{42}$, choice (C).

Notes: (1) The given equation defines the dependent variable y **implicitly** as a function of x.

This just means that the variable y is *not* by itself on one side of the equation.

An example of an **explicitly** defined function is $y = 2x$.

This same function can be defined implicitly as $2x - y = 0$.

(2) When the dependent variable y is defined implicitly as a function of x, we can use **implicit differentiation** to find the derivative $\frac{dy}{dx}$.

This is just an application of the chain rule. Since y is a function of x, we can write $y = f(x)$ for some function f. So if we want to differentiate $g(y)$, simply note that this is $g(f(x))$, and so the derivative is $g'(f(x)) \cdot f'(x) = g'(y) \cdot \frac{dy}{dx}$.

For example, the derivative of y^5 is $5y^4 \frac{dy}{dx}$, and the derivative of y^4 is $4y^3 \frac{dy}{dx}$.

(3) To get the derivative in this problem we needed to use the product rule twice: once for the product xy^5, and once for the product $-x^3y^4$.

(4) Remember that the derivative of a constant is 0. So once we differentiate, we get 0 on the right hand side of the equation. A common mistake is to leave this as 10.

(5) In the solution above after differentiating we plugged in -2 for x and -1 for y first, *and then* solved for $\frac{dy}{dx}$. This is generally much faster than solving for $\frac{dy}{dx}$ first and then plugging in the point.

(6) If we were not given a point in the question, and were simply asked to find $\frac{dy}{dx}$, then we would do the following:

$$x\left(5y^4 \cdot \frac{dy}{dx}\right) + y^5(1) - x^3\left(4y^3 \cdot \frac{dy}{dx}\right) + y^4(-3x^2) = 0$$

$$5xy^4\frac{dy}{dx} + y^5 - 4x^3y^3\frac{dy}{dx} - 3x^2y^4 = 0$$

$$5xy^4\frac{dy}{dx} - 4x^3y^3\frac{dy}{dx} = 3x^2y^4 - y^5$$

$$(5xy^4 - 4x^3y^3)\frac{dy}{dx} = 3x^2y^4 - y^5$$

$$\frac{dy}{dx} = \frac{3x^2y^4-y^5}{5xy^4-4x^3y^3} = \frac{y^4(3x^2-y)}{xy^3(5y-4x^2)} = \frac{y(3x^2-y)}{x(5y-4x^2)}$$

(7) As an alternative solution to this problem (although not recommended), after differentiating, we can first solve for $\frac{dy}{dx}$ as in note (6), and then plug in -2 for x and -1 for y as follows:

$$\frac{dy}{dx} = \frac{y(3x^2-y)}{x(5y-4x^2)} = \frac{(-1)(3(-2)^2-(-1))}{(-2)(5(-1)-4(-2)^2)} = \frac{(-1)(3(4)+1)}{(-2)(-5-4(4))} = \frac{(-1)(12+1)}{(-2)(-5-16)} = \frac{-13}{42}$$

46. Let $f(x) = -3x^2 + x - 5$. A value of c that satisfies the conclusion of the Mean Value Theorem for f on the interval $[-2,2]$ is

(A) -2

(B) $-\frac{1}{2}$

(C) $-\frac{1}{6}$

(D) 0

Solution: $f'(x) = -6x + 1$, so that $f'(c) = -6c + 1$.

$f(2) = -3(2)^2 + 2 - 5 = -3(4) - 3 = -12 - 3 = -15$.

$f(-2) = -3(-2)^2 - 2 - 5 = -3(4) - 7 = -12 - 7 = -19$.

We now solve the equation $f'(c) = \frac{f(2)-f(-2)}{2-(-2)}$ to get

$$-6c + 1 = \frac{-15-(-19)}{2+2} = \frac{-15+19}{4} = \frac{4}{4} = 1$$

So $-6c = 1 - 1 = 0$, and $c = 0$, choice (D).

Notes: (1) The **Mean Value Theorem** says that if f is a function that is continuous on the closed interval $[a, b]$ and differentiable on the open interval (a, b), then there is a real number c with $a < c < b$ such that $f'(c) = \frac{f(b)-f(a)}{b-a}$.

In this problem $a = -2$, $b = 2$, and $f(x) = -3x^2 + x - 5$.

(2) Note that the function $f(x) = -3x^2 + x - 5$ is a polynomial. It is therefore continuous and differentiable everywhere. In particular, it is continuous on $[-2,2]$ and differentiable on $(-2,2)$. Therefore by the Mean Value Theorem, there is a c between -2 and 2 such that

$$f'(c) = \frac{f(2)-f(-2)}{2-(-2)}.$$

(3) Geometrically, $f'(c)$ is the slope of the tangent line to the graph of the function f at c, and $\frac{f(b)-f(a)}{b-a}$ is the slope of the secant line passing through the points $A(a, f(a))$, and $B(b, f(b))$.

The Mean Value Theorem says that the slopes of these two lines are the same. In other words, they are parallel.

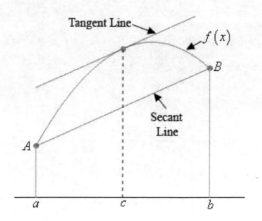

47. If $g(x) = -x^5 + \frac{1}{x} - \sqrt[3]{x} + \frac{1}{\sqrt{x^5}}$, then $g'(1) =$

(A) $-\frac{53}{6}$

(B) $-\frac{58}{15}$

(C) $\frac{58}{15}$

(D) $\frac{53}{6}$

Solution: $g'(x) = -5x^4 - x^{-2} - \frac{1}{3}x^{-\frac{2}{3}} - \frac{5}{2}x^{-\frac{7}{2}}$.

$g'(1) = -5(1)^4 - 1^{-2} - \frac{1}{3}(1)^{-\frac{2}{3}} - \frac{5}{2}(1)^{-\frac{7}{2}} = -5 - 1 - \frac{1}{3} - \frac{5}{2} = -\frac{53}{6}$.

So the answer is choice (A).

Notes: (1) $\frac{1}{x}$ can be written as x^{-1}. So $\frac{d}{dx}\left[\frac{1}{x}\right] = -1x^{-2} = -x^{-2}$.

(2) $\sqrt[3]{x}$ can be written as $x^{\frac{1}{3}}$. So $\frac{d}{dx}\left[\sqrt[3]{x}\right] = \frac{1}{3}x^{-\frac{2}{3}}$.

(3) $\frac{1}{\sqrt{x^5}} = \frac{1}{(x^5)^{\frac{1}{2}}} = \frac{1}{x^{\frac{5}{2}}} = x^{-\frac{5}{2}}$. So $\frac{d}{dx}\left[\frac{1}{\sqrt{x^5}}\right] = -\frac{5}{2}x^{-\frac{7}{2}}$.

(4) $1^a = 1$ for all real numbers a.

In particular, $1^4 = 1$, $1^{-2} = 1$, $1^{-\frac{2}{3}} = 1$, and $1^{-\frac{7}{2}} = 1$

(5) Although it is not needed in this problem, it is useful to be able to rewrite the following:

$$x^{-2} = \frac{1}{x^2}. \text{ So } -x^{-2} = -\frac{1}{x^2}.$$

$$x^{-\frac{2}{3}} = \frac{1}{x^{\frac{2}{3}}} = \frac{1}{\sqrt[3]{x^2}}. \text{ So } \frac{1}{3}x^{-\frac{2}{3}} = \frac{1}{3\sqrt[3]{x^2}}.$$

$$x^{-\frac{7}{2}} = \frac{1}{x^{\frac{7}{2}}} = \frac{1}{\sqrt{x^7}}. \text{ So } -\frac{5}{2}x^{-\frac{7}{2}} = -\frac{5}{2\sqrt{x^7}}.$$

(6) See problem 11 for a review of all of the laws of exponents you should know.

48. The *derivative* of $g(x) = \frac{x^7}{7} - \frac{x^6}{5}$ attains its minimum value at $x =$

(A) $\frac{7}{5}$

(B) $\frac{6}{5}$

(C) 1

(D) 0

Solution: $g'(x) = x^6 - \frac{6}{5}x^5$.

To minimize $g'(x)$ we first take its derivative

$$g''(x) = 6x^5 - 6x^4 = 6x^4(x - 1).$$

We then check when $g''(x)$ is equal to 0 to find the **critical numbers** of g'. The critical numbers of g' are $x = 0$ and $x = 1$.

Now note that for $x < 1$, $g''(x) < 0$, and for $x > 1$, $g''(x) > 0$. So g' is decreasing for $x < 1$ and increasing for $x > 1$. So g' attains its minimum value at $x = 1$, choice (C).

Notes: (1) A **critical number** of a function f is a real number c in the domain of f such that $f'(c) = 0$ or $f'(c)$ is undefined.

(2) A function f attains a **relative minimum** (or **local minimum**) at a real number $x = c$ if there is an interval (a, b) containing c such that $f(c) < f(x)$ for all x in the interval.

If a function is decreasing to the left of c, and increasing to the right of c, then f attains a relative minimum at c.

In terms of derivatives, if $f'(x) < 0$ for $x < c$, and $f'(x) > 0$ for $x > c$, then f attains a relative minimum at c.

This method of finding the relative extrema of a function is called the **first derivative test**.

(3) Take careful note that in this problem we are trying to minimize the *derivative* of g. So we need to be checking $g''(x)$ near $x = c$.

(4) A nice visual way to apply the first derivative test is by creating a **sign chart**. We split up the real line into intervals using the critical numbers of the function (and we also include any points of discontinuity if they exist), and then check the sign of the derivative in each subinterval formed.

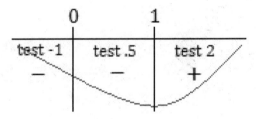

In this case we split up the real line into three pieces. Notice that the cutoff points are 0 and 1, the critical numbers of g'. We then plug a real number from each of these three intervals into g'' to see if the answer is positive or negative. For example, $g''(2) = 6(2)^4(2-1) > 0$. Note that we do not need to finish the computation. We only need to know if the answer is positive or negative. Finally, we make a quick sketch that decreases across the intervals where there is a minus sign, and increases across the intervals where there is a plus sign. We can then clearly see that there is a minimum at $x = 1$.

(5) The sketch of the graph in the sign chart is not meant to be completely accurate (and it is not). It is only being used to demonstrate where the function is increasing and decreasing, so we can determine if there is a minimum or maximum (or neither) at each critical number.

(6) Let's take a look at the expression $g''(x) = 6x^4(x - 1)$.

We see that $g'(x) = 0$ when $x = 0$ and $x = 1$. Note that $x = 0$ is a zero of the equation of multiplicity 4. In particular, it has even multiplicity. It follows that the graph of g'' *does not* pass through the x-axis at $x = 0$. In other words, g'' does not change sign there, and so a maximum or minimum *cannot* occur at $x = 0$.

On the other hand, $x = 1$ is a zero of multiplicity 1. In particular, it has odd multiplicity. It follows that the graph of g' *does* pass through the x-axis at $x = 1$. In other words, g'' does change sign there, and so a maximum or minimum *does* occur at $x = 1$.

(7) Based on the reasoning of note (6) we can get the answer to this question just by looking at the factored form of g''. Since $x = 1$ is the only zero with odd multiplicity, it is the only possible place where a minimum can occur. So the answer must be choice (C).

In other words, in this problem we do not actually need to perform the first derivative test (and in particular, we do not need to draw a sign chart). But it's not a bad idea to do so just to check your work.

LEVEL 2: INTEGRATION

49. $\int_0^2 \frac{3x^2 dx}{\sqrt{8-x^3}} =$

    (A) $-4\sqrt{2}$
    (B) $1 - 4\sqrt{2}$
    (C) $4\sqrt{2} - 1$
    (D) $4\sqrt{2}$

Solution:

$$\int_0^2 \frac{3x^2 dx}{\sqrt{8-x^3}} = -\int_0^2 \frac{(-3x^2)dx}{\sqrt{8-x^3}} = -\int_8^0 u^{-\frac{1}{2}} du = -2u^{\frac{1}{2}} \Big|_8^0 = -2\left(0^{\frac{1}{2}} - 8^{\frac{1}{2}}\right) = 2\sqrt{8} = 2 \cdot 2\sqrt{2} = 4\sqrt{2}.$$

This is choice (D).

Notes: (1) We made the substitution $u = 8 - x^3$, so that $du = -3x^2 dx$.

(2) Since the minus sign is missing (or equivalently, a factor of -1), we multiply by -1 inside and outside the integral. So we have

$$\int_0^2 \frac{3x^2\,dx}{\sqrt{8-x^3}} = -\int_0^2 \frac{(-3x^2)\,dx}{\sqrt{8-x^3}}.$$

When we replace $8 - x^3$ by u and $-3x^2\,dx$ by du we get

$$-\int_0^2 \frac{(-3x^2)\,dx}{\sqrt{8-x^3}} = -\int_8^0 \frac{du}{\sqrt{u}} = -\int_8^0 u^{-\frac{1}{2}}\,du.$$

Notice two things:

First, we changed the limits of integration. We get the new limits by noticing that when $x = 0$, we have $u = 8 - 0^3 = 8$, and when $x = 2$, we have $u = 8 - 2^3 = 8 - 8 = 0$.

Second, $\frac{1}{\sqrt{u}} = \frac{1}{u^{\frac{1}{2}}} = u^{-\frac{1}{2}}$.

(3) To integrate $u^{\frac{1}{2}}$ we use the power rule $\int u^n\,du = \frac{u^{n+1}}{n+1} + C$. In this case

we get $\int u^{-\frac{1}{2}}\,du = \frac{u^{\frac{1}{2}}}{\frac{1}{2}} + C = u^{\frac{1}{2}} \div \frac{1}{2} + C = u^{\frac{1}{2}} \cdot 2 + C = 2u^{\frac{1}{2}} + C.$

(4) $8^{\frac{1}{2}} = \sqrt{8} = \sqrt{4 \cdot 2} = \sqrt{4} \cdot \sqrt{2} = 2\sqrt{2}.$

(5) We can also evaluate the integral without making a formal substitution as follows:

$$\int_0^2 \frac{3x^2\,dx}{\sqrt{8-x^3}} = -\int_0^2 \frac{(-3x^2)\,dx}{\sqrt{8-x^3}} = -2(8 - x^3)^{\frac{1}{2}}\Big|_0^2 = -2\left(0^{\frac{1}{2}} - 8^{\frac{1}{2}}\right) = 4\sqrt{2}.$$

50. $\int_0^{\frac{\pi}{12}} \tan^2 3x\,dx =$

    (A) $4 - \frac{\pi}{4}$

    (B) $\sqrt{3} - \frac{1}{4}$

    (C) $\frac{4-\pi}{12}$

    (D) $\frac{12-3\pi}{4}$

Solution: $\int_0^{\frac{\pi}{12}} \tan^2 3x\,dx = \int_0^{\frac{\pi}{12}} (\sec^2 3x - 1)\,dx = \left(\frac{1}{3}\tan 3x - x\right)\Big|_0^{\frac{\pi}{12}}$

$= \left(\frac{1}{3}\tan\frac{\pi}{4} - \frac{\pi}{12}\right) - (0 - 0) = \frac{1}{3}(1) - \frac{\pi}{12} = \frac{4-\pi}{12}$, choice (C).

Notes: (1) $\cos^2 x + \sin^2 x = 1$ is the most important Pythagorean identity. Make sure you have this one memorized. You may also want to memorize the other two Pythagorean identities:

$$1 + \tan^2 x = \sec^2 x \quad \text{and} \quad \cot^2 x + 1 = \csc^2 x$$

The second Pythagorean identity can be derived from the first by dividing each side of the first equation by $\cos^2 x$ as follows.

$$\frac{\cos^2 x + \sin^2 x}{\cos^2 x} = \frac{1}{\cos^2 x}$$

$$\frac{\cos^2 x}{\cos^2 x} + \frac{\sin^2 x}{\cos^2 x} = \frac{1}{\cos^2 x}$$

$$1 + \tan^2 x = \sec^2 x$$

Similarly, the third Pythagorean identity is derived from the first by dividing each side of the first equation by $\sin^2 x$.

(2) In this problem we solve the second Pythagorean identity for $\tan^2 x$ to get $\tan^2 x = \sec^2 x - 1$. We then replace x by $3x$ to get

$$\tan^2 3x = \sec^2 3x - 1.$$

(3) Since $\frac{d}{dx}[\tan x] = \sec^2 x$, it follows that $\int \sec^2 x \, dx = \tan x + C$.

(4) To evaluate $\int \sec^2 3x \, dx$, we can formally make the substitution $u = 3x$. We then get $du = 3dx$. It follows that

$$\int \sec^2 3x \, dx = \frac{1}{3}\int \sec^2 3x \cdot 3dx = \frac{1}{3}\int \sec^2 u \, du = \frac{1}{3}\tan u + C = \frac{1}{3}\tan 3x + C.$$

51. $\int_1^3 \frac{x^2+x-1}{x^2} \, dx =$

    (A) -3

    (B) $\ln 3 - \frac{4}{3}$

    (C) $\ln 3$

    (D) $\ln 3 + \frac{4}{3}$

Solution: $\int_1^3 \frac{x^2+x-1}{x^2} \, dx = \int_1^3 (\frac{x^2}{x^2} + \frac{x}{x^2} - \frac{1}{x^2}) dx = \int_1^3 \left(1 + \frac{1}{x} - x^{-2}\right) dx$

$= (x + \ln|x| + x^{-1}) \big|_1^3 = \left(3 + \ln 3 + \frac{1}{3}\right) - (1 + 0 + 1) = \ln 3 + \frac{4}{3}$.

This is choice (D).

52. The solution to the differential equation $\frac{dy}{dx} = \frac{x^2}{y^4}$, where $y(3) = 0$, is

(A) $y = \sqrt[5]{\frac{5}{3}x^3 - 45}$

(B) $y = \sqrt[5]{\frac{5}{3}x^3 - 9}$

(C) $y = \sqrt[5]{\frac{5}{3}x^3} - 45$

(D) $y = \sqrt[5]{\frac{5}{3}x^3} - \sqrt[5]{45}$

Solution: We separate variables to get $y^4 dy = x^2 dx$. We then integrate both sides of this equation to get $\frac{y^5}{5} = \frac{x^3}{3} + C$.

Now we substitute in $x = 3$ and $y = 0$ to get $\frac{0^5}{5} = \frac{3^3}{3} + C$. So $C = -9$, and we have $\frac{y^5}{5} = \frac{x^3}{3} - 9$. We multiply each side of this equation by 5 to get $y^5 = \frac{5}{3}x^3 - 45$, and then we take the fifth root of each side of this last equation to get $y = \sqrt[5]{\frac{5}{3}x^3 - 45}$, choice (A).

Notes: (1) A **separable differential equation** (or separable **DE**) has the form $\frac{dy}{dx} = f(x)g(y)$. We can solve this type of differential equation by rewriting it in the form $\frac{1}{g(y)}dy = f(x)dx$. This is called **separating variables**. We then integrate each side to get $\int \frac{1}{g(y)}dy = \int f(x)dx + C$.

In this problem we have $f(x) = x^2$ and $g(y) = \frac{1}{y^4}$.

(2) The condition $y(3) = 0$ is called an **initial condition**. We can use the initial condition to find the constant C.

In this case we substitute in $x = 3$ and $y = 0$, and then solve for C.

(3) It is usually more efficient to find the constant C before solving for the dependent variable y.

(4) Note that when we substitute 3 in for x into the answer choices, only choices (A) and (D) yield $y = 0$. We can use this reasoning to eliminate choices (B) and (C).

53. Each of the following is an antiderivative of $\frac{(\ln x)^2 - 2}{x}$ EXCEPT

(A) $\frac{(\ln x)^3}{3} - \ln x^2$

(B) $\ln x - \ln x^2$

(C) $\frac{(\ln x)^3}{3} - 2\ln|x|$

(D) $1 - \ln x^2 + \frac{(\ln x)^3}{3}$

Solution: $\int \frac{(\ln x)^2 - 2}{x} dx = \frac{(\ln x)^3}{3} - 2\ln|x| + C = \frac{(\ln x)^3}{3} - \ln x^2 + C$

All answer choices have one of the two forms above except choice (B).

Notes: (1) $\frac{(\ln x)^2 - 2}{x} = \frac{(\ln x)^2}{x} - \frac{2}{x}$. So we integrate each of the two terms separately.

(2) To evaluate $\int \frac{(\ln x)^2}{x} dx$, we can formally make the substitution $u = \ln x$. It then follows that $du = \frac{1}{x} dx$. So we have

$$\int \frac{(\ln x)^2}{x} dx = \int (\ln x)^2 \cdot \frac{1}{x} dx = \int u^2 du = \frac{u^3}{3} + C = \frac{(\ln x)^3}{3} + C.$$

(3) With a little practice, we can evaluate an integral like this very quickly with the following reasoning: The derivative of $\ln x$ is $\frac{1}{x}$. So to integrate $\frac{(\ln x)^2}{x}$ we simply pretend we are integrating x^2 but as we do it we leave the $\ln x$ where it is. This is essentially what was done in the above solution.

Note that the $\frac{1}{x}$ "goes away" because it is the derivative of $\ln x$. We need it there for everything to work.

(4) You should know $\int \frac{1}{x} dx = \ln|x| + C$ (See problem 22 for details.)

It follows that $\int \frac{2}{x} dx = 2 \int \frac{1}{x} dx = 2\ln|x| + C$.

(5) Putting notes (1) through (4) together gives us

$$\int \frac{(\ln x)^2 - 2}{x} dx = \int \frac{(\ln x)^2}{x} dx - \int \frac{2}{x} dx = \frac{(\ln x)^3}{3} - 2\ln|x| + C.$$

(6) $n \ln x = \ln x^n$. So we have $2\ln|x| = \ln|x|^2 = \ln x^2$

(7) $|x|^2 = x^2$ because x^2 is always nonnegative.

(8) We can also solve this problem by differentiating the answer choices.

For example, looking at choice (A), we have

$$\frac{d}{dx}\left[\frac{(\ln x)^3}{3} - \ln x^2\right] = \frac{3(\ln x)^2}{3}\cdot\frac{1}{x} - \frac{1}{x^2}\cdot 2x = \frac{(\ln x)^2}{x} - \frac{2}{x} = \frac{(\ln x)^2 - 2}{x}.$$

This shows that we can eliminate choice (A), and a moment's thought allows us to eliminate choice (D) as well.

Let's look at choice (C) next. We have

$$\frac{d}{dx}\left[\frac{(\ln x)^3}{3} - 2\ln|x|\right] = \frac{3(\ln x)^2}{3}\cdot\frac{1}{x} - 2\cdot\frac{1}{x} = \frac{(\ln x)^2}{x} - \frac{2}{x} = \frac{(\ln x)^2 - 2}{x}.$$

So we can eliminate choice (C) and the answer must be choice (B).

(Note that $\frac{d}{dx}[\ln|x|] = \frac{1}{x}$.)

For completeness, let's differentiate the expression in choice (B).

$$\frac{d}{dx}[\ln x - \ln x^2] = \frac{1}{x} - \frac{1}{x^2}\cdot 2x = \frac{1}{x} - \frac{2}{x} = -\frac{1}{x}.$$

Since $-\frac{1}{x} \neq \frac{(\ln x)^2 - 2}{x}$, the answer is definitely choice (B).

54. $\int \frac{8}{1+x^2}\, dx =$

   (A) $8\ln(1 + x^2) + C$

   (B) $8x - \frac{8}{x} + C$

   (C) $8\tan^{-1} x + C$

   (D) $-\frac{16x}{(1+x^2)^2}$

Solution: $\int \frac{8}{1+x^2}\, dx = 8\int \frac{1}{1+x^2}\, dx = 8\tan^{-1} x + C$, choice (C).

Notes: (1) You should know the following basic inverse trig integrals:

$$\int \frac{1}{\sqrt{1-x^2}}\, dx = \sin^{-1} x + C$$

$$\int \frac{1}{1+x^2}\, dx = \tan^{-1} x + C$$

$$\int \frac{1}{|x|\sqrt{x^2-1}}\, dx = \sec^{-1} x + C$$

(2) If you already know the derivatives corresponding to each of the integrals given in note (1), then there is no need to memorize anything new. See problem 75 for the six inverse trig derivatives.

55. The area of the region bounded by the lines $x = 1$, $x = 4$, and $y = 0$ and the curve $y = e^{3x}$ is

(A) $\frac{1}{3}e^3(e^9 - 1)$

(B) $e^3(e^9 - 1)$

(C) $e^{12} - 1$

(D) $3e^3(e^9 - 1)$

Solution: $\int_1^4 e^{3x}\, dx = \frac{1}{3}e^{3x}\Big|_1^4 = \frac{1}{3}e^{12} - \frac{1}{3}e^3 = \frac{1}{3}e^3(e^9 - 1).$

This is choice (A).

Notes: (1) To compute the area under the graph of a function that lies entirely above the x-axis (the line $y = 0$) from $x = a$ to $x = b$, we simply integrate the function from a to b.

In this problem, the function is $y = e^{3x}$, $a = 1$, and $b = 4$.

Note that $e^x > 0$ for all x. So $e^{3x} > 0$ for all x. It follows that the graph of $y = e^{3x}$ lies entirely above the x-axis.

(2) Although it is not needed in this problem, here is a sketch of the area we are being asked to find.

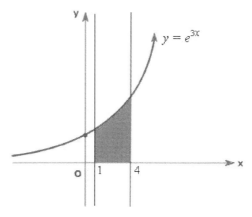

(3) To evaluate $\int e^{3x} dx$, we can formally make the substitution $u = 3x$. It then follows that $du = 3dx$.

67

We place the 3 next to dx where it is needed, and we leave the $\frac{1}{3}$ outside of the integral sign as follows:

$$\int e^{3x}\,dx = \frac{1}{3}\int e^{3x} \cdot 3\,dx$$

We now have

$$\int e^{3x}\,dx = \frac{1}{3}\int e^{3x} \cdot 3\,dx = \frac{1}{3}\int e^u\,du = \frac{1}{3}e^u + C = \frac{1}{3}e^{3x} + C.$$

We get the second equality by replacing $3x$ by u, and $3dx$ by du.

We get the third equality by the basic integration formula

$$\int e^u\,du = e^u + C.$$

And we get the rightmost equality by replacing u with $3x$.

(4) With a little practice, we can evaluate an integral like this very quickly with the following reasoning: The derivative of $3x$ is 3. So we artificially insert a factor of 3 next to dx, and $\frac{1}{3}$ outside the integral sign. Now to integrate $3e^{3x}$ we simply pretend we are integrating e^x but as we do it we leave the $3x$ where it is. This is essentially what was done in the above solution.

Note that the 3 "goes away" because it is the derivative of $3x$. We need it to be there for everything to work.

(5) If we are doing the substitution formally, we can save some time by changing the limits of integration. We do this as follows:

$$\int_1^4 e^{3x}\,dx = \frac{1}{3}\int_1^4 e^{3x} \cdot 3\,dx = \frac{1}{3}\int_3^{12} e^u\,du = \frac{1}{3}e^u\,\Big|_3^{12} = \frac{1}{3}e^{12} - \frac{1}{3}e^3.$$

Notice that the limits 1 and 4 were changed to the limits 3 and 12. We made this change using the formula that we chose for the substitution: $u = 3x$. When $x = 1$, we have $u = 3(1) = 3$. And when $x = 4$, we have $u = 3(4) = 12$.

Note that this method has the advantage that we do not have to change back to a function of x at the end.

56. A population of protozoa is growing at a rate of $400e^{\frac{5t}{2}}$ protozoa per second. At $t = 0$ seconds, the number of protozoa present was 160. Find the number present after 2 seconds.

(A) $320e^5$

(B) $160e^5$

(C) $160e^2$

(D) $80e^2$

Solution: If we let y be the number of protozoa present at time t, then we are given that $\frac{dy}{dt} = 400e^{\frac{5t}{2}}$. We integrate to get

$$y = \int 400e^{\frac{5t}{2}}\, dt = 400\left(\frac{2}{5}\right)e^{\frac{5t}{2}} + C = 160e^{\frac{5t}{2}} + C\,.$$

We now use the initial condition $y(0) = 160$ to get $160 = 160 + C$, so that $C = 0$, and $y = 160e^{\frac{5t}{2}}$.

The number of protozoa present after 2 seconds is $160e^{\frac{5\cdot 2}{2}} = 160e^5$. This is choice (B).

Notes: (1) Always be on the lookout for the word **rate**. The word "rate" generally indicates a derivative. The first sentence in this problem may as well just say "the derivative is $400e^{\frac{5t}{2}}$." Symbolically we write this as

$$\frac{dy}{dt} = 400e^{\frac{5t}{2}}$$

(2) To evaluate $\int e^{\frac{5t}{2}}\,dt$, we can formally make the substitution $u = \frac{5t}{2}$. It then follows that $du = \frac{5}{2}\,dt$.

Since there is no $\frac{5}{2}$ multiplying dt we place $\frac{5}{2}$ next to dt, and we place $\frac{2}{5}$ outside of the integral sign as follows:

$$\int e^{\frac{5t}{2}}\,dt = \frac{2}{5}\int e^{\frac{5t}{2}} \cdot \frac{5}{2}\,dt$$

We now have

$$\int e^{\frac{5t}{2}}\,dt = \frac{2}{5}\int e^{\frac{5t}{2}}\cdot\frac{5}{2}\,dt = \frac{2}{5}\int e^u\,du = \frac{2}{5}e^u + C = \frac{2}{5}e^{\frac{5t}{2}} + C.$$

57. What is $\lim\limits_{h \to 0} \dfrac{\tan\left(\frac{\pi}{4}+h\right)-\tan\left(\frac{\pi}{4}\right)}{h}$?

   (A) 0
   (B) 1
   (C) 2
   (D) The limit does not exist.

Solution 1: If we let $f(x) = \tan x$, then $f'(x) = \lim\limits_{h \to 0} \dfrac{\tan(x+h)-\tan(x)}{h}$. So

$f'\left(\frac{\pi}{4}\right) = \lim\limits_{h \to 0} \dfrac{\tan\left(\frac{\pi}{4}+h\right)-\tan\left(\frac{\pi}{4}\right)}{h}$.

Now, the derivative of $\tan x$ is $\sec^2 x$. So we have

$$\lim\limits_{h \to 0} \frac{\tan\left(\frac{\pi}{4}+h\right)-\tan\left(\frac{\pi}{4}\right)}{h} = f'\left(\frac{\pi}{4}\right) = \sec^2\left(\frac{\pi}{4}\right) = \left(\sqrt{2}\right)^2 = 2.$$

This is choice (C).

Notes: (1) The derivative of the function f is defined by

$$f'(x) = \lim\limits_{h \to 0} \frac{f(x+h)-f(x)}{h}$$

In this problem $f(x) = \tan x$, so that $f'(x) = \lim\limits_{h \to 0} \dfrac{\tan(x+h)-\tan(x)}{h}$

(2) See problem 9 for the basic trig derivatives. In particular,

$$\frac{d}{dx}[\tan x] = \sec^2 x.$$

(3) $\cos\left(\frac{\pi}{4}\right) = \frac{1}{\sqrt{2}}$. Therefore $\sec\left(\frac{\pi}{4}\right) = \dfrac{1}{\cos\left(\frac{\pi}{4}\right)} = 1 \div \frac{1}{\sqrt{2}} = 1 \cdot \sqrt{2} = \sqrt{2}.$

(4) $\sec^2\left(\frac{\pi}{4}\right) = \left(\sec\frac{\pi}{4}\right)^2 = \left(\sqrt{2}\right)^2 = 2.$

Solution 2: We use L'Hôpital's rule to get

$$\lim\limits_{h \to 0} \frac{\tan\left(\frac{\pi}{4}+h\right)-\tan\left(\frac{\pi}{4}\right)}{h} = \lim\limits_{h \to 0} \frac{\sec^2\left(\frac{\pi}{4}+h\right)}{1} = \sec^2\left(\frac{\pi}{4}\right) = \left(\sqrt{2}\right)^2 = 2.$$

This is choice (C).

Note: L'Hôpital's rule says the following: Suppose that

(i) g and k are differentiable on some interval containing c (except possibly at c itself).

(ii) $\lim\limits_{h \to c} g(h) = \lim\limits_{h \to c} k(h) = 0$ or $\lim\limits_{h \to c} g(h) = \lim\limits_{h \to c} k(h) = \pm\infty$

(iii) $\lim\limits_{h \to c} \frac{g'(h)}{k'(h)}$ exists, and

(iv) $k'(h) \neq 0$ for all x in the interval (except possibly at c itself).

Then $\lim\limits_{h \to c} \frac{g(h)}{k(h)} = \lim\limits_{h \to c} \frac{g'(h)}{k'(h)}$.

In this problem $g(h) = \tan\left(\frac{\pi}{4} + h\right) - \tan\left(\frac{\pi}{4}\right)$ and $k(h) = h$.

   58.   What is $\lim\limits_{x \to \infty} \frac{5 - x^2 + 3x^3}{x^3 - 2x + 3}$?

   (A) 1

   (B) $\frac{5}{3}$

   (C) 3

   (D) The limit does not exist.

Solution: $\lim\limits_{x \to \infty} \frac{5 - x^2 + 3x^3}{x^3 - 2x + 3} = \lim\limits_{x \to \infty} \frac{3x^3}{x^3} = 3$, choice (C).

Notes: (1) If p and q are polynomials, then $\lim\limits_{x \to \infty} \frac{p(x)}{q(x)} = \lim\limits_{x \to \infty} \frac{a_n x^n}{b_m x^m}$ where we have

$$p(x) = a_n x^n + a_{n-1} x^{n-1} + \cdots + a_1 x + a_0 \text{ and}$$

$$q(x) = a_m x^m + a_{m-1} x^{m-1} + \cdots + a_1 x + a_0.$$

(2) If $n = m$, then $\lim\limits_{x \to \infty} \frac{a_n x^n}{b_m x^m} = \frac{a_n}{b_m}$.

(3) Combining notes (1) and (2), we could have gotten the answer to this problem immediately by simply taking the coefficients of x^3 in the numerator and denominator and dividing.

The coefficient of x^3 in the numerator is 3, and the coefficient of x^3 in the denominator is 1. So the final answer is $\frac{3}{1} = 3$.

(4) For a more rigorous solution, we can multiply both the numerator and denominator of the fraction by $\frac{1}{x^3}$ to get

$$\frac{5-x^2+3x^3}{x^3-2x+3} = \frac{\left(\frac{1}{x^3}\right)}{\left(\frac{1}{x^3}\right)} \cdot \frac{(5-x^2+3x^3)}{(x^3-2x+3)} = \frac{\frac{5}{x^3}-\frac{1}{x}+3}{1-\frac{2}{x^2}+\frac{3}{x^3}} \cdot$$

It follows that $\lim\limits_{x\to\infty} \dfrac{5-x^2+3x^3}{x^3-2x+3} = \dfrac{5\lim\limits_{x\to\infty}\left(\frac{1}{x^3}\right)-\lim\limits_{x\to\infty}\left(\frac{1}{x}\right)+\lim\limits_{x\to\infty}3}{\lim\limits_{x\to\infty}1-2\lim\limits_{x\to\infty}\left(\frac{1}{x^2}\right)+3\lim\limits_{x\to\infty}\left(\frac{1}{x^3}\right)} = \dfrac{5\cdot0-0+3}{1-2\cdot0+3\cdot0} = 3.$

(5) L'Hôpital's rule can also be used to solve this problem since the limit has the form $\frac{\infty}{\infty}$:

$$\lim\limits_{x\to\infty} \frac{5-x^2+3x^3}{x^3-2x+3} = \lim\limits_{x\to\infty} \frac{-2x+9x^2}{3x^2-2} = \lim\limits_{x\to\infty} \frac{-2+18x}{6x} = \lim\limits_{x\to\infty} \frac{18}{6} = 3.$$

Observe that we applied L'Hôpital's rule three times. Each time we differentiated the numerator and denominator with respect to x to get another expression of the form $\frac{\infty}{\infty}$.

59. $\lim\limits_{h\to0} \frac{1}{h} \ln\left(\frac{10+h}{10}\right)$ is equal to

(A) $\frac{1}{10}$

(B) 10

(C) e^{10}

(D) The limit does not exist.

Solution 1: If we let $f(x) = \ln x$, then

$$f'(x) = \lim\limits_{h\to0} \frac{\ln(x+h)-\ln(x)}{h} = \lim\limits_{h\to0} \frac{1}{h} \ln\left(\frac{x+h}{x}\right).$$

So $f'(10) = \lim\limits_{h\to0} \frac{1}{h} \ln\left(\frac{10+h}{10}\right)$.

Now, the derivative of $\ln x$ is $\frac{1}{x}$. So we have

$$\lim\limits_{h\to0} \frac{1}{h} \ln\left(\frac{10+h}{10}\right) = f'(10) = \frac{1}{10}, \text{ choice (A)}.$$

Notes: (1) The derivative of the function f is defined by

$$f'(x) = \lim\limits_{h\to0} \frac{f(x+h)-f(x)}{h}.$$

72

In this problem $f(x) = \ln x$, so that $f'(x) = \lim\limits_{h \to 0} \frac{\ln(x+h) - \ln(x)}{h}$.

(2) Recall that $\ln a - \ln b = \ln\left(\frac{a}{b}\right)$. So $\ln(x+h) - \ln(x) = \ln\left(\frac{x+h}{x}\right)$, and therefore $\frac{\ln(x+h) - \ln(x)}{h} = \frac{1}{h}[\ln(x+h) - \ln(x)] = \frac{1}{h}\ln\left(\frac{x+h}{x}\right)$.

(3) See the notes at the end of problem 8 for a review of the laws of logarithms.

Solution 2: We use L'Hôpital's rule to get

$$\lim_{h \to 0} \frac{1}{h}\ln\left(\frac{10+h}{10}\right) = \lim_{h \to 0} \frac{\ln\left(\frac{10+h}{10}\right)}{h} = \lim_{h \to 0} \frac{\left(\frac{1}{\frac{10+h}{10}}\right)\left(\frac{1}{10}\right)}{1} = \frac{1}{10}, \text{ choice (A)}.$$

Note: (1) See problem 25 or 57 for more information on L'Hôpital's rule.

(2) To apply L'Hôpital's rule we separately took the derivative of $g(x) = \ln\left(\frac{10+h}{10}\right)$ and $k(x) = h$.

(3) $g(x) = \ln\left(\frac{10+h}{10}\right)$ is a composition of the functions $\ln x$ and $\frac{10+h}{10}$. We therefore need to use the Chain Rule to differentiate it.

The first part of the Chain Rule gives us $\frac{1}{\frac{10+h}{10}}$.

For the second part, it may help to rewrite $\frac{10+h}{10}$ as $\frac{1}{10}(10+h)$. It is now easy to see that the derivative of this expression with respect to h is $\frac{1}{10}(0+1) = \frac{1}{10}$.

60. Let the function f be defined by $f(x) = \begin{cases} \frac{\tan x}{x}, & \text{for } x \neq 0. \\ 0, & \text{for } x = 0. \end{cases}$

Which of the following are true about f?

I. $\lim\limits_{x \to 0} f(x)$ exists.
II. $f(0)$ exists.
III. f is continuous at $x = 0$.

(A) None
(B) I only
(C) 1I only
(D) I and II only

73

Solution: $\lim\limits_{x\to 0} f(x) = \lim\limits_{x\to 0} \frac{\tan x}{x} = 1$. In particular, $\lim\limits_{x\to 0} f(x)$ exists. So I is true.

$f(0) = 0$ by the definition of f. So II is true.

Since $\lim\limits_{x\to 0} \frac{\tan x}{x} = 1 \neq 0 = f(0)$, f is *not* continuous at $x = 0$. So III is false.

The answer is therefore choice (D).

Notes: (1) f is a **piecewise defined function**. It is equal to $\frac{\tan x}{x}$ for nonzero values of x, and it is equal to 0 for $x = 0$.

(2) Two basic limits worth memorizing are

$$\lim\limits_{x\to 0} \frac{\sin x}{x} = 1 \text{ and } \lim\limits_{x\to 0} \frac{\tan x}{x} = 1.$$

(3) Each of the limits in note (2) is actually very easy to compute using L'Hôpital's rule. See problems 29 and 30 for details.

(4) A function f is continuous at $x = a$ if and only if

$$\lim\limits_{x\to a} f(x) = f(a).$$

In this problem $\lim\limits_{x\to 0} f(x) = 1$ and $f(0) = 0$. Since these two numbers disagree, f is not continuous at $x = 0$.

61. Let the function k satisfy $\lim\limits_{h\to 0} \frac{k(7+h)-k(7)}{h} = 12$. Which of the following must be true ?

    I. k is continuous at $x = 7$
    II. $k'(7)$ exists
    III. k' is continuous at $x = 7$

    (A) I only
    (B) II only
    (C) I and II only
    (D) I, II, and III

Solution: The equation $\lim\limits_{h\to 0} \frac{k(7+h)-k(7)}{h} = 12$ can be rewritten as $k'(7) = 12$. In particular $k'(7)$ exists so that II is true.

74

Since k is differentiable at $x = 7$, it must also be continuous at $x = 7$. So I is true.

There is nothing here to suggest that k' is continuous at $x = 7$. So III does not need to be true (coming up with a specific counterexample is difficult, but one is given in note (3) below).

Therefore, the answer is choice (C).

Notes: (1) Differentiability of a function always implies continuity of the function.

More precisely, if f is differentiable at $x = c$, then f must be continuous at $x = c$.

(2) By definition, $f'(x) = \lim\limits_{h \to 0} \dfrac{f(x+h)-f(x)}{h}$.

So $k'(7) = \lim\limits_{h \to 0} \dfrac{k(7+h)-k(7)}{h}$.

(3) **[Advanced Material]:** Let $k(x) = \begin{cases} (x-7)^2 \sin\frac{1}{x-7}, & x \neq 7 \\ 0, & x = 7 \end{cases}$

Then $k'(x) = \begin{cases} 2(x-7)\sin\frac{1}{x-7} - \cos\frac{1}{x-7}, & x \neq 7 \\ 0, & x = 7 \end{cases}$

Observe that $k'(7) = 0$ (see note (4) below) so that $k'(7)$ exists.

Also observe that $\lim\limits_{x \to 7} k'(x)$ does not exist, because as x approaches 7, $\frac{1}{x-7}$ tends toward $+$ or $-\infty$, and so $\cos\frac{1}{x-7}$ oscillates between -1 and 1. So k' is not continuous at $x = 7$.

(4) $k'(7) = \lim\limits_{h \to 0} \dfrac{k(7+h)-k(7)}{h} = \lim\limits_{h \to 0} \dfrac{h^2 \sin\frac{1}{h}-0}{h} = \lim\limits_{h \to 0} h \sin\frac{1}{h} = 0$

because $\lim\limits_{h \to 0} h = 0$ and $\sin\frac{1}{h}$ is bounded (this can be proved using the squeeze theorem – details are left to the interested reader).

62. $\lim\limits_{x \to 0} \dfrac{\sin 7x}{\sin 4x} = $

Solution: $\lim\limits_{x \to 0} \dfrac{\sin 7x}{\sin 4x} = \lim\limits_{x \to 0} \dfrac{7 \cdot 4x \sin 7x}{4 \cdot 7x \sin 4x} = \dfrac{7}{4}\lim\limits_{x \to 0} \dfrac{\sin 7x}{7x} \cdot \dfrac{4x}{\sin 4x}$

75

$$= \frac{7}{4} \left(\lim_{7x \to 0} \frac{\sin 7x}{7x} \right) \left(\lim_{4x \to 0} \frac{4x}{\sin 4x} \right) = \frac{7}{4} \left(\lim_{u \to 0} \frac{\sin u}{u} \right) \frac{1}{\left(\lim_{v \to 0} \frac{\sin v}{v} \right)} = \frac{7}{4} \cdot 1 \cdot \frac{1}{1} = \frac{7}{4}.$$

Notes: (1) Once again it is worth knowing $\lim_{x \to 0} \frac{\sin x}{x} = 1$.

(2) It is not hard to see that $x \to 0$ if and only if $4x \to 0$ if and only if $7x \to 0$. This is why we can replace x by $4x$ and $7x$ in the subscripts of the limits above.

(3) $\frac{\sin 7x}{\sin 4x}$ can be rewritten as $\frac{7 \cdot 4x \sin 7x}{4 \cdot 7x \sin 4x}$.

It follows that we can rewrite $\frac{\sin 7x}{\sin 4x}$ as $\frac{7}{4} \cdot \frac{\sin 7x}{7x} \cdot \frac{4x}{\sin 4x}$.

(4) Using the substitution $u = 7x$, we have

$$\lim_{7x \to 0} \frac{\sin 7x}{7x} = \lim_{u \to 0} \frac{\sin u}{u}.$$

Using the substitution $v = 4x$, we have

$$\lim_{4x \to 0} \frac{4x}{\sin 4x} = \frac{1}{\lim_{4x \to 0} \frac{\sin 4x}{4x}} = \frac{1}{\lim_{v \to 0} \frac{\sin v}{v}}.$$

(5) We can also solve this problem using L'Hôpital's rule as follows:

$$\lim_{x \to 0} \frac{\sin 7x}{\sin 4x} = \lim_{x \to 0} \frac{7 \cos 7x}{4 \cos 4x} = \frac{7(1)}{4(1)} = \frac{7}{4}.$$

63. $\lim_{x \to 11} \frac{x}{(x-11)^2} =$

Solution: The function $f(x) = \frac{x}{(x-11)^2}$ has a vertical asymptote of $x = 11$.

If x is "near" 11, then $\frac{x}{(x-11)^2}$ is positive. Therefore, $\lim_{x \to 11} \frac{x}{(x-11)^2} = +\infty$.

Notes: (1) When we substitute 11 in for x into $f(x) = \frac{x}{(x-11)^2}$, we get $\frac{11}{0}$. This is *not* an indeterminate form.

For a rational function, the form $\frac{a}{0}$ where a is a nonzero real number *always* indicates that $x = a$ is a vertical asymptote. This means that at least one of $\lim_{x \to a^-} f(x)$ or $\lim_{x \to a^+} f(x)$ is $+$ or $-\infty$. If both limits agree, then $\lim_{x \to a} f(x)$ is the common value. If the two limits disagree, then $\lim_{x \to a} f(x)$ does not exist.

(2) A nice visual way to find the left hand and right hand limits is by creating a **sign chart**. We split up the real line into intervals using the x-values where the numerator and the denominator of the fraction are zero, and then check the sign of the function in each subinterval formed.

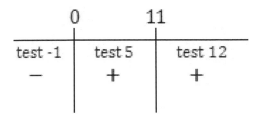

In this case we split up the real line into three pieces. Notice that the cutoff points are 0 and 11 because the numerator of the function is zero when $x = 0$, and the denominator of the function is zero when $x = 11$. We then plug a real number from each of these three intervals into the function to see if the answer is positive or negative. For example, $f(5) = \frac{5}{(5-11)^2} > 0$. Note that we do not need to finish the computation. We only need to know if the answer is positive or negative. Since there are + signs on both sides of $x = 11$, we have that $\lim\limits_{x \to 11} \frac{x}{(x-11)^2} = +\infty$.

(3) We actually do not care about the minus sign to the left of 0. We could have left that part out of the sign chart. It is however important that we include the zero as a cutoff point. This tells us that we can test any value between 0 and 11 to find $\lim\limits_{x \to a^-} f(x)$.

64. Let f be the function defined by

$$f(x) = \begin{cases} \dfrac{5e^{x-7}}{1 + \ln|x - 8|}, & x \le 7 \\ \dfrac{15\cos(x - 7)}{\sin(7 - x) + 3}, & x > 7 \end{cases}$$

Show that f is continuous at $x = 7$.

Solution:

$$\lim\limits_{x \to 7^-} f(x) = \frac{5e^{7-7}}{1 + \ln|7 - 8|} = \frac{5e^0}{1 + \ln 1} = \frac{5}{1+0} = 5.$$

$$\lim\limits_{x \to 7^+} f(x) = \frac{15\cos(7-7)}{\sin(7-7)+3} = \frac{15\cos 0}{\sin 0 + 3} = \frac{15(1)}{0+3} = \frac{15}{3} = 5.$$

So $\lim\limits_{x\to 7} f(x) = 5$.

Also, $f(7) = \dfrac{5e^{7-7}}{1+\ln|7-8|} = 5$. So, $\lim\limits_{x\to 7} f(x) = f(7)$.

It follows that f is continuous at $x = 7$.

LEVEL 3: PRECALCULUS

65. Let $t(x) = |\cos(x) + \frac{3}{2}|$. The minimum value attained by t is

(A) $-\dfrac{5}{2}$

(B) $-\dfrac{3}{2}$

(C) 0

(D) $\dfrac{1}{2}$

Solution: The graph of $y = \cos x$ oscillates between -1 and 1. In other words, $|\cos x| \leq 1$, or equivalently $-1 \leq \cos x \leq 1$.

Adding $\frac{3}{2}$, we have $\frac{1}{2} \leq \cos x + \frac{3}{2} \leq \frac{5}{2}$. So $\frac{1}{2} \leq \left|\cos x + \frac{3}{2}\right| \leq \frac{5}{2}$. In particular, the minimum value attained by $t(x) = |\cos(x) + \frac{3}{2}|$ is $\frac{1}{2}$, choice (D).

Notes: (1) Here is a sketch of the graph of $y = \cos x$:

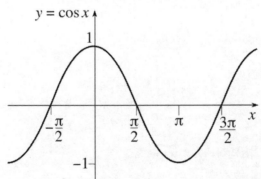

Note that the domain of $y = \cos x$ is $-\infty < x < \infty$. So the graph continues to oscillate between -1 and 1 as x goes to $-\infty$ and ∞.

(2) Since $\cos x + \frac{3}{2}$ is always positive (in fact, it is always *at least* $-1 + \frac{3}{2} = \frac{1}{2}$), it follows that $\left|\cos x + \frac{3}{2}\right| = \cos x + \frac{3}{2}$.

78

This is why we can simply replace $\cos x + \dfrac{3}{2}$ by $\left|\cos x + \dfrac{3}{2}\right|$ in the inequality given in the solution above.

66. For what value of k will the graphs of $y = 3x + k$ and $y^2 = 6x$ intersect in exactly one point?

Solution: We can find the points of intersection of the two graphs by substituting $3x + k$ in for y in the second equation to get

$$(3x + k)^2 = 6x$$
$$9x^2 + 6kx + k^2 = 6x$$
$$9x^2 + 6(k - 1)x + k^2 = 0$$

This quadratic equation has exactly one solution when

$$[6(k - 1)]^2 - 4(9)k^2 = 0$$
$$36(k^2 - 2k + 1) - 36k^2 = 0$$
$$36k^2 - 72k + 36 - 36k^2 = 0$$
$$-72k + 36 = 0$$
$$36 = 72k$$
$$k = \frac{36}{72} = \frac{1}{2} \text{ or } .5.$$

Notes: (1) The **discriminant** of the quadratic equation $ax^2 + bx + c = 0$ is $\Delta = b^2 - 4ac$.

(2) If $\Delta > 0$, the quadratic equation has two *distinct* real roots.

If $\Delta = 0$, the quadratic equation has *exactly* one real root.

If $\Delta < 0$, the quadratic equation has a pair of conjugate complex roots.

(3) In this problem we want the quadratic equation

$$9x^2 + 6(k - 1)x + k^2 = 0$$

to have exactly one real root. We therefore set the discriminant equal to 0.

$$\Delta = b^2 - 4ac = [6(k - 1)]^2 - 4(9)k^2.$$

67. Let $f(x) = 2x^3 - x^2 + 3x$ and $g(x) = x^3 + 4x^2 - 1$. Find the x-coordinates of all points common to the graphs of f and g.

Solution: We set $f(x) = g(x)$ to get $2x^3 - x^2 + 3x = x^3 + 4x^2 - 1$, or equivalently $x^3 - 5x^2 + 3x + 1 = 0$.

By observation we see that $x = 1$ is a zero of $x^3 - 5x^2 + 3x + 1$, and so we can factor $x^3 - 5x^2 + 3x + 1 = (x - 1)(x^2 - 4x - 1)$.

We set $x^2 - 4x - 1 = 0$ and solve for x to get $x = 2 \pm \sqrt{5}$.

So, the three x-coordinates are $1, 2 + \sqrt{5}$, and $2 - \sqrt{5}$.

Notes: (1) The **rational zeros theorem** says that if $\frac{m}{n}$ is a rational zero in reduced form of the polynomial $a_n x^n + a_{n-1} x^{n-1} + \cdots + a_1 x + a_0$, then m must divide a_0 and n must divide a_n.

If we look at the polynomial $x^3 - 5x^2 + 3x + 1$, then $a_0 = 1$ and $a_3 = 1$. So the only possible rational zeros of this polynomial are 1 and -1.

It is easy to see that 1 is *actually* a zero of this polynomial (a quick way to check if 1 is a zero of a polynomial is to simply check if the coefficients add up to 0).

(2) The **factor theorem** says that $x = r$ is a zero of a polynomial if and only if $x - r$ is a factor of the polynomial.

In this problem, we have discovered that $x = 1$ is a zero of the polynomial. It follows that $x - 1$ is a factor of the polynomial.

So $x^3 - 5x^2 + 3x + 1 = (x - 1)(ax^2 + bx + c)$ for some real numbers a, b, and c.

(3) There are several ways to figure out the polynomial $ax^2 + bx + c$. Here are two methods.

Method 1: Since $x \cdot ax^2 = x^3$, it follows that $a = 1$. Since $-1 \cdot c = 1$, it follows that $c = -1$. Finally, we must have $-ax^2 + bx^2 = -5x^2$. So $-1 + b = -5$, and $b = -4$. So the polynomial is $x^2 - 4x - 1$.

Method 2: We use **synthetic division**:

$$
\begin{array}{r|rrrr}
1 & 1 & -5 & 3 & 1 \\
  &   & 1 & -4 & -1 \\
\hline
  & 1 & -4 & -1 & 0
\end{array}
$$

The 1 in the upper left is the zero of the polynomial. We are dividing by $x - 1$. The top line consists of the coefficients of the polynomial $x^3 - 5x^2 + 3x + 1$.

We begin by bringing down the first 1.

$$1|1 \quad -5 \quad 3 \quad 1$$
$$\overline{1}$$

We now multiply this number by the zero in the upper left. So we have $(1)(1) = 1$. We place this number under the -5.

$$1|1 \quad -5 \quad 3 \quad 1$$
$$1$$
$$\overline{1}$$

Next we add -5 and 1.

$$1|1 \quad -5 \quad 3 \quad 1$$
$$1$$
$$\overline{1 \quad -4}$$

We repeat this procedure to get $(-4)(1) = -4$, then add 3 and -4 to get -1.

$$1|1 \quad -5 \quad 3 \quad 1$$
$$1 \quad -4$$
$$\overline{1 \quad -4 \quad -1}$$

Finally, we multiply $(-1)(1) = -1$, then add 1 and -1 to get 0.

$$1|1 \quad -5 \quad 3 \quad 1$$
$$1 \quad -4 \quad -1$$
$$\overline{1 \quad -4 \quad -1 \quad 0}$$

The bottom row gives the coefficients of the quotient which is a polynomial of 1 degree less than the dividend..

So the quotient polynomial is $x^2 - 4x - 1$.

(4) We can solve the equation $x^2 - 4x - 1 = 0$ by completing the square or using the quadratic formula.

Method 1: Here is the solution using the quadratic formula:

$$x = \frac{-b \pm \sqrt{b^2 - 4ac}}{2a} = \frac{4 \pm \sqrt{16 - 4(1)(-1)}}{2(1)} = \frac{4 \pm \sqrt{20}}{2} = \frac{4 \pm \sqrt{4 \cdot 5}}{2} = \frac{4 \pm \sqrt{4}\sqrt{5}}{2}$$

$$= \frac{4 \pm 2\sqrt{5}}{2} = \frac{2(2 \pm \sqrt{5})}{2} = \mathbf{2 \pm \sqrt{5}.}$$

Method 2: Here is the solution by completing the square:

$$x^2 - 4x = 1$$
$$x^2 - 4x + 4 = 1 + 4$$
$$(x - 2)^2 = 5$$
$$x - 2 = \pm\sqrt{5}$$
$$\mathbf{x = 2 \pm \sqrt{5}}$$

In the second line we added 4 to each side of the equation. We get 4 by taking the coefficient of x from the previous step (this is -4), halving this number $(-\frac{4}{2} = -2)$, and then squaring the result $((-2)^2 = 4)$.

Observe that the intermediate result (-2) tells us exactly how to factor in the third line.

In the fourth line we used the **square root property** which says that if $b^2 = a$, then $b = \pm\sqrt{a}$.

68. Find the domain of $k(x) = \frac{1}{\sqrt{x^2-4x-5}}$.

Solution: We need $x^2 - 4x - 5 > 0$, ie. we need $(x - 5)(x + 1) > 0$.

This happens when $x < -1$ or $x > 5$. So the domain of k is

$$(-\infty, -1) \cup (5, \infty).$$

Notes: (1) There are two possible "issues" with the function k.

First, there is a denominator that must be nonzero. So we must have $\sqrt{x^2 - 4x - 5} \neq 0$, or equivalently $x^2 - 4x - 5 \neq 0$.

Second, there is a square root. The expression under the square root must be nonnegative. So we must have $x^2 - 4x - 5 \geq 0$.

Putting these two results together, we must have $x^2 - 4x - 5 > 0$.

(2) $x^2 - 4x - 5 = (x - 5)(x + 1)$.

So we must have $(x - 5)(x + 1) > 0$.

(3) There is a nice **geometric method** for solving the inequality

$$(x - 5)(x + 1) > 0.$$

82

We begin by solving the corresponding equation $(x - 5)(x + 1) = 0$ to get the two solutions $x = 5$ and $x = -1$. We now make a **sign chart**, splitting up the real line into intervals using these two x-values. We then check the sign of the function in each subinterval formed.

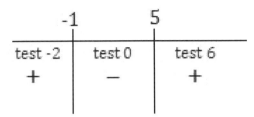

In this case we split up the real line into three pieces. We then plug a real number from each of these three intervals into the expression to see if the answer is positive or negative. For example, $(0 - 5)(0 + 1) < 0$. Note that we do not need to finish the computation. We only need to know if the answer is positive or negative. From this we see $(x - 5)(x + 1) > 0$ when $x < -1$ or $x > 5$.

(4) Here is an alternative **algebraic method** for solving the inequality

$$(x - 5)(x + 1) > 0.$$

A product of two factors is positive if both factors are positive or both factors are negatives. So we must have

$$x - 5 > 0 \text{ and } x + 1 > 0 \qquad \text{or} \qquad x - 5 < 0 \text{ and } x + 1 < 0$$

$$x > 5 \text{ and } x > -1 \qquad \text{or} \qquad x < 5 \text{ and } x < -1$$

$$x > 5 \qquad \qquad \text{or} \qquad \qquad x < -1$$

Note that if $x > 5$ and $x > -1$, then we simply have $x > 5$ because $5 > -1$.

Similarly, "$x < 5$ and $x < -1$" is equivalent to $x < -1$.

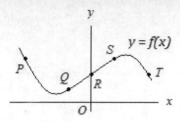

69. At which of the five points on the graph in the figure above is $\frac{dy}{dx}$ negative and $\frac{d^2y}{dx^2}$ positive?

(A) P
(B) Q
(C) S
(D) T

Solution: $\frac{dy}{dx}$ is negative precisely when the graph of y is decreasing, and $\frac{d^2y}{dx^2}$ is positive precisely when the graph of y is concave up. So the answer is point P, choice (A).

Note: For a differentiable function $y = f(x)$,

- $\frac{dy}{dx} > 0$ if and only if the graph of y is increasing.

- $\frac{dy}{dx} < 0$ if and only if the graph of y is decreasing.

- $\frac{d^2y}{dx^2} > 0$ if and only if the graph of y is concave up.

- $\frac{d^2y}{dx^2} < 0$ if and only if the graph of y is concave down.

For point Q we have $\frac{dy}{dx} > 0$ and $\frac{d^2y}{dx^2} > 0$.

For point R we have $\frac{dy}{dx} > 0$ and $\frac{d^2y}{dx^2} = 0$. This point is a **point of inflection** for the graph of y because the graph changes concavity at this point.

For point S we have $\frac{dy}{dx} > 0$ and $\frac{d^2y}{dx^2} < 0$.

For point T we have $\frac{dy}{dx} < 0$ and $\frac{d^2y}{dx^2} < 0$.

70. Given the function defined by $f(x) = 5x^3 - 3x^5$, find all values of x for which the graph of f is concave down.

(A) $-\frac{\sqrt{2}}{2} < x < \frac{\sqrt{2}}{2}$

(B) $x > \frac{\sqrt{2}}{2}$

(C) $-\frac{1}{2} < x < 0$ or $x > \frac{1}{2}$

(D) $-\frac{\sqrt{2}}{2} < x < 0$ or $x > \frac{\sqrt{2}}{2}$

Solution: $f'(x) = 15x^2 - 15x^4$ and

$$f''(x) = 30x - 60x^3 = 30x(1 - 2x^2).$$

The second derivative is 0 when $x = 0$ and $1 - 2x^2 = 0$. We solve this last equation for x to get $2x^2 = 1$, or $x^2 = \frac{1}{2}$, or $x = \pm\frac{1}{\sqrt{2}} = \pm\frac{\sqrt{2}}{2}$

Let's draw a sign chart for f'':

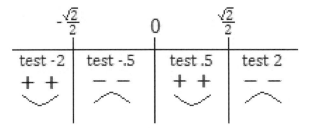

In this case we split up the real line into four pieces. Notice that the cutoff points are $-\frac{\sqrt{2}}{2}$, 0 and $\frac{\sqrt{2}}{2}$, the x-values where $f''(x) = 0$. We then plug a real number from each of these four intervals into f'' to see if the answer is positive or negative. For example, $f''(2) = 30(2)(1 - 2(2)^2) < 0$.

Note that we do not need to finish the computation. We only need to know if the answer is positive or negative. Whenever the answer comes out positive we draw a smiley face with plus signs for eyes. Whenever the answer comes out negative we draw a frowny face with minus signs for eyes. This way we can see the correct concavity right inside the sign chart.

We can then clearly see that the function is concave down when $-\frac{\sqrt{2}}{2} < x < 0$ or $x > \frac{\sqrt{2}}{2}$. This is choice (D).

Notes: (1) In the sign chart above, we drew two plus signs (or two minus signs) for visual purposes only (so that we could draw a face). There is no other reason.

(2) Always remember "positive people are happy, and negative people are sad." This will help you to remember to draw a smiley face with the plus signs, and a frowny face with the minus signs.

(3) When the second derivative of a function is positive, the graph of the function is concave up.

(4) When the second derivative is negative, the graph of the function is concave down.

(5) A point at which a function changes concavity is called a **point of inflection**. In this problem there are three points of inflection. They occur when $x = -\frac{\sqrt{2}}{2}$, $x = 0$, and $x = \frac{\sqrt{2}}{2}$.

(6) At a point of inflection, the second derivative of the function is either 0 or undefined.

(7) If the second derivative of a function is 0 or undefined at $x = c$, then the function may or may not have a point of inflection there. Sometimes the function will change concavity there, and sometimes it will not.

(8) Since each of the three zeros of the second derivative have multiplicity 1 (odd multiplicity), it follows that a point of inflection occurs at each of them.

71. If the line $7x - 4y = 3$ is tangent in the first quadrant to the curve $y = x^3 + x + c$, then c is

   (A) $-\frac{1}{2}$

   (B) $-\frac{1}{4}$

   (C) $\frac{1}{4}$

   (D) $\frac{1}{2}$

Solution: The slope of the line $7x - 4y = 3$ is $\frac{7}{4}$, and the derivative of the given function is $y' = 3x^2 + 1$. So we must have $3x^2 + 1 = \frac{7}{4}$.

We subtract 1 from each side of this equation to get $3x^2 = \frac{7}{4} - 1 = \frac{3}{4}$. We divide by 3 to get $x^2 = \frac{1}{4}$. By the square root property, $x = \pm\frac{1}{2}$.

Since we want the first quadrant solution, we take $x = \frac{1}{2}$.

We substitute $x = \frac{1}{2}$ into the equation of the line to get

$$7\left(\tfrac{1}{2}\right) - 4y = 3.$$

So $4y = \frac{7}{2} - 3 = \frac{1}{2}$, and therefore $y = \frac{1}{2} \cdot \frac{1}{4} = \frac{1}{8}$. It follows that the point of tangency is $\left(\frac{1}{2}, \frac{1}{8}\right)$. We plug $x = \frac{1}{2}$ and $y = \frac{1}{8}$ into the equation for the curve and solve for c.

$$\tfrac{1}{8} = \left(\tfrac{1}{2}\right)^3 + \tfrac{1}{2} + c$$
$$\tfrac{1}{8} = \tfrac{1}{8} + \tfrac{1}{2} + c$$
$$c = -\tfrac{1}{2}$$

This is choice (A).

Notes: (1) One way to find the slope of the line $7x - 4y = 3$ is to put the equation into slope-intercept form by solving for y:

$$7x - 4y = 3$$
$$-4y = -7x + 3$$
$$y = \tfrac{7}{4}x - \tfrac{3}{4}$$

We can now see that the slope is $\frac{7}{4}$.

(2) The slope of a line in the general form $ax + by = c$ is $-\frac{a}{b}$.

In this problem $a = 7$ and $b = -4$, so that the slope is $-\frac{7}{(-4)} = \frac{7}{4}$.

(3) The derivative of a curve at a point is equal to the slope of the tangent line to the curve at that point. This is why we set the derivative equal to $\frac{7}{4}$.

72. Which of the following statements about the function given by $g(x) = x^6 + 4x^5$ is true?

    (A) The function has two relative extrema and the graph of the function has two points of inflection.

    (B) The function has one relative extremum and the graph of the function has two points of inflection

    (C) The function has two relative extrema and the graph of the function has one point of inflection.

    (D) The function has one relative extremum and the graph of the function has one point of inflection.

Solution: $g'(x) = 6x^5 + 20x^4 = 2x^4(3x + 10)$

$g''(x) = 30x^4 + 80x^3 = 10x^3(3x + 8)$

From the factored forms of these derivatives, we see that the function has one relative extremum and the graph of the function has two points of inflection. This is choice (B).

Notes: (1) The critical numbers of g are $x = 0$ and $x = -\frac{10}{3}$. Since $x = 0$ is a zero of g' of multiplicity 4 (even multiplicity), a relative extremum *does not* occur there. Since $x = -\frac{10}{3}$ is a zero of multiplicity 1 (odd multiplicity), a relative extremum *does* occur there.

(2) The zeros of g'' are $x = 0$ and $x = -\frac{8}{3}$. Since both of these zeros have odd multiplicity, a point of inflection occurs at each of them.

(3) You may want to draw sign charts for g' and g'' for practice and as an extra way to check your work.

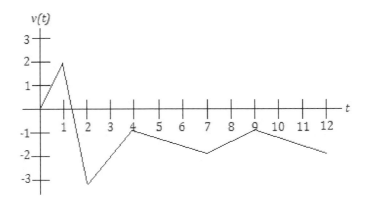

73. A fly is walking along a straight piece of string. The velocity $v(t)$ of the fly at time t, $0 \le t \le 12$, is given in the graph above. According to the graph, at what time t is the speed of the fly greatest?

(A) 1
(B) 1.4
(C) 2
(D) 4

Solution: The speed is the absolute value of the velocity. So the speed is greatest at $t = 2$, choice (C).

Notes: (1) From the graph we see that $v(1) = 2$ and $v(2) = -3$.

(2) The velocity is greatest at time $t = 1$, and the velocity is smallest at $t = 2$. The maximum velocity is 2 and the minimum velocity is -3.

(3) Let's suppose that the string is stretched out in front of us. We can imagine that when the fly is walking along the string to the right that he is moving in the positive direction, and when the fly is walking along the string to the left that he is moving in the negative direction.

From time $t = 0$ to time $t = 1$, the fly is walking to the right and speeding up. He then slows down from $t = 1$ to approximately $t = 1.3$ at which point he changes direction. From time $t = 1.3$ to time $t = 2$, the fly is walking to the left and speeding up. He then slows down from $t = 2$ to $t = 4$ at which point he begins speeding up again.

Note that after time $t = 1.3$, the fly is walking to the left for the duration of his trip.

(4) The speed of the fly at time $t = 1$ is 2, and the speed of the fly at time $t = 2$ is 3.

At time $t = 1$ he is walking to the right, and at time $t = 2$ he is walking to the left.

74. If $g(x) = x^{\frac{1}{3}}(x + 3)^{\frac{1}{2}}$ for all x, then the domain of g' is

(A) $\{x \mid x$ is a real number$\}$
(B) $\{x \mid x \neq 0\}$
(C) $\{x \mid x \neq 0$ and $x \neq 2\}$
(D) $\{x \mid x > -3$ and $x \neq 0\}$

Solution: $g'(x) = x^{\frac{1}{3}} \cdot \frac{1}{2}(x + 3)^{-\frac{1}{2}} + (x + 3)^{\frac{1}{2}} \cdot \frac{1}{3}x^{-\frac{2}{3}}$.

From the form of the derivative, we see that x cannot be equal to 0, and we must have $x + 3 > 0$, or equivalently, $x > -3$.

So the answer is choice (D).

Notes: (1) $x^{\frac{1}{3}} = \sqrt[3]{x}$

(2) $(x + 3)^{\frac{1}{2}} = \sqrt{x + 3}$

(3) $(x + 3)^{-\frac{1}{2}} = \dfrac{1}{(x+3)^{\frac{1}{2}}} = \dfrac{1}{\sqrt{x+3}}$

(4) $x^{-\frac{2}{3}} = \dfrac{1}{x^{\frac{2}{3}}} = \dfrac{1}{\sqrt[3]{x^2}}$.

(5) Using the previous notes, we can rewrite g' as $g'(x) = \dfrac{\sqrt[3]{x}}{2\sqrt{x+3}} + \dfrac{\sqrt{x+3}}{3\sqrt[3]{x^2}}$

(6) Denominators cannot be 0. So we must have $\sqrt[3]{x^2} \neq 0$, and this is equivalent to $x \neq 0$.

(3) Expressions under square roots (and in fact all even roots) must be nonnegative. So we must have $x + 3 \geq 0$. Since we have this square root in the denominator, it also cannot equal zero. So we must, in fact, have $x + 3 > 0$, or equivalently $x > -3$.

(5) Cube roots (and in fact all odd roots) do not cause any problems. So we do not need to worry about $\sqrt[3]{x}$.

75. $\frac{d}{dx}[\sin^{-1}(\frac{x}{2})] =$

(A) $-\frac{1}{\sqrt{4-x^2}}$

(B) $\frac{1}{\sqrt{4-x^2}}$

(C) $-\frac{1}{2\sqrt{1-x^2}}$

(D) $\frac{1}{2\sqrt{1-x^2}}$

Solution:

$$\frac{d}{dx}[\sin^{-1}(\frac{x}{2})] = \frac{1}{\sqrt{1-\left(\frac{x}{2}\right)^2}} \cdot \left(\frac{1}{2}\right) = \frac{1}{2 \cdot \sqrt{1-\frac{x^2}{4}}} = \frac{1}{\sqrt{4} \cdot \sqrt{1-\frac{x^2}{4}}} = \frac{1}{\sqrt{4\left(1-\frac{x^2}{4}\right)}} = \frac{1}{\sqrt{4-x^2}}.$$

This is choice (B).

Notes: (1) Note that $\sin^{-1} x$ is the same thing as $\arcsin x$. This is the *inverse* of the function $\sin x$, $-\frac{\pi}{2} \le x \le \frac{\pi}{2}$.

(2) This notation can actually be confusing. To see why I say this, note that $\sin^2 x$ is an abbreviation for $(\sin x)^2$. But $\sin^{-1} x$ is *not* an abbreviation for $(\sin x)^{-1} = \frac{1}{\sin x}$.

$\sin^{-1} x$ is the inverse function, whereas $(\sin x)^{-1}$ is the reciprocal of $\sin x$.

(3) You should know the derivatives of the six basic inverse trig functions:

$$\frac{d}{dx}[\sin^{-1} x] = \frac{1}{\sqrt{1-x^2}} \qquad \frac{d}{dx}[\csc x] = -\frac{1}{|x|\sqrt{x^2-1}}$$

$$\frac{d}{dx}[\cos^{-1} x] = -\frac{1}{\sqrt{1-x^2}} \qquad \frac{d}{dx}[\sec x] = \frac{1}{|x|\sqrt{x^2-1}}$$

$$\frac{d}{dx}[\tan^{-1} x] = \frac{1}{1+x^2} \qquad \frac{d}{dx}[\cot^{-1} x] = -\frac{1}{1+x^2}$$

(4) Let $f(x) = \sin^{-1}(\frac{x}{2})$. Then $f(x) = g(h(x))$, where $g(x) = \sin^{-1} x$ and $h(x) = \frac{x}{2}$.

To take the derivative of f requires the chain rule. We have

$$f'(x) = g'(h(x)) \cdot h'(x) = \frac{1}{\sqrt{1-\left(\frac{x}{2}\right)^2}} \cdot \left(\frac{1}{2}\right).$$

91

(5) To get from $\dfrac{1}{\sqrt{1-\left(\frac{x}{2}\right)^2}} \cdot \left(\dfrac{1}{2}\right)$ to the expression $\dfrac{1}{2\cdot\sqrt{1-\frac{x^2}{4}}}$ we simply multiplied the two numerators together ($1 \cdot 1 = 1$), and we multiplied the two denominators together ($\sqrt{1-\left(\frac{x}{2}\right)^2} \cdot 2 = 2 \cdot \sqrt{1-\frac{x^2}{4}}$).

(6) We would now like to move the 2 in the denominator inside of the square root. to do this we write $2 = \sqrt{4}$, and use the fact that for any nonnegative real numbers a and b, we have $\sqrt{a}\sqrt{b} = \sqrt{ab}$.

So we have $\dfrac{1}{2\cdot\sqrt{1-\frac{x^2}{4}}} = \dfrac{1}{\sqrt{4}\cdot\sqrt{1-\frac{x^2}{4}}} = \dfrac{1}{\sqrt{4\left(1-\frac{x^2}{4}\right)}}$.

(7) Finally, we distribute the 4 to get $4\left(1-\dfrac{x^2}{4}\right) = 4 - 4\left(\dfrac{x^2}{4}\right) = 4 - x^2$.

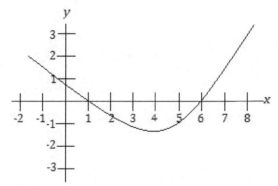

76. The **derivative** of g is graphed above. Give a value of x where g has a local minimum.

    (A) 0
    (B) 1
    (C) 4
    (D) 6

Solution: From the graph of g' we see that $g'(6) = 0$, so that $x = 6$ is a critical number of g.

We have $g'(x) < 0$ for x near 6 and to the left of 6, and $g'(x) > 0$ for x near 6 and to the right of 6.

It follows that $g(x)$ is decreasing for x a little less than 6, and $g(x)$ is increasing for x a little greater than 6. Therefore g has a local minimum at $x = 6$, choice (D).

Notes: (1) Recall that a **critical number** of a function f is a real number c in the domain of f such that $f'(c) = 0$ or $f'(c)$ is undefined.

The function g here has two critical numbers: $x = 1$ and $x = 6$.

(2) If a function is decreasing to the left of c, and increasing to the right of c, then f attains a local minimum at c.

In terms of derivatives, if $f'(x) < 0$ for $x < c$, and $f'(x) > 0$ for $x > c$, then f attains a local minimum at c.

This happens at $x = 6$.

(3) If a function is increasing to the left of c, and decreasing to the right of c, then f attains a local maximum at c.

In terms of derivatives, if $f'(x) > 0$ for $x < c$, and $f'(x) < 0$ for $x > c$, then f attains a local maximum at c.

This happens at $x = 1$.

(4) This method of finding the local minima and maxima of a function is called the **first derivative test**.

(5) Let's make a sign chart

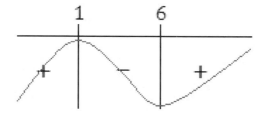

In this case we split up the real line into three pieces. Notice that the cutoff points are 1 and 6, the critical numbers of g. We then note that $g'(x) > 0$ for $x < 1$ and $x > 6$, and $g'(x) < 0$ for $1 < x < 6$ (just look at the given graph of g'). Finally, we make a quick sketch that decreases across the interval where there is a minus sign, and increases across the intervals where there is a plus sign. We can then clearly see that there is a local maximum at $x = 1$ (not needed in this problem) and a local minimum at $x = 6$.

(5) The sketch of the graph in the sign chart is not meant to be completely accurate. It is only being used to demonstrate where the function is increasing and decreasing, so we can determine if there is a minimum or maximum (or neither) at each critical number.

(6) Many students get confused about the distinction between g and g'. The graph that is given in the problem is the graph of g', the *derivative* of g, whereas the graph that we sketched in the sign chart gives the general shape of the graph of g.

Note that the graph of g in the sign chart is increasing precisely when the given graph of g' is above the x-axis, and the graph of g in the sign chart is decreasing precisely when the given graph of g' is below the x-axis.

The maximum and minimum points of g in the sign chart at $x = 1$ and $x = 6$, respectively, correspond to the zeros of g', ie. where the given graph of g' crosses the x-axis.

77. If $\sec(x^2 y) = y$, then $\frac{dy}{dx} =$

(A) $\dfrac{-2y \sec(x^2 y)}{1 - x \sec(x^2 y)}$

(B) $\dfrac{2xy \tan(x^2 y)}{\cos(x^2 y) - x^2 \tan(x^2 y)}$

(C) $\dfrac{1}{\sec(x^2 y) \tan(x^2 y)}$

(D) $\dfrac{1 - y \tan^2(x^2 y)}{x \tan^2(x^2 y)}$

Solution: We have

$$\sec(x^2 y) \tan(x^2 y) \left(x^2 \frac{dy}{dx} + 2xy \right) = \frac{dy}{dx}$$

$$x^2 \sec(x^2 y) \tan(x^2 y) \frac{dy}{dx} + 2xy \sec(x^2 y) \tan(x^2 y) = \frac{dy}{dx}$$

$$2xy \sec(x^2 y) \tan(x^2 y) = \frac{dy}{dx} - x^2 \sec(x^2 y) \tan(x^2 y) \frac{dy}{dx}$$

$$2xy \sec(x^2 y) \tan(x^2 y) = \frac{dy}{dx} (1 - x^2 \sec(x^2 y) \tan(x^2 y))$$

$$\frac{2xy \sec(x^2 y) \tan(x^2 y)}{1 - x^2 \sec(x^2 y) \tan(x^2 y)} = \frac{dy}{dx}$$

$$\frac{2xy\tan(x^2y)}{\cos(x^2y)-x^2\tan(x^2y)}=\frac{dy}{dx}$$

This is choice (B).

Notes: (1) The given equation defines the dependent variable y **implicitly** as a function of x. We therefore used implicit differentiation to find the derivative $\frac{dy}{dx}$. See problem 45 for more information on implicit differentiation.

(2) Recall that the derivative of $\sec x$ is $\sec x\tan x$.

To differentiate x^2y, we use the product rule to get $x^2\frac{dy}{dx}+2xy$.

We then used the chain rule to get the derivative of $\sec(x^2y)$.

(3) After differentiating we must solve for $\frac{dy}{dx}$.

We first distributed on the left as follows:

$$\sec(x^2y)\tan(x^2y)\left(x^2\frac{dy}{dx}+2xy\right)=x^2\sec(x^2y)\tan(x^2y)\frac{dy}{dx}+2xy\sec(x^2y)\tan(x^2y)$$

We then brought the term on the left with $\frac{dy}{dx}$ over to the right hand side of the equation, and then factored out $\frac{dy}{dx}$. This gave the following:

$$2xy\sec(x^2y)\tan(x^2y)=\frac{dy}{dx}(1-x^2\sec(x^2y)\tan(x^2y)).$$

We then got $\frac{dy}{dy}$ by itself by dividing by $1-x^2\sec(x^2y)\tan(x^2y)$:

$$\frac{2xy\sec(x^2y)\tan(x^2y)}{1-x^2\sec(x^2y)\tan(x^2y)}=\frac{dy}{dx}$$

Unfortunately, this expression doesn't look like any of the answer choices. This is easily fixed however by multiplying both the numerator and denominator by $\cos(x^2y)$.

Note that $\cos(x^2y)\sec(x^2y)=1$ (because $\sec(x^2y)=\frac{1}{\cos(x^2y)}$).

So we have

$$\frac{\cos(x^2y)[2xy\sec(x^2y)\tan(x^2y)]}{\cos(x^2y)[1-x^2\sec(x^2y)\tan(x^2y)]}=\frac{2xy\tan(x^2y)}{\cos(x^2y)-x^2\tan(x^2y)}.$$

Alternative solution using partial derivatives:

Let $F(x, y) = \sec(x^2 y) - y$. Then

$$\frac{dy}{dx} = -\frac{\frac{\partial F}{\partial x}}{\frac{\partial F}{\partial y}} = -\frac{\sec(x^2 y)\tan(x^2 y)(2xy)}{\sec(x^2 y)\tan(x^2 y)(x^2) - 1} = \frac{\sec(x^2 y)\tan(x^2 y)(2xy)}{1 - \sec(x^2 y)\tan(x^2 y)(x^2)}$$

$$= \frac{\tan(x^2 y)(2xy)}{\cos(x^2 y) - \tan(x^2 y)(x^2)} = \frac{2xy\tan(x^2 y)}{\cos(x^2 y) - x^2\tan(x^2 y)}.$$

This is choice (B).

Note: Partial differentiation is *not* an AP Calculus topic, and therefore a full explanation of this solution lies outside of the scope of this book.

78. A point moves in a straight line so that its distance at time t from a fixed point of the line is $2t^3 - 9t^2 + 12t$. The *total* distance that the point travels from $t = 0$ to $t = 4$ is

    (A) 32
    (B) 33
    (C) 34
    (D) 35

Solution: The velocity of the point is

$$v(t) = 6t^2 - 18t + 12 = 6(t^2 - 3t + 2) = 6(t - 1)(t - 2).$$

So the point might change direction at $t = 1$ and $t = 2$.

Let $s(t) = 2t^3 - 9t^2 + 12t$.

We have $s(0) = 0$, $s(1) = 5$, $s(2) = 4$, and $s(4) = 32$.

So the total distance traveled is

$$(5 - 0) + (5 - 4) + (32 - 4) = 5 + 1 + 28 = 34.$$

This is choice (C).

Notes: (1) A common mistake here would be to compute $s(4) - s(0)$. This gives the *total displacement* of the point. In other words it tells us how far the point is from its starting point ($t = 0$) at the time $t = 4$.

If the point is travelling to the right, and never changes direction, then this computation would give the correct answer. In this problem however the point *does* change direction.

(2) To find out when the point changes direction, we set the velocity $v(t) = s'(t)$ equal to 0.

In this case the position function is $s(t) = 2t^3 - 9t^2 + 12t$. It follows that the velocity function is $v(t) = s'(t) = 6t^2 - 18t + 12$.

(3) Just because $v(t) = 0$, it is not necessarily true that the point changes direction. For this particular problem it is not necessary to determine if the point actually changes direction, so we will *not* need to make a sign chart.

(4) Once we find out that the velocity is 0 at $t = 1$ and $t = 2$, we can just compute the distance traveled from $t = 0$ to $t = 1$, then from $t = 1$ to $t = 2$, and then from $t = 2$ to $t = 4$. Adding up these three distances gives us the total distance traveled by the point.

So we wish to compute

$$|s(1) - s(0)| + |s(2) - s(1)| + |s(4) - s(2)|.$$

The quickest way to do this is to first compute $s(0)$, $s(1)$, $s(2)$, and $s(4)$, then perform the three subtractions, dropping any minus signs, and finally adding up the three resulting distances.

79. * Two particles start at the origin and move along the x-axis. For $0 \le t \le 10$, their position functions are given by $x = \cos t$ and $y = \ln(2t) + 1$. For how many values of t do the particles have the same velocity?

  (A) None
  (B) One
  (C) Two
  (D) Three

Solution: $x' = -\sin t$ and $y' = \frac{2}{2t} = \frac{1}{t}$. We want to find out for how many values of t between 0 and 5 that $x' = y'$, ie. $-\sin t = \frac{1}{t}$. Now we use our graphing calculator. Make sure that your calculator is in radian mode (Press MODE and select Radian). Press Y= and next to Y_1 enter −sin X, and next to Y_2 enter 1/X. Then press WINDOW and set Xmin to 0 and Xmax to 10. Press GRAPH to display the graph (if you do not see the graph well, you may have to adjust Ymin and Ymax as well, perhaps Ymin = −2, and Ymax = 2).

You will see that the two graphs intersect three times, choice (D).

80. Consider the equation $x^2 + e^{xy} + y^2 = 2$. Find $\frac{d^2y}{dx^2}$ at $(0,1)$.

Solution: We differentiate implicitly to get

$$2x + e^{xy}\left(x\frac{dy}{dx} + y\right) + 2y\frac{dy}{dx} = 0$$

$$2x + xe^{xy}\frac{dy}{dx} + ye^{xy} + 2y\frac{dy}{dx} = 0$$

$$xe^{xy}\frac{dy}{dx} + 2y\frac{dy}{dx} = -2x - ye^{xy}$$

$$\frac{dy}{dx}(xe^{xy} + 2y) = -2x - ye^{xy}$$

$$\frac{dy}{dx} = \frac{-2x - ye^{xy}}{xe^{xy} + 2y}.$$

So we have $\frac{d^2y}{dx^2}$

$$= \frac{(xe^{xy}+2y)\left(-2-\left[ye^{xy}\left(x\frac{dy}{dx}+y\right)+e^{xy}\cdot\frac{dy}{dx}\right]\right)-(-2x-ye^{xy})\left(xe^{xy}\left(x\frac{dy}{dx}+y\right)+e^{xy}+2\frac{dy}{dx}\right)}{(xe^{xy}+2y)^2}$$

At $(0,1)$, we have $\frac{dy}{dx} = -\frac{1}{2}$, and so

$$\frac{d^2y}{dx^2} = \frac{(2)\left(-2-\left[1(1)+1(-\frac{1}{2})\right]\right)-(-1)\left(1+2(-\frac{1}{2})\right)}{2^2} = \frac{2\left(-2-\frac{1}{2}\right)+(0)}{4} = -\frac{5}{4}.$$

LEVEL 3: INTEGRATION

81. The area of the region in the first quadrant bounded by the graph of $y = x^2\sqrt{1 - x^3}$, the line $x = 1$, and the x-axis is

(A) $\frac{2}{9}$

(B) $\frac{2\sqrt{2}}{9}$

(C) $\frac{2\sqrt{3}}{9}$

(D) $\frac{4}{9}$

Solution: $\int_0^1 x^2\sqrt{1 - x^3}\, dx = -\frac{1}{3}\cdot\frac{2}{3}(1 - x^3)^{\frac{3}{2}}\Big|_0^1 = \frac{2}{9}$, choice (A).

Notes: (1) To compute the area under the graph of a function that lies entirely above the x-axis (the line $y = 0$) from $x = a$ to $x = b$, we simply integrate the function from a to b.

In this problem, the function is $y = x^2\sqrt{1 - x^3}$, $a = 0$, and $b = 1$.

Note that $x^2 \geq 0$ for all x, $\sqrt{1 - x^3} \geq 0$ for all x in the interval $[0,1]$, and therefore $x^2\sqrt{1 - x^3} \geq 0$ for all x in the interval $[0,1]$. It follows that the graph of $y = x^2\sqrt{1 - x^3}$ lies entirely above the x-axis for $0 \leq x \leq 1$.

(2) $x = 0$ and $x = 1$ are the only two zeros of $y = x^2\sqrt{1 - x^3}$.

(3) To evaluate $\int x^2\sqrt{1 - x^3}\,dx$, we can formally make the substitution $u = 1 - x^3$. It then follows that $du = -3x^2\,dx$.

Since there is no -3 multiplying $x^2\,dx$ we place -3 to the left of x^2, and we place $-\frac{1}{3}$ outside of the integral sign as follows:

$$\int x^2\sqrt{1 - x^3}\,dx = -\frac{1}{3}\int \sqrt{1 - x^3}(-3)x^2\,dx$$

We now have

$$\int x^2\sqrt{1 - x^3}\,dx = -\frac{1}{3}\int \sqrt{1 - x^3}(-3)x^2\,dx = -\frac{1}{3}\int \sqrt{u}\,du =$$
$$-\frac{1}{3}\int u^{\frac{1}{2}}\,du = -\frac{1}{3}\frac{u^{\frac{3}{2}}}{\frac{3}{2}} + C = -\frac{1}{3}\cdot\frac{2}{3}u^{\frac{3}{2}} + C = -\frac{2}{9}(1 - x^3)^{\frac{3}{2}} + C$$

We get the second equality by replacing $1 - x^3$ by u, and $-3x^2\,dx$ by du.

We get the fourth equality by applying the power rule for integrals

$$\int u^n\,du = \frac{u^{n+1}}{n+1} + C.$$

And we get the rightmost equality by replacing u with $1 - x^3$.

(4) With a little practice, we can evaluate an integral like this very quickly with the following reasoning: The derivative of $1 - x^3$ is $-3x^2$. So we artificially insert a factor of -3 next to x^2, and $-\frac{1}{3}$ outside the integral sign. Now to integrate $-3x^2\sqrt{1 - x^3}$ we simply pretend we are integrating $\sqrt{x}$ but as we do it we leave the $1 - x^3$ where it is. This is essentially what was done in the above solution.

Note that the $-3x^2$ "goes away" because it is the derivative of $1 - x^3$. We need it to be there for everything to work.

(5) If we are doing the substitution formally, we can save some time by changing the limits of integration. We do this as follows:

$$\int_0^1 x^2\sqrt{1-x^3}\,dx = -\frac{1}{3}\int_0^1 \sqrt{1-x^3}\,(-3)x^2dx = -\frac{1}{3}\int_1^0 \sqrt{u}\,du$$

$$= -\frac{1}{3}\cdot\frac{2}{3}u^{\frac{3}{2}}\Big|_1^0 = -\frac{2}{9}(0) - \left(-\frac{2}{9}\right)(1) = \frac{2}{9}.$$

Notice that the limits 0 and 1 were changed to the limits 1 and 0, respectively. We made this change using the formula that we chose for the substitution: $u = 1 - x^3$. When $x = 0$, we have $u = 1 - 0^3 = 1$. And when $x = 1$, we have $u = 1 - 1^3 = 0$.

Note that this method has the advantage that we do not have to change back to a function of x at the end.

82. A particle moves in a straight line with velocity $v(t) = t - \sqrt{t}$ beginning at time $t = 0$. How far is the particle from its starting point at time $t = 4$?

 (A) 0

 (B) 2

 (C) $\frac{8}{3}$

 (D) $\frac{40}{3}$

Solution: $\int_0^4 (t - \sqrt{t})dt = (\frac{t^2}{2} - \frac{2}{3}t^{\frac{3}{2}})\Big|_0^4 = 8 - \frac{16}{3} = \frac{24}{3} - \frac{16}{3} = \frac{8}{3}$

This is choice (C).

Notes: (1) The particle actually changes direction at time $t = 1$. To see this note that $v(1) = 0$, $v(t) < 0$ for $0 < t < 1$, and $v(t) > 0$ for $t > 1$.

We do not actually need to worry about the particle changing direction in this problem since we only want the particle's position relative to its starting point.

(2) If we know the velocity function v of a particle, then we can find its position function s by integrating the velocity v. That is $s(t) = \int v(t)dt$.

100

(3) $\int_a^b v(t)dt = s(b) - s(a)$ gives the distance between the position of the particle at time a and the position of the particle at time b.

(3) If we were asked to find the *total distance* traveled by the particle, then we would need to be more careful. In this case we would compute $\int_0^4 |t - \sqrt{t}| dt$. See problem 92 for an example like this.

83. The acceleration $a(t)$ of a body moving in a straight line is given in terms of time t by $a(t) = 3 - 2t$. If the velocity of the body is 10 at $t = 1$ and if $s(t)$ is the distance of the body from the origin at time t, then $s(5) - s(1) =$

(A) $\dfrac{10}{3}$

(B) $\dfrac{20}{3}$

(C) $\dfrac{40}{3}$

(D) $\dfrac{80}{3}$

Solution: $v(t) = \int a(t)dt = \int (3 - 2t)dt = 3t - t^2 + C$.

We are given that $10 = v(1) = 3(1) - 1^2 + C = 3 - 1 + C = 2 + C$. So $C = 10 - 2 = 8$. It follows that $v(t) = 3t - t^2 + 8$.

$s(5) - s(1) = \int_1^5 v(t)dt = \int_1^5 (3t - t^2 + 8)dt = \left(\frac{3}{2}t^2 - \frac{t^3}{3} + 8t\right)\Big|_1^5$

$= \left(\frac{3}{2}(5)^2 - \frac{5^3}{3} + 8 \cdot 5\right) - \left(\frac{3}{2}(1)^2 - \frac{(1)^3}{3} + 8 \cdot 1\right) = \frac{80}{3}$.

This is choice (D).

Notes: (1) s, v, and a are generally used for *position*, *velocity*, and *acceleration*, respectively.

(2) The velocity function is the derivative of the position function, and the acceleration function is the derivative of the velocity function.

That is $v(t) = s'(t)$ and $a(t) = v'(t) = s''(t)$.

In terms of integrals, $v(t) = \int a(t)dt$ and $s(t) = \int v(t)dt$.

84. The area of the region completely bounded by the curve $y = -x^2 + 2x + 5$ and the line $y = 2$ is

(A) $\frac{32}{3}$

(B) $\frac{24}{3}$

(C) $\frac{16}{3}$

(D) $\frac{8}{3}$

Solution: Let's draw a picture:

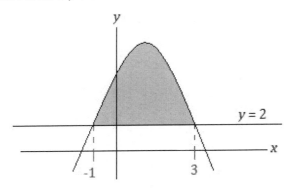

The area of the shaded region is

$$\int_{-1}^{3}[(-x^2 + 2x + 5) - 2]\, dx = \int_{-1}^{3}(-x^2 + 2x + 3)\, dx = \left(-\frac{x^3}{3} + x^2 + 3x\right)\Big|_{-1}^{3}$$

$$= \left(-\frac{3^3}{3} + 3^2 + 3 \cdot 3\right) - \left(-\frac{(-1)^3}{3} + (-1)^2 + 3(-1)\right) = \frac{32}{3}.$$

This is choice (A).

Notes: (1) The area between the curves $y = f(x)$ and $y = g(x)$ from $x = a$ to $x = b$ is $\int_{a}^{b}|f(x) - g(x)|\, dx$. The x-values a and b are usually the x-coordinates of points of intersection of the two graphs.

(2) If we are allowed to use our graphing calculator to solve this problem, we can simply graph the functions $f(x) = -x^2 + 2x + 5$ and $g(x) = 2$ in our calculator, use the intersect feature under the CALC menu to find that $a = -1$ and $b = 3$. We would then see that $f(x)$ lies above $g(x)$, and so we would compute $\int_{-1}^{3}[(-x^2 + 2x + 5) - 2]\, dx$.

We can do this last computation by hand (as was done in the solution above), or by using the integration feature in our calculator.

(3) If we cannot use a calculator, we can find a and b by setting $f(x)$ equal to $g(x)$. We have $-x^2 + 2x + 5 = 2$, so that

$$0 = x^2 - 2x - 3 = (x + 1)(x - 3).$$

This last equation has solutions $x = -1$ and $x = 3$. So $a = -1$ and $b = 3$.

(4) The graph of the quadratic function $q(x) = ax^2 + bx + c$ is a parabola with vertex at $x = -\frac{b}{2a}$. If $a > 0$, the parabola opens upwards. If $a < 0$, the parabola opens downwards.

In this problem we have that the graph of $f(x) = -x^2 + 2x + 5$ is a downward facing parabola with vertex at $x = -\frac{2}{2(-1)} = 1$.

The y-coordinate of this point is then $f(1) = -1^2 + 2(1) + 5 = 6$.

So the vertex of the parabola is the point $(1,6)$.

(5) Notes (3) and (4) allow us to sketch the region shown above without using a calculator.

85. Let f and g be continuous functions such that $f'(x) = g(x)$ for all x. It follows that $\int_a^b g(x)dx =$

   (A) $f(a) - f(b)$
   (B) $f(b) - f(a)$
   (C) $f'(a) - f'(b)$
   (D) $f'(b) - f'(a)$

Solution: $\int_a^b g(x)dx = \int_a^b f'(x)dx = f(x)\,\big|_a^b = f(b) - f(a).$

This is choice (B).

Notes: (1) The second Fundamental Theorem of Calculus says that if f is a Riemann integrable function on $[a, b]$, then $\int_a^b f(x)\,dx = F(b) - F(a)$ where F is any antiderivative of f.

(2) If a function f is continuous on $[a, b]$, then f is Riemann integrable on $[a, b]$.

(3) Since f is an antiderivative of f', by the notes above, we have

103

$$\int_a^b f'(x)dx = f(b) - f(a).$$

86. If $\frac{dy}{dx} = xy + 3y$ and if $y = 5$ when $x = 0$, then $y =$

(A) $5e^{x^2+3x}$

(B) e^{x^2+3x}

(C) $5 + e^{x^2+3x}$

(D) $4 + e^{x^2+3x}$

Solution: We have $\frac{dy}{dx} = xy + 3y = y(x + 3)$. We separate variables to get $\frac{dy}{y} = (x + 3)dx$. Now we integrate both sides of this equation to get $\ln|y| = x^2 + 3x + C$. We change to exponential form to get

$$|y| = e^{x^2+3x+C} = e^{x^2+3x} \cdot e^C.$$

So $y = \pm e^C \cdot e^{x^2+3x} = K \cdot e^{x^2+3x}$ where K is the constant $\pm e^C$.

Now we substitute in $x = 0$ and $y = 5$ to get $5 = K \cdot e^0 = K \cdot 1 = K$. So $K = 5$, and we have $y = 5e^{x^2+3x}$, choice (A).

Note: See problem 52 for more information on separable differential equations.

87. The average value of $\frac{1}{\sqrt{x}}$ over the interval $1 \le x \le 4$ is

(A) $-\frac{1}{2}$

(B) 0

(C) $\frac{1}{2}$

(D) $\frac{2}{3}$

Solution: $\frac{1}{4-1} \int_1^4 \frac{1}{\sqrt{x}} dx = \frac{1}{3} \int_1^4 x^{-\frac{1}{2}} dx = \frac{1}{3} \cdot 2x^{\frac{1}{2}} \Big|_1^4 = \frac{2}{3}(2 - 1) = \frac{2}{3}.$

This is choice (D).

Notes: (1) The **average value** of the function f over the interval $[a, b]$ is

$$\frac{1}{b-a} \int_a^b f(x)\, dx.$$

(2) $\frac{1}{\sqrt{x}} = \frac{1}{x^{\frac{1}{2}}} = x^{-\frac{1}{2}}$.

(3) $\int \frac{1}{\sqrt{x}} dx = \int x^{-\frac{1}{2}} dx = \frac{x^{\frac{1}{2}}}{\frac{1}{2}} + C = x^{\frac{1}{2}} \div \frac{1}{2} + C = x^{\frac{1}{2}} \cdot 2 + C = 2x^{\frac{1}{2}} + C$.

88. Given $h(x) = \begin{cases} \sin \pi x & \text{for } x < 0 \\ x^2 - x & \text{for } x \geq 0 \end{cases}$, we have $\int_{-2}^{1} h(x)dx =$

(A) $-\frac{1}{6} - \frac{1}{\pi}$

(B) $-\frac{1}{6}$

(C) $\frac{1}{6} - \frac{1}{\pi}$

(D) $\frac{1}{6}$

Solution: $\int_{-2}^{1} h(x)dx = \int_{-2}^{0} \sin \pi x \, dx + \int_{0}^{1} (x^2 - x)dx$

$= -\frac{1}{\pi} \cos \pi x \Big|_{-2}^{0} + \left(\frac{x^3}{3} - \frac{x^2}{2} \right) \Big|_{0}^{1} = \left(-\frac{1}{\pi} + \frac{1}{\pi} \right) + \left(\frac{1}{3} - \frac{1}{2} \right) = -\frac{1}{6}$.

This is choice (B).

Notes: (1) h is a **piecewise defined function**. It is equal to $\sin \pi x$ for negative values of x, and it is equal to $x^2 - x$ for nonnegative values of x.

(2) We have the following property of definite integrals:

$$\int_{a}^{b} f(x)dx = \int_{a}^{c} f(x)dx + \int_{c}^{b} f(x)dx$$

for any real number c between a and b.

In this question $a = -2$, $b = 1$, and $c = 0$. Between -2 and 0, we can replace $h(x)$ by $\sin \pi x$, and between 0 and 1, we can replace $h(x)$ by $x^2 - x$.

89. If $\int_{j}^{k} f(x)dx = k^2 - j^2$, then $\int_{j}^{k} (3f(x) - 2x)dx =$

(A) $k^2 - j^2$
(B) $2k^2 - 2j^2$
(C) $2j^2 - 2k^2$
(D) $3k^2 - 3j^2$

Solution: $\int_{j}^{k} (3f(x) - 2x)dx = 3 \int_{j}^{k} f(x) \, dx - 2 \int_{j}^{k} x \, dx$

$$= 3(k^2 - j^2) - \frac{2x^2}{2} \Big|_j^k = 3k^2 - 3j^2 - (k^2 - j^2) = 2k^2 - 2j^2.$$

This is choice (B).

90. If $\int_2^5 f(3x + k)dx = b$ where k and b are real numbers, then $\int_{6+k}^{15+k} f(x)dx =$

(A) $3b$

(B) b

(C) $\frac{b}{3}$

(D) $3b + k$

Solution: If we let $u = 3x + k$, then $du = 3dx$, and we have

$$b = \int_2^5 f(3x + k)\, dx = \frac{1}{3}\int_2^5 f(3x + k)\, 3dx = \frac{1}{3}\int_{6+k}^{15+k} f(u)\, du.$$

But in the expression $\frac{1}{3}\int_{6+k}^{15+k} f(u)\, du$, u is a dummy variable. So it is also equal to $\frac{1}{3}\int_{6+k}^{15+k} f(x)\, dx$.

So we have $\frac{1}{3}\int_{6+k}^{15+k} f(x)\, dx = b$, and so $\int_{6+k}^{15+k} f(x)\, dx = 3b$, choice (A).

91. * Calculate the approximate area under the curve $f(x) = x^2$ and bounded by the lines $x = 2$ and $x = 3$ by the trapezoidal rule, using three equal subintervals.

(A) 1.285

(B) 3.176

(C) 6.352

(D) 12.704

Solution: $\int_2^3 f(x)\, dx \approx \frac{1}{2} \cdot \frac{1}{3}\left[f(2) + 2f\left(\frac{7}{3}\right) + 2f\left(\frac{8}{3}\right) + f(3) \right]$

$$= \frac{1}{6}\left[4 + 2\left(\frac{49}{9}\right) + 2\left(\frac{64}{9}\right) + 9 \right] \approx 6.352$$

This is choice (C).

Notes: (1) The **trapezoidal rule** says

$$\int_a^b f(x)\, dx \approx \frac{1}{2} \cdot \frac{b-a}{n}[f(x_0) + 2f(x_1) + \cdots + 2f(x_{n-1}) + f(x_n)],$$

where the interval $[a, b]$ is partitioned into n equal subintervals with endpoints $a = x_0, x_1,...,x_{n-1}, x_n = b$.

In this problem, we have $a = 2$, $b = 3$, $n = 3$, and $f(x) = x^2$.

So $\frac{b-a}{n} = \frac{1}{3}$ is the length of each subinterval.

(2) Recall the formula for the area of a trapezoid: $A = (\frac{b_1+b_2}{2})h$. In other words we take the average of the bases times the height.

(3) Here is a picture of the trapezoidal rule being used in this problem:

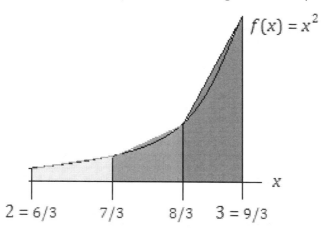

Note that all three trapezoids have a height of $\frac{1}{3}$ (the height runs along the x-axis).

The two bases of the leftmost trapezoid are $f(2)$ and $f(\frac{7}{3})$. It follows that the area of the leftmost trapezoid is $\frac{f(2)+f(\frac{7}{3})}{2} \cdot \frac{1}{3}$.

The two bases of the middle trapezoid are $f(\frac{7}{3})$ and $f(\frac{8}{3})$. It follows that the area of the middle trapezoid is $\frac{f(\frac{7}{3})+f(\frac{8}{3})}{2} \cdot \frac{1}{3}$.

The two bases of the rightmost trapezoid are $f(\frac{8}{3})$ and $f(3)$. It follows that the area of the rightmost trapezoid is $\frac{f(\frac{8}{3})+f(3)}{2} \cdot \frac{1}{3}$.

Finally, we get the area of the shaded region by adding these three areas:

$$\int_2^3 f(x)\,dx \approx \frac{f(2)+f\left(\frac{7}{3}\right)}{2}\cdot\frac{1}{3} + \frac{f\left(\frac{7}{3}\right)+f\left(\frac{8}{3}\right)}{2}\cdot\frac{1}{3} + \frac{f\left(\frac{8}{3}\right)+f(3)}{2}\cdot\frac{1}{3}$$

$$= \frac{1}{2}\cdot\frac{1}{3}\left[f(2) + 2f\left(\frac{7}{3}\right) + 2f\left(\frac{8}{3}\right) + f(3)\right].$$

92. A point moves in a straight line so that its velocity at time t is $2t^3 - 5t^2 + 2t$. What is the *total* distance that the point travels from $t = 0$ to $t = 3$?

Solution: The velocity of the point is

$$v(t) = 2t^3 - 5t^2 + 2t = t(2t^2 - 5t + 2) = t(2t - 1)(t - 2)$$

So the point might change direction at $t = \frac{1}{2}$ and $t = 2$.

$$\int v(t)\,dt = \int (2t^3 - 5t^2 + 2t)\,dt = \frac{t^4}{2} - \frac{5t^3}{3} + t^2 + C.$$

Let $x(t) = \frac{t^4}{2} - \frac{5t^3}{3} + t^2$.

We have $x(0) = 0$, $x\left(\frac{1}{2}\right) = \frac{7}{96}$, $x(2) = -\frac{4}{3}$, $x(3) = \frac{9}{2}$.

The total distance traveled by the point is

$$\int_0^3 |v(t)|\,dt = \left|x\left(\frac{1}{2}\right) - x(0)\right| + \left|x(2) - x\left(\frac{1}{2}\right)\right| + |x(3) - x(2)|$$

$$= \frac{7}{96} + \frac{45}{32} + \frac{35}{6} = \frac{117}{16}, \textbf{7.312 or 7.313}.$$

Notes: (1) A common mistake here would be to simply compute $\int_0^3 (2t^3 - 5t^2 + 2t)\,dt$. This gives the *total displacement* of the point. In other words it tells us how far the point is from its starting point ($t = 0$) at the time $t = 3$.

If the point is travelling to the right, and never changes direction, then this computation would give the correct answer. In this problem however the point *does* change direction.

(2) To find out when the point might change direction, we set the velocity $v(t)$ (the given function) equal to 0.

(3) Just because $v(t) = 0$, it is not necessarily true that the point changes direction. For this particular problem it is not necessary to determine if the point actually changes direction, so we will *not* need to make a sign chart.

(4) Once we find out that the velocity is 0 at $t = \frac{1}{2}$ and $t = 2$, we can just compute the distance traveled from $t = 0$ to $t = \frac{1}{2}$, then from $t = \frac{1}{2}$ to $t = 2$, and then from $t = 2$ to $t = 3$. Adding up these three distances gives us the total distance traveled by the point.

So we wish to compute

$$\left| x\left(\tfrac{1}{2}\right) - x(0) \right| + \left| x(2) - x\left(\tfrac{1}{2}\right) \right| + |x(3) - x(2)|.$$

The quickest way to do this is to first compute $x(0)$, $x\left(\tfrac{1}{2}\right)$, $x(2)$, and $x(3)$, then perform the three subtractions, dropping any minus signs, and finally adding up the three resulting distances.

(5) If we can use a calculator for this problem, we can compute $\int_0^3 |v(t)|\, dt = \int_0^3 |2t^3 - 5t^2 + 2t|\, dt$ using our TI-84 calculator by first selecting fnInt((or pressing 9) under the MATH menu, and then going to the MATH menu again, moving right once to NUM and selecting abs((or pressing 1). The display will show the following:

fnInt(abs(

We then type the following: fnInt(abs(2X^3 − 5X^2 + 2X), X, 0, 3), and press ENTER.

The display will show 7.312502794. So we can answer **7.312** or **7.313**.

LEVEL 3: LIMITS AND CONTINUITY

93. If $\lim_{x \to c} f(x) = f(\lim_{x \to c} x)$ for all c in the interval (a, b), which of the following *must* be true?

   (A) f is continuous on (a, b).
   (B) f is differentiable on (a, b).
   (C) f is a polynomial.
   (D) $f'(x) = 0$ for some $x \in (a, b)$.

Solution: $\lim\limits_{x \to c} x = c$. Therefore $f(\lim\limits_{x \to c} x) = f(c)$. So the given condition can be rewritten as $\lim\limits_{x \to c} f(x) = f(c)$. This is precisely the definition for f to be continuous at $x = c$.

Since we are given that this condition is true for all c in (a, b), the answer is choice (A).

94. Let f be defined by $f(x) = \frac{1}{\sqrt{17-x^2}} + \sqrt{x-3}$ for $-2 \le x \le 10$.

Let g be defined by $g(x) = \begin{cases} f(x) + 2 & \text{for } -2 \le x \le 4 \\ |x-8| & \text{for } \quad 4 < x \le 10 \end{cases}$

Is g continuous at $x = 4$? Use the definition of continuity to explain your answer.

Solution:

$$\lim_{x \to 4^-} g(x) = f(4) + 2 = \frac{1}{\sqrt{17-4^2}} + \sqrt{4-3} + 2 = 1 + 1 + 2 = 4.$$

$$\lim_{x \to 4^+} g(x) = |4 - 8| = |-4| = 4$$

So $\lim\limits_{x \to 4} g(x) = 4$.

Also, $g(4) = f(4) + 2 = 4$. So, $\lim\limits_{x \to 4} g(x) = g(4)$.

It follows that g is continuous at $x = 4$.

95. A 5000 gallon tank is filled to capacity with water. At time $t = 0$, water begins to leak out of the tank at a rate modeled by $R(t)$, measured in gallons per hour, where

$$R(t) = \begin{cases} \dfrac{300t}{t+1}, & 0 \le t \le 4 \\ 500e^{-0.5t}, & t > 4 \end{cases}$$

Is R continuous at $t = 4$? Show the work that leads to your answer.

Solution:

$$\lim_{t \to 4^-} R(t) = \frac{300(4)}{4+1} = 240.$$

$$\lim_{t \to 4^+} R(t) = 500e^{-0.5(4)} = 500e^{-2}$$

Since $\lim\limits_{t\to 4^-} R(t) \ne \lim\limits_{t\to 4^+} r(t)$, $\lim\limits_{t\to 4} R(t)$ does not exist.

It follows that R is *not* continuous at $t = 4$.

96. The function $g(x) = \dfrac{x^2+4x-12}{x^2+3x-10}$ has a removable discontinuity at $x = c$. Find c, and define a function G such that G is continuous at $x = c$ and $G(x) = g(x)$ for all x in the domain of g.

Solution: $g(x) = \dfrac{x^2+4x-12}{x^2+3x-10} = \dfrac{(x-2)(x+6)}{(x-2)(x+5)} = \dfrac{x+6}{x+5}$, $x \ne 2$.

So $\lim\limits_{x\to 2} g(x) = \dfrac{2+6}{2+5} = \dfrac{8}{7}$.

It follows that g has a removable discontinuity at $x = 2$. So $c = 2$.

Define G by $G(x) = \begin{cases} \dfrac{x^2+4x-12}{x^2+3x-10}, & x \ne 2 \\ \dfrac{8}{7}, & x = 2 \end{cases}$.

Notes: (1) If f is not continuous at $x = c$, then the discontinuity is **removable** if $\lim\limits_{x\to c} f(x)$ exists (and is a finite number). Otherwise the discontinuity is **nonremovable**.

In this problem $x = 2$ is a removable discontinuity of g because $\lim\limits_{x\to 2} g(x) = \dfrac{8}{7}$. On the other hand, $x = -5$ is a nonremovable discontinuity of g because $\lim\limits_{x\to -5} g(x)$ does not exist (see problem 63 for more information on how to compute this limit).

(2) If $x = c$ is a removable discontinuity of f, then we can **extend** f to a function F such that F is continuous at $x = c$, and $F(x) = f(x)$ for all x in the domain of f. We simply set $F(c) = \lim\limits_{x\to c} f(x)$, and we let $F(x) = f(x)$ for all $x \ne c$.

111

97. Suppose that f is an even function (so that $f(-x) = f(x)$ for all x), and that $f'(c)$ exists. Then $f'(-c)$ must be equal to

    (A) $f'(c)$

    (B) $-f'(c)$

    (C) $\dfrac{1}{f'(c)}$

    (D) $-\dfrac{1}{f'(c)}$

Solution: $f'(x) = f'(-x)(-1) = -f'(-x)$. So $f'(-x) = -f'(x)$, and therefore $f'(-c) = -f'(c)$, choice (B).

Notes: (1) We used the chain rule here. If we let $g(x) = f(-x)$, then g is the composition $g(x) = h(k(x))$, where $h(x) = f(x)$ and $k(x) = -x$.

So $g'(x) = h'(k(x)) \cdot k'(x) = f'(-x)(-1) = -f'(-x)$.

But we also have $g(x) = f(x)$, so that $g'(x) = f'(x)$.

Therefore $f'(x) = -f'(-x)$.

(2) We just showed that if f is an even function, f' is an odd function.

(3) It can also be shown that the derivative of an odd function is an even function.

(4) See problem 5 for more information about even and odd functions.

98. The function $g(x) = 10x^4 - 7e^{x-1}$, $x > \frac{1}{2}$ is invertible. The derivative of g^{-1} at $x = 3$ is

    (A) $-\dfrac{7}{e}$

    (B) $-\dfrac{e}{7}$

    (C) 1

    (D) $\dfrac{1}{33}$

Solution: First note that $g(1) = 10(1)^4 - 7e^{1-1} = 10 - 7 = 3$. It follows that $g^{-1}(3) = 1$.

Now, $g'(x) = 40x^3 - 7e^{x-1}$, so that

$$(g^{-1})'(x) = \frac{1}{g'(g^{-1}(x))} = \frac{1}{40y^3 - 7e^{y-1}}$$

where $y = g^{-1}(x)$.

So $(g^{-1})'(3) = \frac{1}{40(1)^3 - 7e^{1-1}} = \frac{1}{40-7} = \frac{1}{33}$, choice (D).

Notes: (1) Many students find it tricky to find the derivative of an inverse, but the procedure is fairly simple.

Suppose we want to find $(f^{-1})'(x)$. First find $f'(x)$. Then take the reciprocal to get $\frac{1}{f'(x)}$. Finally, replace x by $y = f^{-1}(x)$ to get $\frac{1}{f'(f^{-1}(x))}$.

Now the trickiest part comes when we need to plug in a value. We need to remember that to compute $(f^{-1})'(x)$ we plug in $f^{-1}(x)$, and not x. This is why we started the given problem by figuring out what $g^{-1}(3)$ was.

(2) The question "what is $g^{-1}(3)$?" is equivalent to "g of what is equal to 3?" Equivalently, we need to find x such that $g(x) = 3$.

Often in calculus problems on the AP exam, this value can be found fairly easily by simple observation, or guessing and checking simple numbers. In this example, it is not too hard to see that $g(1) = 3$, so that $g^{-1}(3) = 1$.

(3) If a calculator were allowed to be used for this problem, then we could solve the equation $g(x) = 3$ by graphing $y = 10x^4 - 7e^{x-1}$ and $y = 3$ in our graphing calculator, and using the intersect button to find the x-coordinate of the point of intersection.

Be careful to find the x-value that is greater than $\frac{1}{2}$, since this is the restriction placed on the given function (this was done to ensure that the function passes the horizontal line test, and therefore is invertible).

(4) Another notation that is used that some students find helpful is

$$\frac{dx}{dy} = \frac{1}{\frac{dy}{dx}}.$$

In this problem, $\frac{dy}{dx} = 40x^3 - 7e^{x-1}$.

So $\frac{dx}{dy} = \frac{1}{40x^3 - 7e^{x-1}}$.

But remember that we are plugging in 1 for x (and *not* the given value of 3). So we get $\frac{dx}{dy}\big|_{x=1} = \frac{1}{40(1)^3 - 7e^{1-1}} = \frac{1}{40-7} = \frac{1}{33}$.

99. The radius of a spherical balloon is decreasing at a constant rate of 0.5 centimeters per second. At the instant when the volume V becomes 288π cubic centimeters, what is the rate of decrease, in square centimeters per second, of the surface area of the balloon?

(A) 24π
(B) 48π
(C) 64π
(D) 72π

Solution: Recall that the volume of a sphere with radius r is $V = \frac{4}{3}\pi r^3$, and the surface area of a sphere with radius r is $S = 4\pi r^2$. We are given that $\frac{dr}{dt} = -0.5$, and we are being asked to find $\frac{dS}{dt}$ when $V = 288\pi$.

First note that when $V = 288\pi$, we have

$$288\pi = \frac{4}{3}\pi r^3$$
$$\frac{3}{4} \cdot 288\pi = \pi r^3$$
$$216 = r^3$$
$$6 = r$$

Now,

$$\frac{dS}{dt} = 8\pi r \cdot \frac{dr}{dt} = 8\pi r(-0.5) = -4\pi r.$$
$$\frac{dS}{dt}\big|_{r=6} = -4\pi(6) = -24\pi.$$

So the surface area of the balloon is decreasing at a rate of 24π cm^2/sec. Therefore, the answer is choice (A).

Notes: (1) Observe that one can get the formula for the surface area of a sphere by differentiating the formula for the volume of a sphere. This is just a little trick that can be used to reduce the number of formulas to memorize.

(2) Remember that the word *rate* generally indicates a derivative. "Increasing at a rate of" indicates a positive derivative, and "decreasing at a rate of" indicates a negative derivative.

(3) A radius is a length and is therefore measured in single units (in this case centimeters). Area (and in particular surface area) is measured in square units. Volume is measured in cubic units.

The type of units being mentioned usually gives a big hint as to what measurement is being given or asked for.

(4) This is a **related rates** problem. In a related rates problem we differentiate the independent and dependent variables with respect to a new variable, usually named t, for time.

(5) A *related rates* problem can be pictured as a *dynamic* (moving) process that gets fixed at a specific moment in time.

For this problem we can picture a sphere shaped balloon deflating. We then *freeze time* at the moment when the volume is 288π cm^3.

At this moment in time we want to know what the *rate of decrease* of the surface area is. The word "rate" indicates that we want the derivative of surface area with respect to time, $\frac{dS}{dt}$.

Don't forget to apply the chain rule when differentiating the right hand side. In this case, the derivative of r is $\frac{dr}{dt}$.

100. If $y = e^{kx}$, then $\frac{d^n y}{dx^n} =$

    (A) $n!\, e^{kx}$
    (B) $n^n e^{kx}$
    (C) $n^k e^{kx}$
    (D) $k^n e^{kx}$

Solution: Let's take the first few derivatives and look for a pattern:

$$\frac{dy}{dx} = k e^{kx}$$

$$\frac{d^2 y}{dx^2} = k(k e^{kx}) = k^2 e^{kx}$$

$$\frac{d^3 y}{dx^3} = k^2(k e^{kx}) = k^3 e^{kx}$$

...

That should be enough to see the pattern.

$\frac{d^n y}{dx^n} = k^n e^{kx}$. This is choice (D).

Notes: (1) See problem 12 for an explanation of how the chain rule is used to differentiate $y = e^{kx}$.

(2) In the equation $\frac{d^3 y}{dx^3} = k^3 e^{kx}$, observe how the exponent of k (which is 3) matches the derivative we are taking (the 3rd). So we can generalize this to an nth derivative by changing the power of 3 to a power of n.

101. For small values of h, the function $\frac{1}{\sqrt[3]{27+h}}$ is best approximated by

(A) $\frac{27-h}{81}$

(B) $\frac{81-h}{81}$

(C) $\frac{27-h}{243}$

(D) $\frac{81-h}{243}$

Solution: We are being asked to find the **linear approximation** of $f(x) = \frac{1}{\sqrt[3]{x}} = x^{-\frac{1}{3}}$ when $x = 27$. Well we have $f'(x) = -\frac{1}{3}x^{-\frac{4}{3}}$. So $f'(27) = -\frac{1}{3}(27)^{-\frac{4}{3}} = -\frac{1}{3} \cdot \frac{1}{81} = -\frac{1}{243}$.

Now,

$$f(x+h) - f(x) \approx f'(x) \cdot h$$
$$f(27+h) - f(27) \approx f'(27) \cdot h$$
$$\frac{1}{\sqrt[3]{27+h}} - \frac{1}{3} \approx -\frac{1}{243}h$$
$$\frac{1}{\sqrt[3]{27+h}} \approx \frac{1}{3} - \frac{1}{243}h = \frac{81}{243} - \frac{h}{243} = \frac{81-h}{243}.$$

This is choice (D).

Notes: (1) Recall the definition of the derivative:

$$f'(x) = \lim_{h \to 0} \frac{f(x+h)-f(x)}{h}$$

So for small values of h we have $f'(x) \approx \frac{f(x+h)-f(x)}{h}$. Equivalently,

$$hf'(x) \approx f(x+h) - f(x).$$

116

(2) Geometrically $f'(x)$ is the slope of the tangent line to the graph of f at the point $(x, f(x))$, whereas $\frac{f(x+h)-f(x)}{h}$ is the slope of the secant line passing through the points $(x, f(x))$ and $(x+h, f(x+h))$. For very small values of h these two slopes are *almost* the same. For a picture of this, see the figures in the notes following problem 102.

x	2.5	2.6	2.7	2.8
$f(x)$	7	7.4	7.7	7.9

102. Let f be a function that is concave down for all x in the closed interval $[2,3]$, with selected values shown in the above table. Which of the following inequalities must be true?

(A) $f'(2.7) > 3$
(B) $2 < f'(2.7) < 3$
(C) $1 < f'(2.7) < 2$
(D) $0 < f'(2.7) < 1$

Solution: Since f is concave down in the interval $[2,3]$, the tangent line to f when $x = 2.7$ lies above the graph of f in this interval.

So $f'(2.7) > \frac{f(2.8)-f(2.7)}{2.8-2.7} = \frac{7.9-7.7}{.1} = \frac{.2}{.1} = 2$.

Also $f'(2.7) < \frac{f(2.7)-f(2.6)}{2.7-2.6} = \frac{7.7-7.4}{.1} = \frac{.3}{.1} = 3$.

So $2 < f'(2.7) < 3$, choice (B).

Notes: (1) Here is a sketch of the graph of the function together with the tangent line to the graph at $x = 2.7$.

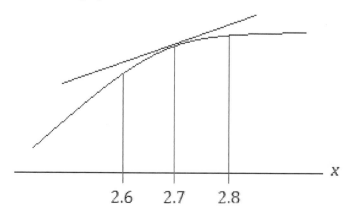

2.6   2.7   2.8

Observe that the graph is below the tangent line in the interval [2,3].

(2) Now let's also look at the secant line through the points (2.7,7.7) and (2.8,7.9).

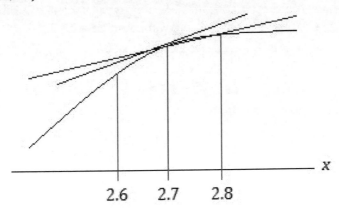

Notice that the tangent line has a greater slope than the secant line.

The slope of the tangent line is $f'(2.7)$, and the slope of the secant line is $\frac{f(2.8)-f(2.7)}{2.8-2.7}$. So we have $f'(2.7) > \frac{f(2.8)-f(2.7)}{2.8-2.7}$.

(3) Now let's also look at the secant line through the points (2.6,7.4) and (2.7,7.7).

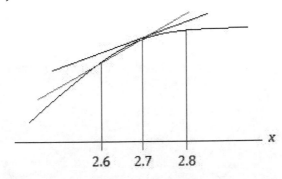

Notice that the tangent line has a smaller slope than the secant line.

The slope of the tangent line is $f'(2.7)$, and the slope of the secant line is $\frac{f(2.7)-f(2.6)}{2.7-2.6}$. So we have $f'(2.7) < \frac{f(2.7)-f(2.6)}{2.7-2.6}$.

103. Consider the differential equation $\frac{dy}{dx} = e^{y-1}(2x^3 - 5)$. Let $y = f(x)$ be the particular solution to the differential equation that passes through $(1,1)$. Write an equation for the line tangent to the graph of f at the point $(1,1)$, and use the tangent line to approximate $f(1.1)$.

Solution: The slope of the tangent line at $(1,1)$ is

$$m = \frac{dy}{dx}\Big|_{(1,1)} = e^{1-1}(2(1)^3 - 5) = e^0(2 - 5) = (1)(-3) = -3.$$

So an equation of the tangent line in point–slope form is

$$y - 1 = -3(x - 1).$$

When $x = 1.1$, we have $y - 1 = -3(1.1 - 1) = -3(.1) = -.3$.

So $y = -.3 + 1 = .7$.

It follows that $f(1.1) \approx .7$.

Notes: (1) To find the slope of the tangent line to a function $y = f(x)$ at a point (x_0, y_0), we take the derivative $\frac{dy}{dx} = f'(x)$, and substitute in x_0 for x and y_0 for y.

In this problem, we were already given $\frac{dy}{dx}$, and so we simply needed to substitute in the x-coordinate of the point for x and the y-coordinate of the point for y.

(2) The **point-slope form of an equation of a line** is

$$y - y_0 = m(x - x_0)$$

where m is the slope of the line and (x_0, y_0) is any point on the line.

It is generally easiest to write an equation of a line in point-slope form once the slope of the line and a point on the line are known.

In this problem, the slope is -3 and the point is $(1,1)$.

t (minutes)	0	1	2	3	4
$G(t)$ (pints)	0	2.2	4.5	6.8	8.3

104. Gasoline is dripping out of a gas pump, filling up a bucket. The amount of gasoline in the bucket at time t, $0 \leq t \leq 4$, is given by a differentiable function G, where t is measured in minutes. Selected values of $G(t)$, measured in pints, are given in the table above. Is there a time t, $1 \leq t \leq 3$, at which $G'(t) = 2.3$? Justify your answer.

Solution: Since G is differentiable, it follows that G is continuous on $[1,3]$.

We have $\frac{G(3)-G(1)}{3-1} = \frac{6.8-2.2}{2} = 2.3.$

By the Mean Value Theorem, there is at least one time t, $1 < t < 3$, for which $G'(t) = 2.3$.

Note: See problem 46 for more information on the Mean Value Theorem.

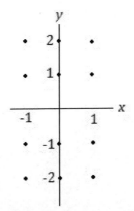

105. Consider the differential equation $\frac{dy}{dx} = -\frac{x^2}{y}$. On the axes provided above, sketch a slope field for the differential equation at the twelve points indicated.

120

Solution:

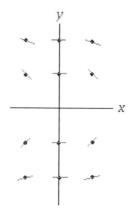

Notes: (1) When $x = 0$, we have $\frac{dy}{dx} = -\frac{0^2}{y} = 0$ (as long as $y \neq 0$). So at each of the four points on the y-axis, the slope is 0. That is, the the tangent line is horizontal. So we draw a horizontal line segment at the points $(0,1)$, $(0,2)$, $(0,-1)$, and $(0,-2)$.

(2) At the points $(1,1)$ and $(-1,1)$, we have $\frac{dy}{dx} = -\frac{1}{1} = -1$.

(3) At the points $(1,-1)$ and $(-1,-1)$, we have $\frac{dy}{dx} = -\frac{1}{-1} = 1$.

(4) At the points $(1,2)$ and $(-1,2)$, we have $\frac{dy}{dx} = -\frac{1}{2}$.

(5) At the points $(1,-2)$ and $(-1,-2)$, we have $\frac{dy}{dx} = -\frac{1}{-2} = \frac{1}{2}$.

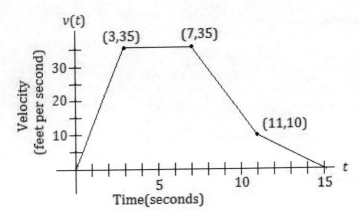

106. A bus is traveling on a straight road. For $0 \le t \le 15$ seconds, the bus's velocity $v(t)$, in feet per second, is modeled by the function shown in the graph above. For each of $v'(3)$, $v'(8)$, and $v'(11)$, find the value or explain why it does not exist. Indicate units of measure.

Solution: $\lim\limits_{x \to 3^-} \left(\frac{v(t)-v(3)}{t-3} \right) = \frac{35}{3}$ and $\lim\limits_{x \to 3^+} \left(\frac{v(t)-v(3)}{t-3} \right) = 0.$

Since $\lim\limits_{x \to 3^-} \left(\frac{v(t)-v(3)}{t-3} \right) \ne \lim\limits_{x \to 3^+} \left(\frac{v(t)-v(3)}{t-3} \right)$, $v'(3)$ **does not exist.**

$v'(8) = \frac{10-35}{11-7} = -\frac{25}{4}$ **ft/sec².**

$\lim\limits_{x \to 11^-} \left(\frac{v(t)-v(11)}{t-11} \right) = -\frac{25}{4}$ and $\lim\limits_{x \to 11^+} \left(\frac{v(t)-v(11)}{t-11} \right) = \frac{-10}{4} = -\frac{5}{2}.$

Since $\lim\limits_{x \to 11^-} \left(\frac{v(t)-v(3)}{t-3} \right) \ne \lim\limits_{x \to 11^+} \left(\frac{v(t)-v(3)}{t-3} \right)$, $v'(11)$ **does not exist.**

Notes: (1) At $t = 3$ and $t = 11$ (as well as $t = 7$) there are "sharp edges." A function of t is *not* differentiable at any such t-value. The reason is that these "sharp edges" indicate a disagreement in the slope of the graph from the left and from the right.

For example, to the left of 3, the slope of the line is positive (in fact it is $\frac{35-0}{3-0} = \frac{35}{3}$), whereas, to the right of 3, the slope of the line is 0.

Symbolically, we can write $v'(3)^- = \frac{35}{3}$ and $v'(3)^+ = 0$. Since the slopes from the left and right disagree, there is no well-defined slope at $t = 3$.

122

Note that $v'(3)^-$ is just a shorthand notation for $\lim\limits_{x\to 3^-}\left(\frac{v(t)-v(3)}{t-3}\right)$, and similarly $v'(3)^+$ is shorthand for $\lim\limits_{x\to 3^+}\left(\frac{v(t)-v(3)}{t-3}\right)$.

(2) To compute $v'(3)^-$, we simply compute the slope of the leftmost line segment. This line segment passes through the points $(0,0)$ and $(3,35)$. So the slope is $v'(3)^- = \frac{35-0}{3-0} = \frac{35}{3}$.

Similarly, to compute $v'(8)$, we simply compute the slope of the third line segment from the left. This line segment passes through the points $(7,35)$ and $(11,10)$. So the slope is $v'(8) = \frac{10-35}{11-7} = -\frac{25}{4}$.

We can compute all the other slopes in a similar fashion.

107. Two particles are moving along the x-axis. For $0 \le t \le 10$, the position of particle A at time t is given by $a(t) = 3\sin t$, and the position of particle B at time t by $b(t) = t^3 - 12t^2 + 21t - 1$. For $0 \le t \le 10$, find all times t during which the two particles travel in opposite directions.

Solution: $a'(t) = 3\cos t$ and

$$b'(t) = 3t^2 - 24t + 21 = 3(t^2 - 8t + 7) = 3(t-1)(t-7).$$

Now, $a'(t) = 0$ when $t = \frac{\pi}{2}, \frac{3\pi}{2}$, and $\frac{5\pi}{2}$ on the interval $[0,10]$, and $b'(t) = 0$ when $t = 1$, and 7.

$a'(t) > 0$ for $0 \le t < \frac{\pi}{2}$, and $\frac{3\pi}{2} < t < \frac{5\pi}{2}$

$a'(t) < 0$ for $\frac{\pi}{2} < t < \frac{3\pi}{2}$, and $\frac{5\pi}{2} < t \le 10$

$b'(t) > 0$ for $0 \le t < 1$, and $7 < t \le 10$

$b'(t) < 0$ for $1 < t < 7$

Therefore, the particles are travelling in opposite directions for $1 < t < \frac{\pi}{2}, \frac{3\pi}{2} < t < 7$, and $\frac{5\pi}{2} < t \le 10$.

In interval notation, the two particles are travelling in opposite directions for t in $\left(1,\frac{\pi}{2}\right) \cup \left(\frac{3\pi}{2},7\right) \cup \left(\frac{5\pi}{2},10\right]$.

123

Notes: (1) We can determine which direction a particle is moving by looking at its velocity function. If the velocity is positive, the particle is moving to the right. If the velocity is negative, the particle is moving to the left.

(2) The velocity function of a particle is the derivative of its position function. So in this problem we want to determine when a' and b' have opposite signs.

(3) We start by finding the **critical numbers** of a and b. In other words we want to find all real numbers t such that $a'(t) = 0$ and $b'(t) = 0$.

Finding the critical numbers of b is straightforward.

To find the critical numbers of a, recall that $\cos t = 0$ whenever t is an odd multiple of $\frac{\pi}{2}$. In other words, $t = \pm\frac{\pi}{2}, \pm\frac{3\pi}{2}, \pm\frac{5\pi}{2}, \dots$

It follows that the critical numbers of a on $[0,10]$ are $t = \frac{\pi}{2}, \frac{3\pi}{2}$, and $\frac{5\pi}{2}$ (use your calculator if allowed, or estimate π as a little more than 3 to see this).

See problem 65 for the graph of $y = \cos x$.

(4) Here is a sign chart for a':

0	$\pi/2$	$3\pi/2$	$5\pi/2$	10
test $\pi/4$	test π	test 2π	test 3π	
+	−	+	−	

And here is a sign chart for b':

0	1	7	10
test .5	test 2	test 9	
+	−	+	

Let's combine these two sign charts into a single chart:

124

	0	1	π/2		3π/2	7	5π/2		10
a'	+	+		−		+	+	−	
b'	+	−		−		−	+	+	

From this last chart it is easy to see where a' and b' have opposite signs.

x	0	$0 < x < 1$	1	$1 < x < 2$	2	$2 < x < 3$	3
$f(x)$	−4	−	−3	−	−1	−	−2
$f'(x)$	3	+	0	+	0	−	−5

108. The differentiable function f is defined for all real numbers x. Values of f and f' for various values of x are given in the table above. Find the x-coordinate of each relative maximum of f on the interval $[0,3]$. Justify your answers.

Solution: The critical numbers of f are $x = 1$ and $x = 2$. But $x = 2$ is the only critical number at which f' changes sign from positive to negative. Therefore $x = 2$ is the only x-coordinate where f has a relative maximum.

Notes: (1) See problem 48 for more detailed information on the first derivative test and how to interpret the chart above.

In particular observe that $f'(x) > 0$ for $1 < x < 2$. It follows that f is increasing for $1 < x < 2$.

Similarly, $f'(x) < 0$ for $2 < x < 3$ implies that f is decreasing for $2 < x < 3$.

So f has a relative maximum at $x = 2$.

At the critical number $x = 1$ there is no sign change ($f'(x) > 0$ both to the left and right of $x = 1$). It follows that f is increasing before and after $x = 1$. So there is no relative minimum or maximum at $x = 1$.

109. Consider a differentiable function g with domain all positive real numbers, satisfying $g'(x) = \frac{2-x}{x^3}$ for $x > 0$. Find the x-coordinates of all relative minima and maxima, find all intervals on which the graph of g is concave up, and find all intervals on which the graph of g is concave down. Justify your answers.

Solution: $g'(x) = 0$ at $x = 2$, $g'(x) > 0$ for $0 < x < 2$, and $g'(x) < 0$ for $x > 2$. It follows that g has a relative maximum at $x = 2$.

$$g''(x) = \frac{x^3(-1)-(2-x)\cdot 3x^2}{x^6} = \frac{x^2[-x-3(2-x)]}{x^6} = \frac{2(x-3)}{x^4}.$$

$g''(x) = 0$ at $x = 3$.

$g''(x) < 0$ for $0 < x < 3$, and $g''(x) > 0$ for $x > 3$.

So the graph of graph of g is **concave down for $0 < x < 3$** and the graph of g is **concave up for $x > 3$**.

Notes: (1) $x = 2$ is a critical number of g since $g'(2) = 0$.

(2) See problem 48 for more detailed information on the first derivative test and how to interpret the information about g'.

(3) At $x = 3$ the graph of g has a point of inflection because g changes concavity there (from concave down to concave up).

(4) See problem 70 for more detailed information on how to interpret the information about g''.

t (minutes)	0	1	2	3	4
$G(t)$ (pints)	0	2.2	4.5	6.8	8.3

110. Gasoline is dripping out of a gas pump, filling up a bucket. The amount of gasoline in the bucket at time t, $0 \leq t \leq 4$, is given by a differentiable function G, where t is measured in minutes. Selected values of $G(t)$, measured in pints, are given in the table above. Use the data in the table to approximate $G'(1.5)$. Show the computations that lead to your answer, and indicate units of measure.

126

Solution: $G'(1.5) \approx \frac{G(2)-G(1)}{2-1} = \frac{4.5-2.2}{1} = \mathbf{2.3}$ **pints/minute.**

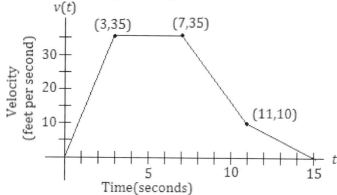

111. A bus is traveling on a straight road. For $0 \le t \le 15$ seconds, the bus's velocity $v(t)$, in feet per second, is modeled by the function defined by the graph above. Let $a(t)$ be the bus's acceleration at time t, in feet per second per second. For $0 < t < 15$, write a piecewise-defined function for $a(t)$.

Solution: $a(t) = \begin{cases} \frac{35}{3} & \text{if } 0 < t < 3 \\ 0 & \text{if } 3 < t < 7 \\ -\frac{25}{4} & \text{if } 7 < t < 11 \\ -\frac{5}{2} & \text{if } 11 < t < 15 \end{cases}$

$a(t)$ does not exist at $t = 3$, $t = 7$, and $t = 11$.

Notes: (1) The acceleration function $a(t)$ is the derivative of the velocity function $v(t)$. That is, $a(t) = v'(t)$.

(2) See the notes after the the solution to problem 106 for more detailed information.

(3) If $0 < t < 3$, then $a(t)$ is simply the slope of the leftmost line segment. This line segment passes through the points $(0,0)$ and $(3,35)$. So the slope is $a(t) = \frac{35-0}{3-0} = \frac{35}{3}$.

(4) If $3 < t < 7$, then $a(t)$ is the slope of the second line segment from the left. This line segment is horizontal and therefore has a slope of $a(t) = 0$.

(5) If $7 < t < 11$, then $a(t)$ is the slope of the third line segment from the left. This line segment passes through the points $(7,35)$ and $(11,10)$. So the slope is $a(t) = \frac{10-35}{11-7} = -\frac{25}{4}$.

(6) If $11 < t < 15$, then $a(t)$ is the slope of the rightmost line segment. This line segment passes through the points $(11,10)$ and $(15,0)$. So the slope is $a(t) = \frac{0-10}{15-11} = \frac{-10}{4} = -\frac{5}{2}$.

x	0	$0 < x < 1$	1	$1 < x < 2$	2	$2 < x < 3$	3
$f(x)$	5	+	2	+	3	+	0
$f'(x)$	-2	$-$	0	+	0	$-$	-8

112. The twice-differentiable function f is defined for all real numbers x. Values of f and f' for various values of x are given in the table above. Explain why there must be a value c, for $0 < c < 3$, such that $f''(c) = -2$.

Solution: Since f' is differentiable, it follows that f' is continuous on the interval $[0,3]$.

We have $\frac{f'(3)-f'(0)}{3-0} = \frac{-8-(-2)}{3-0} = \frac{-6}{3} = -2$.

By the Mean Value Theorem, there is at least one real number c with $0 < c < 3$ such that $f''(c) = -2$.

Note: See problem 46 for more information on the Mean Value Theorem.

113. The region in the xy-plane bounded by the graph of $y = \frac{\ln(x)}{\sqrt{x}}$, $x = 1$, $x = 4$, and the x-axis is rotated about the x-axis. What is the volume of the solid generated?

(A) $\frac{(\ln 4)^3}{3} - 1$

(B) $\frac{\pi (\ln 4)^3}{3} - 1$

(C) $\frac{\pi (\ln 4)^3 - 1}{3}$

(D) $\frac{\pi (\ln 4)^3}{3}$

Solution:

$$\pi \int_1^4 \left(\frac{\ln(x)}{\sqrt{x}}\right)^2 dx = \pi \int_1^4 \frac{(\ln x)^2}{x} dx = \pi \frac{(\ln x)^3}{3} \Big|_1^4 = \frac{\pi}{3}((\ln 4)^3 - (\ln 1)^3)$$

$$= \frac{\pi}{3}((\ln 4)^3 - (0)^3) = \frac{\pi}{3}(\ln 4)^3 = \frac{\pi(\ln 4)^3}{3}, \text{ choice (D)}.$$

Notes: (1) It is helpful to begin by drawing a picture of the region. We do not need an accurate sketch of the function. We need only show where it lies above and below the x-axis. In this case, we have $\frac{\ln(1)}{\sqrt{1}} = 0$, and for all $x > 1$, we have $\frac{\ln(x)}{\sqrt{x}} > 0$.

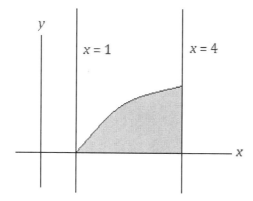

(2) We will use the **disk method** to find the requested volume. A *disk* is a circle together with its interior. A typical disk can be described as follows:

First we take a value x between 1 and 4. Find this number on the x-axis.

We then draw the radius of the disk by drawing a vertical segment from the x-axis straight up until we hit the curve.

Next we draw a circle from the top of this line segment that sweeps below the x-axis, and who's radius is as specified in the last step.

Here is a picture:

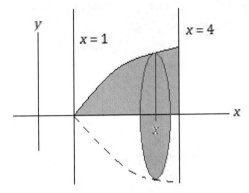

The radius of this disk is $\frac{\ln(x)}{\sqrt{x}}$. It follows that the area of this disk is $\pi r^2 = \pi(\frac{\ln(x)}{\sqrt{x}})^2$.

The disk method requires us to integrate this area over the given interval, in this case from 1 to 4.

$$V = \pi \int_1^4 r^2 \, dx = \pi \int_1^4 (\frac{\ln(x)}{\sqrt{x}})^2 \, dx = \pi \int_1^4 \frac{(\ln x)^2}{x} \, dx$$

(3) To evaluate $\int \frac{(\ln x)^2}{x} \, dx$, we can formally make the substitution $u = \ln x$. It then follows that

$$du = \frac{1}{x} dx$$

We now have

$$\int \frac{(\ln x)^2}{x} \, dx = \int (\ln x)^2 \cdot \frac{1}{x} \, dx = \int u^2 \, du = \frac{u^3}{3} + C = \frac{(\ln x)^3}{3} + C$$

It follows that $\pi \int \frac{(\ln x)^2}{x} \, dx = \pi \frac{(\ln x)^3}{3} + C$.

130

(4) If we are doing the substitution formally, we can save some time by changing the limits of integration. We do this as follows:

$$\pi \int_1^4 \frac{(\ln x)^2}{x} \, dx = \pi \int_0^{\ln 4} u^2 \, du = \pi \frac{u^3}{3} \Big|_0^{\ln 4} = \frac{\pi}{3}((\ln 4)^3 - 0^3) = \frac{\pi(\ln 4)^3}{3}.$$

Notice that the limits 1 and 4 were changed to the limits 0 and $\ln 4$, respectively. We made this change using the formula that we chose for the substitution: $u = \ln x$. When $x = 1$, we have $u = 0$ and when $x = 4$, we have $u = \ln 4$.

114. * Water is leaking from an air conditioning unit at the rate of $f(t) = 750e^{-\frac{t}{3}}$ quarts per hour, where t is measured in hours. Approximately how much water has leaked out of the unit after 5 hours?

(A) 47
(B) 142
(C) 608
(D) 1825

Solution:

$$\int_0^5 750e^{-\frac{t}{3}} \, dt = 750(-3)e^{-\frac{t}{3}} \Big|_0^5 = -2250 \left(e^{-\frac{5}{3}} - e^0\right) \approx 1825.$$

This is choice (D).

Notes: (1) The word "rate" indicates a derivative.

(2) f gives the *rate* at which the amount of water in the air conditioning unit is decreasing. So we can find the *amount* of water in the tank by integrating $F(t) = \int f(t) \, dt$ to get $F(t) = -2250e^{-\frac{t}{3}} + C$.

Note that we do not have enough information to figure out what C is. We therefore cannot determine the amount of water in the unit at a specific time t.

(3) Although we do not have enough information to figure out the amount of water in the unit at a specific time, we *can* figure out how much water has leaked out over any specified interval of time.

The amount of water that has leaked out from time $t = a$ to time $t = b$ is the difference between the amount in the unit at time a and time b. So we would simply compute $\int_a^b f(t) \, dt$.

In this problem we want to find the amount of water that has leaked out after 5 hours, ie. from $t = 0$ to $t = 5$. So we compute $\int_0^5 f(t)\, dt$.

(4) To evaluate $\int 750e^{-\frac{t}{3}}dt$, we can formally make the substitution $u = -\frac{t}{3} = -\frac{1}{3}t$. It then follows that $du = -\frac{1}{3}dt$

We now have

$$\int 750e^{-\frac{t}{3}}dt = 750(-3)\int e^{-\frac{t}{3}}\left(-\frac{1}{3}\right)dt = -2250\int e^u du$$

$$= -2250e^u + C = -2250e^{-\frac{t}{3}} + C$$

(5) If we are doing the substitution formally, we can save some time by changing the limits of integration. We do this as follows:

$$\int_0^5 750e^{-\frac{t}{3}}\, dt = -2250\int_0^{-\frac{5}{3}} e^u\, du = -2250e^u\Big|_0^{-\frac{5}{3}} = -2250(e^{-\frac{5}{3}} - e^0)$$

$$\approx 1825.$$

Notice that the limits 0 and 5 were changed to the limits 0 and $-\frac{5}{3}$, respectively. We made this change using the formula that we chose for the substitution: $u = -\frac{1}{3}t$. When $t = 0$, we have $u = 0$ and when $t = 5$, we have $u = -\frac{5}{3}$.

115. * The average value of $(\ln x)^5$ on the interval $[2,5]$ is

(A) 0.584
(B) 1.299
(C) 3.896
(D) 11.687

Solution: $\frac{1}{5-2}\int_2^5 (\ln x)^5\, dx \approx 3.896$, choice (C).

Notes: (1) The **average value** of the function f over the interval $[a, b]$ is

$$\frac{1}{b-a}\int_a^b f(x)\, dx.$$

(2) We can compute $\int_2^5 (\ln x)^5\, dx$ directly in our TI-84 calculator as follows:

132

Press MATH, followed by 9 (or scroll up 2 times and select 9:fnInt( ). Type ((ln(X))^5, X, 2, 5) followed by ENTER. The display will show 11.6865333.

(2) Remember to multiply 11.6865333 by $\frac{1}{5-2} = \frac{1}{3}$ to get

$$\frac{1}{3}\int_2^5 (\ln x)^5 \, dx \approx 3.896.$$

116. * If $f'(x) = \cos(\frac{\ln(x+1)}{4})$ and $f(0) = 2$, then $f(3) =$

   (A) 4.919
   (B) 2.919
   (C) −0.75
   (D) −1.5

Solution: $f(3) = 2 + \int_0^3 f'(x) \, dx = 2 + \int_0^3 \cos(\frac{\ln(x+1)}{4}) \, dx \approx 4.919.$

This is choice (A).

Notes: (1) Given a continuous function g with G an antiderivative of g, and initial condition $G(a) = k$, it follows that

$$G(b) = k + \int_a^b g(x) \, dx.$$

To see why this is true, simply observe that $\int_a^b g(x) \, dx = G(b) - G(a)$, so that $k + \int_a^b g(x) \, dx = G(a) + (G(b) - G(a)) = G(b)$.

The formula given above is especially useful when you cannot easily find a closed form for G. In other words, this form is very useful when solving this type of problem with a calculator.

(2) In this problem, we have $g = f'$, $G = f$, $a = 0$, $b = 3$, and $k = 2$, so that

$$f(3) = 2 + \int_0^3 f'(x) \, dx.$$

117. * Let D be the region enclosed by $y = \sin x$ and $y = \cos x$ for $0 \le x \le \frac{\pi}{4}$. The volume of the solid generated when D is revolved around the line $x = 4$ is

   (A) 9.715
   (B) 4.857
   (C) 1.793
   (D) 0.897

Solution: $2\pi \int_0^{\frac{\pi}{4}} (4-x)(\cos x - \sin x)\, dx \approx 9.715$, choice (A).

Notes: (1) It is helpful to begin by drawing a picture of the region D and the line $x = 4$.

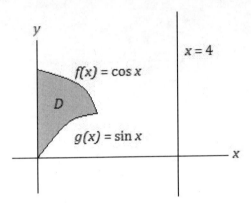

(2) We will use the **shell method** to find this volume. A *shell* is cylinder. A typical shell can be described as follows:

First we take a value x between 0 and $\frac{\pi}{4}$. Find this number on the x-axis.

We then draw the height of the shell directly above this number between the two graphs.

Next we draw circles from the top and bottom of this line segment (the height) that sweep across the line $x = 4$, and who's radius is the distance from the height to the line $x = 4$.

Here is a picture:

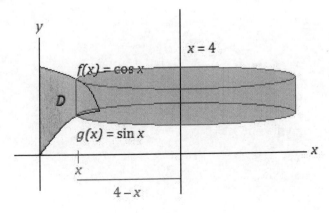

The height of this cylinder is $f(x) - g(x) = \cos x - \sin x$, and the radius of this cylinder is $4 - x$. It follows that the volume of this cylinder is $2\pi rh = 2\pi(4 - x)(\cos x - \sin x)$.

The shell method requires us to integrate this volume over the given interval, in this case from 0 to $\frac{\pi}{4}$.

$$V = 2\pi \int_0^{\frac{\pi}{4}} rh\, dx = 2\pi \int_0^{\frac{\pi}{4}}(4 - x)(\cos x - \sin x)\, dx.$$

118. * Let the function F be defined by $F(x) = \int_0^x \cos(u^4)\, du$ on the closed interval $[0,1.5]$. F has a local maximum at $x =$

(A) 0
(B) 1.120
(C) 1.571
(D) 1.473

Solution: $F'(x) = \cos(x^4)$. Now we use our graphing calculator. First make sure that your calculator is in radian mode (Press MODE and select Radian). Next press Y= and next to Y_1 enter cos (X^4). Then press WINDOW and set Xmin to 0 and Xmax to 1.5. Press GRAPH to display the graph (if you do not see the graph well, you may have to adjust Ymin and Ymax as well).

Press CALC (2nd TRACE), select zero (or press 2). Move the cursor to the left of the zero and press ENTER. Then move the cursor to the right of the zero and press ENTER. Press ENTER one more time, and you will get an answer of $x = 1.120$ (rounded). This is choice (B).

Notes: (1) We need to find the critical numbers of F in the interval $[0,1.5]$. To do this we set $F'(x) = 0$.

(2) To compute $F'(x)$ we use the first Fundamental Theorem of Calculus which says that if $F(x) = \int_a^x f(t)\, dt$, for some constant a, then $F'(x) = f(x)$.

So in this problem we must solve the equation $\cos(x^4) = 0$.

(3) Note that the graph of F' is above the x-axis to the left of the critical number, and below the x-axis to the right of the critical number. So $F'(x) > 0$ for $x < 1.120$ and $F'(x) < 0$ for $x > 1.120$.

135

It follows that F is increasing for $0 < x < 1.120$ and decreasing for $1.120 < x < 1.473$. So F has a local maximum at $x = 1.120$.

(4) $x = 1.473$ is also a critical number of F. But by an argument similar to that used in note (3), F has a local minimum at $x = 1.473$.

119. The expression $\frac{1}{100}(\sqrt[3]{\frac{1}{100}} + \sqrt[3]{\frac{2}{100}} + \sqrt[3]{\frac{3}{100}} + \cdots + \sqrt[3]{\frac{100}{100}})$ is a Riemann sum approximation for

(A) $\frac{1}{100}\int_0^{100} \sqrt[3]{x}\, dx$

(B) $\frac{1}{100}\int_0^1 \sqrt[3]{x}\, dx$

(C) $\frac{1}{100}\int_0^1 \sqrt[3]{\frac{x}{100}}\, dx$

(D) $\int_0^1 \sqrt[3]{x}\, dx$

Solution: Let $f(x) = \sqrt[3]{x}$ and partition the interval $[0,1]$ into 100 equal subintervals as follows:

Let $x_0 = \frac{0}{100} = 0$, $x_1 = \frac{1}{100}$, $x_2 = \frac{2}{100}$, ..., $x_{99} = \frac{99}{100}$, $x_{100} = \frac{100}{100} = 1$.

We get the corresponding subintervals $[0, \frac{1}{100}]$, $[\frac{1}{100}, \frac{2}{100}]$, ..., $[\frac{99}{100}, 1]$.

The length of each subinterval (and therefore the base of each rectangle) is $\frac{1-0}{100} = \frac{1}{100}$.

For the height of each rectangle we choose the right endpoint of each subinterval x^*, and compute $f(x^*)$.

So the height of the leftmost rectangle will be $f\left(\frac{1}{100}\right) = \sqrt[3]{\frac{1}{100}}$. It follows that the area of the leftmost rectangle is $\frac{1}{100} \cdot \sqrt[3]{\frac{1}{100}}$.

Similarly, the area of the next rectangle will be $\frac{1}{100} \cdot \sqrt[3]{\frac{2}{100}}$.

Continuing in this fashion, we get that the area of the rightmost rectangle is $\frac{1}{100} \cdot \sqrt[3]{\frac{100}{100}}$.

So we are approximating the area under the graph of $f(x) = \sqrt[3]{x}$ from $x = 0$ to $x = 1$ by

$$\frac{1}{100} \cdot \sqrt[3]{\frac{1}{100}} + \frac{1}{100} \cdot \sqrt[3]{\frac{2}{100}} + \cdots + \frac{1}{100} \cdot \sqrt[3]{\frac{100}{100}}$$

$$= \frac{1}{100} \left(\sqrt[3]{\frac{1}{100}} + \sqrt[3]{\frac{2}{100}} + \cdots + \sqrt[3]{\frac{100}{100}} \right).$$

This is precisely the expression given in the problem. So the answer is choice (D).

Notes: (1) A **Riemann Sum Approximation** of f over the interval $I = [a, b]$ with partition $P = \{[x_0, x_1], [x_1, x_2], \dots, [x_{n-1}, x_n]\}$ where $a = x_0 < x_1 < x_2 < \cdots < x_n = b$ is given by

$$S = \sum_{i=1}^{n} f(x_i^*)(x_i - x_{i-1}) , \text{ where } x_{i-1} \le x^* \le x_i$$

or equivalently

$$S = f(x_1^*)(x_1 - x_0) + f(x_2^*)(x_2 - x_1) + \cdots + f(x_n^*)(x_n - x_{n-1}).$$

where $x_0 \le x_1^* \le x_1$, $x_1 \le x_2^* \le x_2$, ..., $x_{n-1} \le x_n^* \le x_n$.

(2) Geometrically (and in English), what note (1) says is that we first chop up the interval $[a, b]$ into n pieces, called subintervals.

For each subinterval we then choose an x-value in that subinterval, and draw a rectangle whose base is the length of the subinterval, and whose height is the corresponding y-value on the graph (more precisely, if we choose x^* in the subinterval, then the height is $f(x^*)$).

Finally we add up the areas of all of these rectangles.

(3) Very often (such as in this problem) we want all of the subintervals in our partition to have equal length. In this case, the length of each subinterval is $\frac{b-a}{n}$ (remember that a and b are the left and right endpoints of the original interval, and n is the number of pieces we are chopping it up into). The formula for the Riemann Sum Approximation then simplifies to

$$S = \frac{b-a}{n} \sum_{i=1}^{n} f(x_i^*)$$

or equivalently

$$S = \frac{b-a}{n}[f(x_1^*) + f(x_2^*) + \cdots + f(x_n^*)].$$

(4) Here is a sketch of the Riemann Sum approximation for this problem:

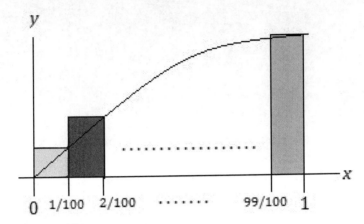

Note that only part of the picture is drawn here. In reality there should be 100 rectangles, each with a base of $\frac{1}{100}$.

Also note that for each subinterval we chose the right endpoint of the interval to form the height of the rectangle. For example, the height of the leftmost rectangle is $f\left(\frac{1}{100}\right) = \sqrt[3]{\frac{1}{100}}$. It follows that the area of the leftmost rectangle is $\frac{1}{100} \cdot \sqrt[3]{\frac{1}{100}}$.

Similarly, the area of the second rectangle is $\frac{1}{100} \cdot \sqrt[3]{\frac{2}{100}}$.

Continuing in this fashion, we get that the area of the rightmost rectangle is $\frac{1}{100} \cdot \sqrt[3]{\frac{100}{100}}$.

It follows that the sum of all of these rectangles is

$$\frac{1}{100} \cdot \sqrt[3]{\frac{1}{100}} + \frac{1}{100} \cdot \sqrt[3]{\frac{2}{100}} + \cdots + \frac{1}{100} \cdot \sqrt[3]{\frac{100}{100}}$$

$$= \frac{1}{100}\left(\sqrt[3]{\frac{1}{100}} + \sqrt[3]{\frac{2}{100}} + \cdots + \sqrt[3]{\frac{100}{100}}\right).$$

138

Observe that this computation led to an approximation of the area under the graph of $f(x) = \sqrt[3]{x}$ from $x = 0$ to $x = 1$. In other words, we approximated $\int_0^1 \sqrt[3]{x}\,dx$.

t (minutes)	0	1	2	3	4
$G(t)$ (pints)	0	2.2	4.5	6.8	8.3

120. Gasoline is dripping out of a gas pump, filling up a bucket. The amount of gasoline in the bucket at time t, $0 \leq t \leq 4$, is given by a continuous function G, where t is measured in minutes. Selected values of $G(t)$, measured in pints, are given in the table above. Use a midpoint sum with two subintervals of equal length indicated by the given data to approximate $\frac{1}{4}\int_0^4 G(t)\,dt$. Using correct units, explain the meaning of $\frac{1}{4}\int_0^4 G(t)\,dt$ in the context of the problem.

Solution:

$$\frac{1}{4}\int_0^4 G(t)\,dt \approx \frac{1}{4}[2G(1) + 2G(3)] = \frac{1}{4}(2 \cdot 2.2 + 2 \cdot 6.8) = \mathbf{4.5\ pints}.$$

$\frac{1}{4}\int_0^4 G(t)\,dt$ is the average amount of gasoline in the bucket, in pints, over the time interval $0 \leq t \leq 4$ minutes.

Notes: (1) Here is a picture of the midpoint sum in this problem:

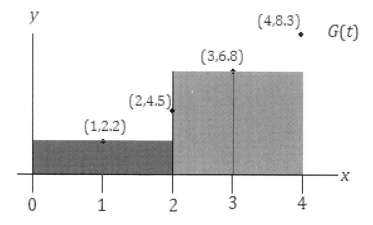

Note that both rectangles have a width of 2.

139

The leftmost rectangle has a length (or height) of $G(1) = 2.2$. It follows that the area of the leftmost rectangle is $(2)(2.2) = 4.4$

The rightmost rectangle has a length (or height) of $G(3) = 6.8$. It follows that the area of the rightmost rectangle is $(2)(6.8) = 13.6$

Finally, we get the area of the shaded region by adding these two areas:

$$\int_0^4 G(t)dt \approx 4.4 + 13.6 = 18.$$

(2) Remember we actually want $\frac{1}{4}\int_0^4 G(t)dt \approx \frac{18}{4} = 4.5$.

(3) Recall that the average value of a function f over the interval $[a, b]$ is

$$\frac{1}{b-a}\int_a^b f(x)\,dx.$$

So the average value of G over the interval $[0,4]$ is

$$\frac{1}{4-0}\int_0^4 G(t)\,dt = \frac{1}{4}\int_0^4 G(t)\,dt.$$

121. Consider the differential equation $\frac{dy}{dx} = e^{y-1}(2x^3 - 5)$. Let $y = f(x)$ be the particular solution to the differential equation that passes through $(1,1)$. Find $y = f(x)$.

Solution: We separate variables to get $e^{1-y}dy = (2x^3 - 5)dx$. Now we integrate both sides of this equation to get $-e^{1-y} = \frac{x^4}{2} - 5x + C$.

Now we substitute in $x = 1$ and $y = 1$ to get $-e^0 = \frac{1}{2} - 5 + C$. So $C = -1 - \frac{1}{2} + 5 = \frac{7}{2}$, and we have $-e^{1-y} = \frac{x^4}{2} - 5x + \frac{7}{2}$. We multiply each side of this equation by -1 to get $e^{1-y} = -\frac{x^4}{2} + 5x - \frac{7}{2}$, and then we take the natural logarithm of each side of this last equation to get $1 - y = \ln(-\frac{x^4}{2} + 5x - \frac{7}{2})$, We subtract 1 to get

$$-y = \ln\left(-\frac{x^4}{2} + 5x - \frac{7}{2}\right) - 1$$

Finally, we multiply by -1 to get $y = 1 - \ln\left(-\frac{x^4}{2} + 5x - \frac{7}{2}\right)$.

Notes: See problem 52 for more information on separable differential equations.

140

x	0	1	2	3
$f(x)$	2	7	-1	1
$f'(x)$	3	0	0	-5
$g(x)$	-2	-5	-2	4
$g'(x)$	8	9	-6	0

122. The differentiable functions f and g are defined for all real numbers x. Values of f, f', g, and g' for various values of x are given in the table above. Evaluate $\int_0^3 g'(f(x))f'(x)\,dx$.

Solution: $\int_0^3 g'(f(x))f'(x)\,dx = [g(f(x))]_{x=0}^{x=3} = g(f(3)) - g(f(0))$

$$= g(1) - g(2) = -5 - (-2) = -5 + 2 = -3.$$

Notes: (1) By the chain rule, the derivative of $g(f(x))$ is $g'(f(x))f'(x)$. It follows that $\int g'(f(x))f'(x)\,dx = g(f(x)) + C$.

(2) To evaluate $\int g'(f(x))f'(x)\,dx$, we can formally make the substitution $u = f(x)$. It then follows that $du = f'(x)dx$.

We now have

$$\int g'(f(x))f'(x)\,dx = \int g'(u)du = g(u) + C = g(f(x)) + C.$$

(3) If we are doing the substitution formally, we can save some time by changing the limits of integration. We do this as follows:

$$\int_0^3 g'(f(x))f'(x)\,dx = \int_{f(0)}^{f(3)} g'(u)\,du = \int_2^1 g'(u)\,du = g(u)\,\Big|_2^1$$

$$= g(1) - g(2) = -5 - (-2) = -5 + 2 = -3.$$

Notice that the limits 0 and 3 were changed to the limits $f(0)$ and $f(3)$, respectively. We made this change using the formula that we chose for the substitution: $u = f(x)$. When $x = 0$, we have $u = f(0)$ and when $x = 3$, we have $u = f(3)$.

(4) Using the table we see that $f(0) = 2$ and $f(3) = 1$. This is how we got the third equality in the main solution above, and also the second equality in note (3) above.

141

(5) Using the table we see that $g(1) = -5$ and $g(2) = -2$. This is how we got the fourth equality in the main solution above, and also the fifth equality in note (3) above.

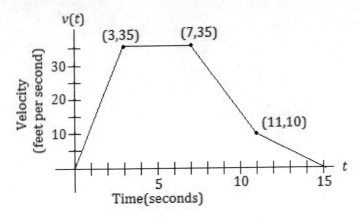

123. A bus is traveling on a straight road. For $0 \leq t \leq 15$ seconds, the bus's velocity $v(t)$, in feet per second, is modeled by the function defined by the graph above. Find $\int_0^{15} v(t)\, dt$. Using correct units, explain the meaning of $\int_0^{15} v(t)\, dt$.

Solution:

$$\int_0^{15} v(t)\, dt = \frac{1}{2}(3)(35) + (4)(35) + \left(\frac{35+10}{2}\right)(4) + \frac{1}{2}(4)(10)$$

$$= 302.5.$$

The bus travels 302.5 feet in these 15 seconds.

Notes: (1) Geometrically we can interpret $\int_0^{15} v(t)\, dt$ as the area under the graph of $v(t)$ from $t = 0$ to $t = 15$. We split this area into four pieces as follows:

142

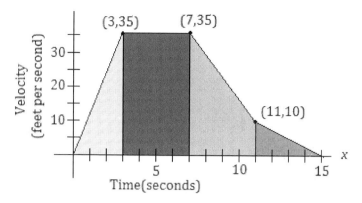

(2) The area of the leftmost triangle is $\frac{1}{2}bh = \frac{1}{2}(3)(35)$.

(3) The area of the rectangle is $bh = (7 - 3)(35) = (4)(35)$.

(4) The area of the trapezoid is

$$\frac{(b_1+b_2)}{2} \cdot h = \left(\frac{35+10}{2}\right)(11 - 7) = \left(\frac{35+10}{2}\right)(4).$$

Note that for the trapezoid, the height lies along the x-axis.

(5) The area of the last triangle is $\frac{1}{2}bh = \frac{1}{2}(15 - 11)(10) = \frac{1}{2}(4)(10)$.

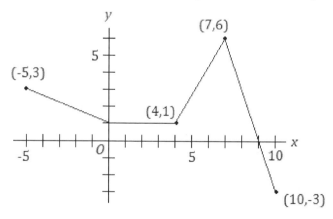

124. The function g is defined on the closed interval $[-5,10]$. The graph of g consists of four line segments and is shown in the figure above. Let G be defined by $G(x) = \int_0^x g(x)\, dx$. Compute $\frac{G(-5)+G(4)}{G(10)-G(7)}$.

143

Solution: $G(-5) = \int_0^{-5} g(x)\,dx = -\int_{-5}^0 g(x)\,dx = -\left(\frac{3+1}{2}\right) \cdot 5 = -10.$

$G(4) = \int_0^4 g(x)\,dx = (4)(1) = 4.$

$G(10) - G(7) = \int_7^{10} g(x)\,dx = \int_7^9 g(x)\,dx + \int_9^{10} g(x)\,dx$

$$= \frac{1}{2}(2)(6) - \frac{1}{2}(1)(3) = 6 - \frac{3}{2} = \frac{9}{2}.$$

So $\frac{G(-5)+G(4)}{G(10)-G(7)} = (-10+4) \div \frac{9}{2} = -6 \cdot \frac{2}{9} = -\frac{12}{9} = -\frac{4}{3}.$

Notes: (1) $\int_a^b f(x)\,dx = -\int_b^a f(x)\,dx.$

We used this theorem in the first computation to get

$$\int_0^{-5} g(x)\,dx = -\int_{-5}^0 g(x)\,dx.$$

(2) If $a < c < b$, then $\int_a^b f(x)\,dx = \int_a^c f(x)\,dx + \int_c^b f(x)\,dx.$

We used this theorem in the third computation to get

$$\int_7^{10} g(x)\,dx = \int_7^9 g(x)\,dx + \int_9^{10} g(x)\,dx.$$

(3) Geometrically, if the graph of f lies above the x-axis between a and b, then $\int_a^b f(x)\,dx$ is the area under the graph of f between $x = a$ and $x = b$.

If the graph of f lies below the x-axis between a and b, then $\int_a^b f(x)\,dx$ is the negative of the area above the graph of f between a and b.

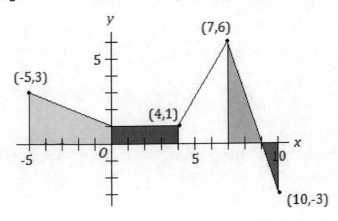

144

So $\int_{-5}^{0} g(x)\, dx$ is the leftmost area of the trapezoid with bases of length 3 and 1, and height 5 (note that the height lies along the x-axis). So we have $\int_{-5}^{0} g(x)\, dx = \left(\frac{b_1+b_2}{2}\right) h = \left(\frac{3+1}{2}\right) \cdot 5 = \frac{4}{2} \cdot 5 = 2 \cdot 5 = 10$.

$\int_{0}^{4} g(x)\, dx$ is the area of the rectangle with base 4 and height 1. So we have $\int_{0}^{4} g(x)\, dx = bh = (4)(1) = 4$.

$\int_{7}^{9} g(x)\, dx$ is the area of the first shaded triangle with base 2 and height 6. So we have $\int_{7}^{9} g(x)\, dx = \frac{1}{2}bh = \frac{1}{2}(2)(6) = 6$.

$\int_{9}^{10} g(x)\, dx$ is the negative of the area of the rightmost triangle with base 1 and height 3. So we have $\int_{9}^{10} g(x)\, dx = -\frac{1}{2}bh = -\frac{1}{2}(1)(3) = -\frac{3}{2}$.

125. * A 5000 gallon tank is filled to capacity with water. At time $t = 0$, water begins to leak out of the tank at a rate modeled by $R(t)$, measured in gallons per hour, where

$$R(t) = \begin{cases} \dfrac{300t}{t+1}, & 0 \le t \le 4 \\ 500e^{-0.5t}, & t > 4 \end{cases}$$

Find the average rate at which water is leaking from the tank between time $t = 0$ and time $t = 10$ hours. Then write, but do not solve, an equation involving an integral to find the time T when the amount of water in the tank is 1000 gallons.

Solution: The average rate at which water is leaking from the tank between time $t = 0$ and time $t = 10$ hours is

$$\frac{1}{10-0}\int_{0}^{10} R(t)\, dt = \frac{1}{10}\left(\int_{0}^{4}\frac{300t}{t+1}\, dt + \int_{4}^{10} 500e^{-0.5t}\, dt\right) \approx \mathbf{84.577}.$$

To find the time T when the amount of water in the tank is 1000 gallons, we would solve the equation $\mathbf{5000 - \int_{0}^{T} R(t)\, dt = 1000}$.

Notes: (1) Recall that the average value of a function f over the interval $[a, b]$ is $\frac{1}{b-a}\int_{a}^{b} f(x)\, dx$.

So the average value of R over the interval $[0,10]$ is $\frac{1}{10-0}\int_{0}^{10} R(t)\, dt$.

(2) The use of the word "rate" in this problem can be confusing. In general we associate the word "rate" with a derivative (as we should). In this problem, note that the function R is a rate function. So when we are asked to find the average rate at which water is leaking from the tank, we are being asked to find the average value of R.

(3) If $a < c < b$, then $\int_a^b f(x)\, dx = \int_a^c f(x)\, dx + \int_c^b f(x)\, dx$.

We used this theorem to write

$$\int_0^{10} R(t)\, dt = \int_0^4 R(t)\, dt + \int_4^{10} R(t)\, dt.$$

(4) We can compute $\int_0^4 \frac{300t}{t+1}\, dt$ directly in our TI-84 calculator as follows:

Press MATH, followed by 9 (or scroll up 2 times and select 9:fnInt( ). Type (300X/(X + 1), X, 0, 4) followed by ENTER. The display will show 717.1686263.

Similarly, we can compute $\int_4^{10} 500e^{-0.5t}\, dt$ in our TI-84 calculator:

Press MATH, followed by 9 (or scroll up 2 times and select 9:fnInt( ). Type (500e^(-.5X), X, 4, 10) followed by ENTER. The display will show 128.5973362.

(5) Since $R(t)$ gives the rate at which water is leaking out of the tank, it follows that $\int_0^T R(t)\, dt$ gives the total amount of water that has leaked out of the tank at time T.

Since we started with 5000 gallons of water in the tank, it follows that $5000 - \int_0^T R(t)\, dt$ is the amount of water in the tank at time T.

Since we want to find the time T when the amount of water in the tank is 1000 gallons, we set $5000 - \int_0^T R(t)\, dt$ equal to 1000.

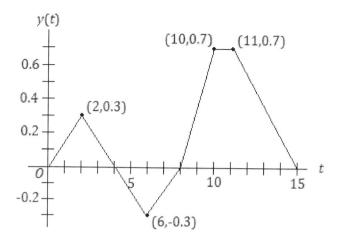

126. Joe is driving his car along a straight road. For $0 \le t \le 15$ seconds, his velocity $v(t)$, in miles per minute, is modeled by the function defined by the graph above. Using correct units, explain the meaning of $\int_0^{15} |v(t)| \, dt$ in terms of Joe's trip. Then find the value of $\int_0^{15} |v(t)| \, dt$.

Solution: $\int_0^{15} |v(t)| \, dt$ is the total distance, in miles, that Joe drove during the 15 minutes from $t = 0$ to $t = 15$.

$$\int_0^{15} |v(t)| \, dt = \int_0^4 v(t) \, dt - \int_4^8 v(t) \, dt + \int_8^{15} v(t) \, dt$$

$$= 0.6 + 0.6 + 4(0.7) = \textbf{4 miles}.$$

Notes: (1) $\int_0^{15} |v(t)| \, dt$ is equal to the following shaded area:

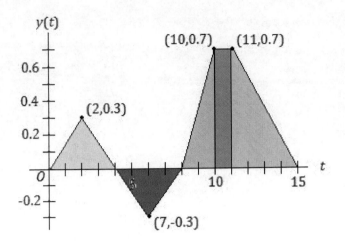

The leftmost triangle has area $\frac{1}{2}bh = \frac{1}{2}(4)(0.3) = 0.6$.

The second triangle also has an area of 0.6.

The third triangle has area $\frac{1}{2}bh = \frac{1}{2}(2)(0.7) = 0.7$.

The rectangle has area $bh = (1)(0.7) = 0.7$.

The rightmost triangle has area $\frac{1}{2}bh = \frac{1}{2}(4)(0.7) = 1.4$.

So the total area is $0.6 + 0.6 + 0.7 + 0.7 + 1.4 = 4$.

x	1	5	6	8	11
$f(x)$	3	5	1	-3	4

127. Let f be a function that is continuous for all real numbers. The table above gives values of f for selected points in the closed interval $[1,11]$. Use a left Riemann Sum with subintervals indicated by the data in the table to approximate $\int_1^{11} f(x)\, dx$. Show the work that leads to your answer.

Solution: $\int_1^{11} f(x)\, dx \approx (3)(4) + (5)(1) + (1)(2) + (-3)(3) = \mathbf{10}$.

Notes: (1) See problem 119 for general information about Riemann Sum Approximations.

(2) In this problem we are partitioning the interval $[1,11]$ into $n = 4$ subintervals: $P = \{[1,5], [5,6], [6,8], [8,11]\}$.

We have $a = x_0 = 1$, $x_1 = 5$, $x_2 = 6$, $x_3 = 8$, $x_4 = b = 11$.

(3) We are choosing x_i^* to be the left endpoint.

So $x_1^* = 1$, $x_2^* = 5$, $x_3^* = 6$, and $x_4^* = 8$.

(4) We have $S = \sum_{i=1}^{4} f(x_i^*)(x_i - x_{i-1})$

$$= f(x_1^*)(x_1 - x_0) + f(x_2^*)(x_2 - x_1) + f(x_3^*)(x_3 - x_2) + f(x_4^*)(x_4 - x_3)$$

$$= f(1)(5 - 1) + f(5)(6 - 5) + f(6)(8 - 6) + f(8)(11 - 8)$$

$$= (3)(4) + (5)(1) + (1)(2) + (-3)(3) = 12 + 5 + 2 - 9 = 10.$$

(5) Geometrically (and in English), we are chopping up the interval $[1,11]$ into $n = 4$ subintervals. Note that in this case the subintervals are *not* equal.

For each subinterval we then choose the left endpoint of that interval, and draw a rectangle whose base is the length of the subinterval, and whose height is the corresponding y-value on the graph (more precisely, the height is $f(x^*)$, where x^* is the left endpoint of the interval).

Finally we add up the areas of all of these rectangles.

(6) Here is a sketch of the Riemann Sum approximation for this problem:

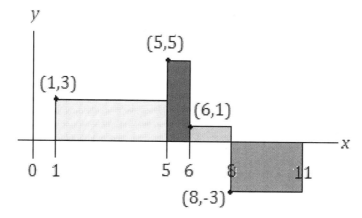

Note that for each subinterval we chose the left endpoint of the interval to form the height of the rectangle. For example, the height of the leftmost rectangle is $f(1) = 3$. It follows that the area of the leftmost rectangle is $(3)(5 - 1) = (3)(4) = 12$.

149

Similarly, the area of the second rectangle is $(5)(1) = 5$, the area of the third rectangle is $(1)(8 - 6) = (1)(2) = 2$, and the area of the rightmost rectangle is $(3)(11 - 8) = (3)(3) = 9$.

Note that when we compute the Riemann Sum, we subtract the area of the rightmost rectangle since it lies below the x-axis.

The Riemann Sum is then $12 + 5 + 2 - 9 = 10$.

128. * Let R be the region in the first and second quadrants bounded above by the graph of $y = \frac{48}{2+x^4}$ and below by the horizontal line $y = 4$. The region R is the base of a solid whose cross sections perpendicular to the x-axis are semicircles. Find the volume of this solid.

Solution: We first find the x-values where the graph of $y = \frac{48}{2+x^4}$ intersects the line $y = 4$. To do this we solve the equation $\frac{48}{2+x^4} = 4$. Multiplying by the denominator on the left hand side gives the equation $48 = 8 + 4x^4$. We subtract 8 to get $40 = 4x^4$, divide by 4 to get $10 = x^4$, and finally take the fourth root of each side to get $x = \pm\sqrt[4]{10}$.

So the volume we are looking for is

$$\frac{\pi}{2}\int_{-\sqrt[4]{10}}^{\sqrt[4]{10}} \left[\frac{1}{2}\left(\frac{48}{2+x^4} - 4\right)\right]^2 dx \approx \textbf{284.202}.$$

Notes: (1) It is helpful to begin by drawing a picture of the region R

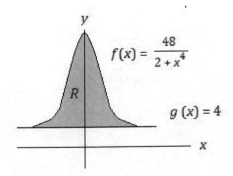

(2) Let's draw a cross section that is perpendicular to the x-axis.

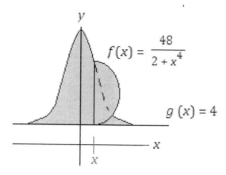

$$f(x) = \frac{48}{2 + x^4}$$

$$g(x) = 4$$

First we take a value x between $-\sqrt[4]{10}$ and $\sqrt[4]{10}$ and find this number on the x-axis.

We then draw the diameter of the semicircle. This diameter has a length of $f(x) - g(x) = \frac{48}{2+x^4} - 4$. It follows that the length of a radius of this semicircle is $r = \frac{1}{2}(\frac{48}{2+x^4} - 4)$. So the area of the semicircle is

$$A = \frac{\pi}{2}r^2 = \frac{\pi}{2}\left[\frac{1}{2}\left(\frac{48}{2+x^4} - 4\right)\right]^2.$$

To get the desired volume, we now simply integrate this expression over the interval $[-\sqrt[4]{10}, \sqrt[4]{10}]$:

$$V = \frac{\pi}{2}\int_{-\sqrt[4]{10}}^{\sqrt[4]{10}} \left[\frac{1}{2}\left(\frac{48}{2+x^4} - 4\right)\right]^2 dx.$$

(3) We can compute $\int_{-\sqrt[4]{10}}^{\sqrt[4]{10}} \left[\frac{1}{2}\left(\frac{48}{2+x^4} - 4\right)\right]^2 dx$ directly in our TI-84 calculator as follows:

Press MATH, followed by 9 (or scroll up 2 times and select 9:fnInt( ). Type ((1 / 2(48 / (2 + X^4) − 4))^2, X, −4$\sqrt[x]{}$10, 4$\sqrt[x]{}$10) followed by ENTER. The display will show 180.9284648. Multiply this result by π / 2, and the display will show 284.201768.

(4) We can compute $\sqrt[4]{10}$ in our TI-84 calculator by typing 4, then selecting $\sqrt[x]{}$ from the MATH menu, then typing 10 followed by ENTER. We needed to do this for the calculator computation in note (3).

151

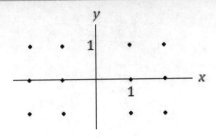

129 – 132 Consider the differential equation $\frac{dy}{dx} = \frac{y+1}{x}$ and the figure above.

129. On the axes provided, sketch a slope field for the differential equation at the twelve points indicated, and for $y > -1$, sketch the solution curve passing through the point $(-1,0)$. Then describe all points in the xy-plane, $x \neq 0$, for which $\frac{dy}{dx} = -1$.

Solution:

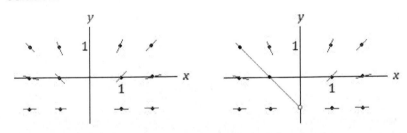

$$\frac{dy}{dx} = -1 \Leftrightarrow \frac{y+1}{x} = -1 \Leftrightarrow y+1 = -x \Leftrightarrow y = -x - 1.$$

Notes: (1) The figure above on the left gives the slope field for the differential equation at the twelve indicated points. For more information on how to draw this slope field see problem 105.

(2) The figure on the right shows the solution curve that passes through the point $(-1,0)$. Observe that at any point of the form $(x, -x-1)$, the slope is $\frac{dy}{dx} = \frac{(-x-1)+1}{x} = \frac{-x}{x} = -1$. So the solution curve is a line with slope -1.

130. Write an equation for the line tangent to the solution curve at the point $(-2,0)$. Use the equation to approximate $f(-1.5)$ where $y = f(x)$ is the particular solution of the differential equation with initial condition $f(-2) = 0$.

Solution: The slope of the tangent line at $(-2,0)$ is

$$m = \frac{dy}{dx}\Big|_{(-2,0)} = \frac{0+1}{-2} = -\frac{1}{2}.$$

So an equation of the tangent line in point–slope form is

$$y - 0 = -\frac{1}{2}(x - (-2)), \text{ or equivalently}$$

$$y = -\frac{1}{2}x - 1$$

When $x = -1.5$, we have $y = -\frac{1}{2}(-1.5) - 1 = -\frac{1}{4}$.

It follows that $f(-1.5) \approx -\frac{1}{4}$ or $-.25$.

Notes: (1) To find the slope of the tangent line to a function $y = f(x)$ at a point (x_0, y_0), we take the derivative $\frac{dy}{dx} = f'(x)$, and substitute in x_0 for x and y_0 for y.

In this problem, we were already given $\frac{dy}{dx}$, and so we simply need to substitute in the x-coordinate of the point for x and the y-coordinate of the point for y.

(2) The **point-slope form of an equation of a line** is

$$y - y_0 = m(x - x_0)$$

where m is the slope of the line and (x_0, y_0) is any point on the line.

It is generally easiest to write an equation of a line in point-slope form once the slope of the line and a point on the line are known.

In this problem, the slope is $-\frac{1}{2}$ and the point is $(-2,0)$.

131. Find $y = f(x)$, the particular solution to the differential equation with the initial condition $f(-2) = 0$.

Solution: We separate variables to get $\frac{dy}{y+1} = \frac{dx}{x}$. Now we integrate both sides of this equation to get $\ln|y + 1| = \ln|x| + C$. So we have that $\ln|y + 1| - \ln|x| = C$, and so $\ln\left|\frac{y+1}{x}\right| = C$. Changing to exponential form yields $\frac{y+1}{x} = \pm e^C$. We can simply rename the constant $\pm e^C$ as D.

So we have $\frac{y+1}{x} = D$.

Now we substitute in $x = -2$ and $y = 0$ to get $\frac{1}{-2} = D$. So we have $\frac{y+1}{x} = -\frac{1}{2}$, and so $y + 1 = -\frac{1}{2}x$, and finally, $y = -\frac{1}{2}x - 1$.

So $f(x) = -\frac{1}{2}x - 1$.

Notes: (1) See problem 52 for more information on separable differential equations.

(2) Observe that in this problem, the solution curve is a line, and therefore it is equal to its tangent line (so the approximation found in problem 130 is actually the exact value).

132. Describe the region in the xy-plane in which all solution curves to the differential equation are concave down.

Solution: $\frac{d^2y}{dx^2} = \frac{x\frac{dy}{dx} - (y+1)(1)}{x^2} = \frac{x\left(\frac{y+1}{x}\right) - (y+1)}{x^2} = \frac{(y+1) - (y+1)}{x^2} = \frac{0}{x^2} = 0.$

Since $\frac{d^2y}{dx^2}$ is always 0, it follows that there are no solution curves which are concave down. So the region is empty.

Notes: (1) The graph of a function $y = f(x)$ is concave down at x-values such that $\frac{d^2y}{dx^2} = f''(x) < 0$. Therefore, we are looking for solutions y to the differential equation for which $\frac{d^2y}{dx^2} < 0$.

(2) We get the third expression above by replacing $\frac{dy}{dx}$ with $\frac{y+1}{x}$.

(3) Since $\frac{d^2y}{dx^2} = 0$, all solutions to this differential equation are in fact linear. Only linear functions have second derivatives that are 0 everywhere.

To see this, we integrate each side of $\frac{d^2y}{dx^2} = 0$ to get $\frac{dy}{dx} = C$ where C is some constant. We integrate again to get $y = Cx + D$, where D is another constant.

133 – 136 * Suppose that the average annual salary of an NBA player is modeled by the function $S(t) = 161.4(1.169^t)$, where $S(t)$ is measured in thousands of dollars and t is measured in years since 1980 (for example, since $S(0) = 161.4$, the average salary of an NBA player in 1980 was $161,400).

133. * Find the average rate of change of $S(t)$ over the interval $0 \leq t \leq 20$. Interpret this answer and indicate units of measure.

Solution: The average rate of change of $S(t)$ over $0 \leq t \leq 20$ is

$$\frac{S(20)-S(0)}{20-0} = \mathbf{175.230} \text{ (or } \mathbf{175.231})$$

So the average rate of change in the annual salary of an NBA player from 1980 through 2000 was $175,230 (or $175,231) per year

Notes: (1) The **average rate of change** of the function f on the interval $a \leq x \leq b$ is $\frac{f(b)-f(a)}{b-a}$.

(2) $S(20) = 161.4(1.169^{20})$ and $S(0) = 161.4(1.169^0) = 161.4$.

(3) We perform the computation $\frac{S(20)-S(0)}{20-0}$ right in our calculator.

(4) When $t = 0$ the year is 1980, and when $t = 20$ the year is 2000.

(5) Since $S(t)$ is measured in *thousands of dollars*, we interpret the answer 175.230 as $175,230.

134. * Find the value of $S'(10)$. Using correct units, interpret the meaning of the value in the context of the problem.

Solution: We use our calculator to compute

$$S'(10) = \mathbf{120.112}$$

So the average annual salary of an NBA player is increasing at a rate of $120,112 per year at the beginning of 1990.

Notes: (1) We can compute $S'(10)$ directly in our TI-84 calculator as follows:

Press MATH, followed by 8 (or scroll up 3 times and select 8:nDeriv( ). Type 161.4(1.169^X), X, 10) followed by ENTER. The display will show 120.1121575. We truncate this number to 120.112.

(2) As an alternative, we can first compute the derivative

$$S'(x) = 161.4(1.169^t)(\ln(1.169))$$

and then use our calculator to get

$$S'(10) = 161.4(1.169^{10})(\ln(1.169))$$

(3) Since $S'(10)$ is positive, it follows that the average annual salary of an NBA player is *increasing* when $t = 10$.

(4) $t = 10$ at the beginning of the year 1990.

(5) Since $S(t)$ is measured in *thousands of dollars*, we interpret the answer 120.112 as \$120,112.

135. * Use a right Riemann sum with five equal subintervals to approximate $\frac{1}{20}\int_0^{20} S(t)dt$. Does this approximation overestimate or underestimate the average salary from the beginning of 1980 through the end of 2000? Explain your reasoning.

Solution:

$$\frac{1}{20}\int_0^{20} S(t)dt \approx \frac{1}{20} \cdot 4[S(4) + S(8) + S(12) + S(16) + S(20)]$$

$$\approx 1508.911 \text{ or } 1508.912.$$

This approximation is an overestimate, because a right Riemann sum is used and the function S is strictly increasing.

Note: See problem 119 for general information about Riemann Sum Approximations, and problem 127 for more details about this type of problem.

136. * Find the year in which it occurs that the average annual salary is equal to the average salary from the beginning of 1980 through the end of 2000.

Solution: The average salary from the beginning of 1980 through the end of 2000 is

156

$$\frac{1}{20-0}\int_0^{20} S(t)dt \approx 1122.203$$

So we solve the equation $S(t) = \frac{1}{20}\int_0^{20} S(t)dt$ and get $t \approx 12.418$ or $t \approx 12.419$.

It follows that the average annual salary is equal to the average salary from the beginning of 1980 through the end of 2000 in **1992**.

Notes: (1) We can compute $\int_0^{20} S(t)dt$ directly in our TI-84 calculator as follows:

Press MATH, followed by 9 (or scroll up 2 times and select 9:fnInt( ). Type 161.4(1.169^X), X, 0, 20) followed by ENTER. The display will show 22444.0633.

(2) Remember to multiply 22444.0633 by $\frac{1}{20}$ to get

$$\frac{1}{20}\int_0^{20} S(t)dt = 1122.203165.$$

(3) We can solve the equation $S(t) = \frac{1}{20}\int_0^{20} S(t)dt$ using the graphing features of our TI-84 calculator as follows:

Press Y=, and next to Y_1 type 161.4(1.169^X), and next to Y_2 type 1122.203. Then press WINDOW, set Xmin to 0, Xmax to 20, Ymin to 0, and Ymax to a number greater than 1122.203 (such as 1500). Next press GRAPH. After the two graphs appear press CALC (2nd TRACE), followed by 5 (or scroll down and select 5:intersect). Press ENTER three times, and we see that X is approximately 12.418.

(4) $t = 12$ at the beginning of the year 1992. It follows that the average annual salary is equal to the average salary from the beginning of 1980 through the end of 2000 in 1992.

157

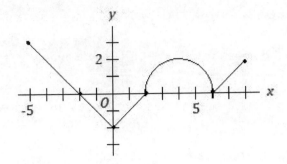

137 – 144 Let f be the continuous function defined on $[-5,8]$ whose graph, consisting of three line segments and a semicircle centered at $(4,0)$, is shown above. Let F be the function that is defined by $F(x) = \int_2^x f(t)\, dt$.

137. Find the values of $F(8)$ and $F(-1)$.

Solution: $F(8) = \int_2^8 f(t)\, dt = \int_2^6 f(t)\, dt + \int_6^8 f(t)\, dt$

$$= \frac{\pi}{2}(2)^2 + \frac{1}{2}(2)(2) = 2\pi + 2.$$

$F(-1) = \int_2^{-1} f(t)\, dt = -\int_{-1}^2 f(t)\, dt = -[\int_{-1}^0 f(t)\, dt + \int_0^2 f(t)\, dt]$

$$= -\left[-\left(\frac{1+2}{2}\right)(1) - \frac{1}{2}(2)(2)\right] = -\left(-\frac{3}{2} - 2\right) = \frac{7}{2}.$$

Notes: (1) $\int_2^6 f(t)\, dt$ is the area under the semicircle of radius 2 shown. The area of this semicircle is $\frac{\pi}{2}r^2 = \frac{\pi}{2}(2)^2 = 2\pi$.

(2) $\int_6^8 f(t)\, dt$ is the area under the rightmost triangle shown. The area of this triangle is $\frac{1}{2}bh = \frac{1}{2}(2)(2) = 2$.

(3) $\int_{-1}^0 f(t)\, dt$ is the *negative* of the area of the trapezoid from -1 to 0 with bases of length 1 and 2, and a height of length 1 (note that the height is along the x-axis). This area is $\frac{b_1 + b_2}{2} \cdot h = \left(\frac{1+2}{2}\right)(1) = \frac{3}{2}$.

(4) $\int_0^2 f(t)\, dt$ is the *negative* of the area of the triangle from 0 to 2 with bases and height both 2. This area is $\frac{1}{2}bh = \frac{1}{2}(2)(2) = 2$.

158

138. For each of $F'(-4)$, $F''(-4)$, $F'(6)$, and $F''(6)$, find the value or explain why it does not exist.

Solution: $F'(-4) = f(-4) = 2$.

$F''(-4) = f'(-4) = -1$.

$F'(6) = f(6) = 0$.

$F''(6) = f'(6)$ which does not exist because the graph of f has a "cusp" at $x = 6$.

Notes: (1) To compute $F'(x)$ we use the first Fundamental Theorem of Calculus which says that if $F(x) = \int_a^x f(t)\, dt$, for some constant a, then $F'(x) = f(x)$.

(2) To compute $f(x)$ we can simply use the given graph of f. For example, $f(6) = 0$ because the point $(6,0)$ is on the graph of f.

(3) $f'(x)$ is the slope of the tangent line to the graph of f at x.

At $x = -4$, the graph of f is a line with slope -1. So $f'(-4) = -1$.

At $x = 6$, the slope from the left is ∞ and the slope from the right is 1. That is $f'(6)^- = \infty$ and $f'(6)^+ = 1$. Since these two values disagree, $f'(6)$ does not exist.

(4) See problem 106 for more detailed information about the notation $f'(x)^-$ and $f'(x)^+$.

139. On what open intervals contained in $-5 < x < 8$ is the graph of F both increasing and concave up? Justify your answer.

Solution: The graph of F is increasing when $F' = f > 0$ (or equivalently, the graph of f is above the x-axis). The graph of F is concave up when $F'' = f' > 0$, or equivalently when f is increasing.

f is above the x-axis and increasing on the intervals $2 < x < 4$ and $6 < x < 8$.

140. Find the x-coordinate of each point at which the graph of F has a horizontal tangent line. For each of these points, determine whether F has a relative minimum, relative maximum, or neither a minimum nor a maximum at the point. Justify your answer.

Solution: $F'(x) = f(x) = 0$ when $x = -2$, $x = 2$, and $x = 6$.

159

$F' = f$ changes sign from positive to negative at $x = -2$. Therefore F has a **relative maximum** at $x = -2$.

$F' = f$ changes sign from negative to positive at $x = 2$. Therefore F has a **relative minimum** at $x = 2$.

$F' = f$ does not change sign at $x = 6$. Therefore F has **neither** a relative minimum nor a relative maximum at $x = 6$.

    141. For $-5 < x < 8$, find all values of x for which the graph of F has a point of inflection. Explain your reasoning.

Solution: The graph of F has a point of inflection at $x = 0$, $x = 4$, and $x = 6$ because $F'' = f'$ changes sign at each of these values.

Note: Recall that $f' < 0$ is equivalent to f decreasing, and $f' > 0$ is equivalent to f increasing.

So f' changing sign is equivalent to f changing from increasing to decreasing, or from decreasing to increasing. We can check this easily by looking at the graph of f.

    142. Find the absolute minimum and absolute maximum of F over the closed interval $[-5,8]$. Explain your reasoning.

Solution: We will evaluate F at each critical number of F and the two endpoints of the interval.

$F(-5) = \int_2^{-5} f(t)\, dt = -\left[\left(\frac{3+2}{2}\right) \cdot 1 + 0 - \frac{1}{2}(2)(2)\right] = -\left(\frac{5}{2} - 2\right) = -\frac{1}{2}$

$F(-2) = \int_2^{-2} f(t)\, dt = -\int_{-2}^{2} f(t)\, dt = \left(\frac{1}{2}\right)(4)(2) = 4$

$F(2) = \int_2^2 f(t)\, dt = 0$

$F(6) = \int_2^6 f(t)\, dt = \frac{\pi}{2}(2)^2 = 2\pi$

$F(8) = \int_2^8 f(t)\, dt = 2\pi + \frac{1}{2}(2)(2) = 2\pi + 2$

The absolute minimum of F on $[-5,8]$ is $F(-5) = -\frac{1}{2}$.

The absolute maximum of F on $[-5,8]$ is $F(8) = 2\pi + 2$.

    143. The function G is defined by $G(x) = \ln\frac{F(x)}{2x}$. Find $G'(-4)$.

Solution: $G'(x) = \left(\frac{2x}{F(x)}\right)\left(\frac{2xF'(x)-2F(x)}{4x^2}\right)$.

So $G'(-4) = \left(\frac{-8}{F(-4)}\right)\left(\frac{-8F'(-4)-2F(-4)}{64}\right) = \left(\frac{-8}{2}\right)\left(\frac{-8\cdot2-2\cdot2}{64}\right) = \frac{5}{4}$ or **1.25**.

Notes: (1) $F(-4) = \int_2^{-4} f(t)\,dt = -\int_{-4}^2 f(t)\,dt$

$$= -\left[\int_{-4}^0 f(t)\,dt + \int_0^2 f(t)\,dt\right] = -\left[0 - \frac{1}{2}(2)(2)\right] = 2.$$

(2) $F'(-4) = f(-4) = 2$ because the point $(-4,2)$ is on the graph of f.

144. The function H is defined by $H(x) = f(\frac{3x^2-2x}{e^{x-1}})$. Find an equation of the tangent line to the graph of H at the point where $x = 1$.

Solution: $H(1) = f\left(\frac{3(1)^2-2\cdot1}{e^{1-1}}\right) = f\left(\frac{3-2}{e^0}\right) = f(1) = -1$.

$H'(x) = f'(\frac{3x^2-2x}{e^{x-1}})\left(\frac{e^{x-1}(6x-2)-(3x^2-2x)e^{x-1}}{e^{2x-2}}\right)$.

So $H'(1) = f'(1)\left(\frac{4-1}{1}\right) = 3f'(1) = 3\cdot1 = 3$.

So the line passes through the point $(1,-1)$ and has slope $m = 3$. An equation of the line in point-slope form is then

$$y + 1 = 3(x - 1).$$

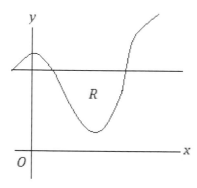

145 – 148 * Let R be the region in the first quadrant enclosed by the graph of $f(x) = x^6 - 3.5x^4 + 7$ and the horizontal line $y = 5$, as shown in the figure above.

161

145. * Write an equation for the tangent line to the graph of f at $x = -0.5$.

Solution: $f(-0.5) = (-0.5)^6 - 3.5(-0.5)^4 + 7 \approx 6.797$.

$f'(x) = 6x^5 - 14x^3$.

So $f'(-0.5) = 6(-0.5)^5 - 14(-0.5)^3 \approx 1.563$.

So the line passes through $(-0.5, 6.797)$ and has slope $m = 1.563$. An equation of the line in point-slope form is then

$$y - 6.797 = 1.563(x + 0.5).$$

146. * Find the volume of the solid generated when R is rotated about the horizontal line $y = -3$.

Solution: $V = \pi \int_{.934}^{1.822} [(5 - (-3))^2 - (x^6 - 3.5x^4 + 7 - (-3))^2] \, dx$

$= \pi \int_{.934}^{1.822} [64 - (x^6 - 3.5x^4 + 10)^2] \, dx \approx \mathbf{93.216}$.

Notes: (1) We begin by finding the x-values where f intersects the line $y = 5$. We can do this in our calculator as follows:

Press Y=, and next to Y$_1$ type X^6 − 3.5X^4 + 7 and next to Y$_2$ type 5. Then press WINDOW, set Xmin to 0, Xmax to 5, Ymin to 0, and Ymax to 10 (other windows will work, of course – you may need to experiment a bit to find the right window). Next press GRAPH. After the two graphs appear press CALC (2nd TRACE), followed by 5 (or scroll down and select 5:intersect).Press ENTER twice, then place the cursor close to the leftmost point of intersection and press ENTER again. The display will show that $x \approx .934$. Repeat the procedure again, but this time place the cursor close to the rightmost point of intersection before pressing ENTER the third time. This time the display will show that $x \approx 1.822$.

(2) We will use the **washer method** to find the requested volume. A *washer* is a disk with a hole in it. A typical washer can be described as follows:

First we take a value x between .934 and 1.822 Find this number on the x-axis.

We then draw the outer radius of the washer by drawing a vertical segment from the line $y = -3$ straight up until we hit the line $y = 5$.

Next we draw a circle from the top of this line segment that sweeps below the line $x = -3$, and who's radius is as specified in the last step.

We draw the inner radius of the washer by drawing a vertical line segment from the line $y = -3$ straight up until we hit the graph of f.

We then draw a circle from the top of this line segment that sweeps below the line $x = -3$, and who's radius is as specified in the last step.

Here is a picture:

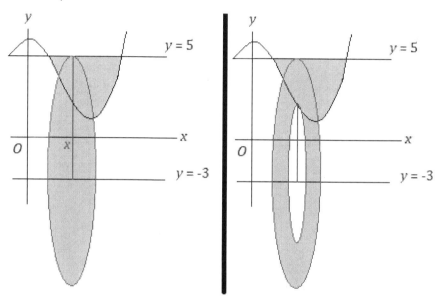

The picture on the left shows the disk formed from the outer radius. This radius is $R = 5 - (-3) = 5 + 3 = 8$. It follows that the area of this disk is $\pi R^2 = \pi(8)^2 = 64\pi$.

The picture on the right shows the formation of the hole from the inner radius. This radius is $r = f(x) - (-3) = f(x) + 3$. It follows that the area of this disk is $\pi r^2 = \pi(f(x) + 3)^2$

So the area of the washer is "outer disk" − "inner hole." This is

$$\pi R^2 - \pi r^2 = 64\pi - \pi(f(x) + 8)^2 = \pi[64 - (f(x) + 3)^2]$$

The washer method requires us to integrate this area over the given interval, in this case from .934 to 1.822.

$$V = \pi \int_{.934}^{1.822} [64 - (f(x) + 3)^2] \, dx$$

$$= \pi \int_{.934}^{1.822} [64 - (x^6 - 3.5x^4 + 10)^2] \, dx$$

(3) We can compute $\int_{.934}^{1.822} [64 - (x^6 - 3.5x^4 + 10)^2] \, dx$ directly in our TI-84 calculator as follows:

Press MATH, followed by 9 (or scroll up 2 times and select 9:fnInt( ). Type 64 − (X^6 − 3.5X^4 + 10)^2, X, .934, 1.822) followed by ENTER. The display will show 29.67169214.

Remember to multiply this result by π to get approximately **93.216.**

    147. * The region R is the base of a solid. For this solid, each cross section perpendicular to the x-axis is an equilateral triangle. Find the volume of the solid.

Solution: $V = \frac{\sqrt{3}}{4} \int_{.934}^{1.822} (-x^6 + 3.5x^4 - 2)^2 \, dx \approx \mathbf{3.420}.$

Notes: (1) To see where the limits of integration come from, see note (1) from problem 146.

(2) Let's draw a cross section that is perpendicular to the x-axis.

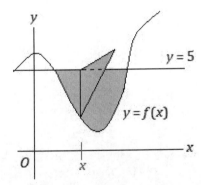

First we take a value x between .934 and 1.822 and find this number on the x-axis.

We then draw a side of the triangle between $y = f(x)$ and $y = 5$. This side has length $5 - f(x) = 5 - (x^6 - 3.5x^4 + 7) = -x^6 + 3.5x^4 - 2$.

The area of an equilateral triangle with side length s is $A = \frac{\sqrt{3}}{4} s^2$ (see note (4) below).

It follows that the area of this triangle is $\frac{\sqrt{3}}{4}(-x^6 + 3.5x^4 - 2)^2$.

To get the desired volume, we now simply integrate this expression over the interval [.934,1.822]:

$$= \frac{\sqrt{3}}{4} \int_{.934}^{1.822} (-x^6 + 3.5x^4 - 2)^2 \, dx.$$

(3) We can compute $\int_{.934}^{1.822} (-x^6 + 3.5x^4 - 2)^2 \, dx$ directly in our TI-84 calculator as follows:

Press MATH, followed by 9 (or scroll up 2 times and select 9:fnInt( ). Type (-X^6 + 3.5X^4 − 2)^2, X, .934, 1.822) followed by ENTER. The display will show 7.89719.

Remember to multiply this result by $\frac{\sqrt{3}}{4}$ to get approximately **3.420.**

(4) Most students do not know the formula for the area of an equilateral triangle, so here is a quick derivation.

Let's start by drawing a picture of an equilateral triangle with side length s, and draw an **altitude** from a vertex to the opposite base. Note that an altitude of an equilateral triangle is the same as the **median** and **angle bisector** (this is in fact true for any isosceles triangle).

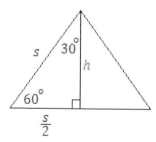

So we get two 30, 60, 90 right triangles with a leg of length $\frac{s}{2}$ and hypotenuse of length s.

We can find h by recalling that the side opposite the 60 degree angle has length $\sqrt{3}$ times the length of the side opposite the 30 degree angle. So $h = \frac{\sqrt{3}s}{2}$.

Alternatively, we can use the Pythagorean Theorem to find h:

$$h^2 = s^2 - \left(\frac{s}{2}\right)^2 = s^2 - \frac{s^2}{4} = \frac{3s^2}{4}. \text{ So } h = \frac{\sqrt{3}s}{2}.$$

It follows that the area of the triangle is

$$A = \frac{1}{2}\left(\frac{s}{2} + \frac{s}{2}\right)\left(\frac{\sqrt{3}s}{2}\right) = \frac{1}{2}s\left(\frac{\sqrt{3}s}{2}\right) = \frac{\sqrt{3}}{4}s^2.$$

148. The vertical line $x = a$ divides R into two regions with equal areas. Write, but do not solve, an equation involving integral expressions whose solution gives the value a.

Solution:

$$\int_{.934}^{a}[5 - f(x)]\,dx = \int_{a}^{1.822}[5 - f(x)]\,dx$$

$$\int_{.934}^{a}[5 - (x^6 - 3.5x^4 + 7\,)]\,dx = \int_{a}^{1.822}[5 - (x^6 - 3.5x^4 + 7\,)]\,dx$$

$$\int_{.934}^{a}(-x^6 + 3.5x^4 - 2\,)\,dx = \int_{a}^{1.822}(-x^6 + 3.5x^4 - 2\,)\,dx$$

149 – 152 Let h and k be twice-differentiable functions such that $h(1) = -4$, $h(8) = 6$, $k(-3) = 1$, and $k(2) = 8$. Let f be the function given by $f(x) = h(k(x))$.

149. Let b satisfy $-4 < b < 6$. Explain why there must be a value a for $-3 < a < 2$ such that $f(a) = b$.

Solution: Since h and k are twice-differentiable, they are continuous. It follows that f is continuous.

$f(-3) = h(k(-3)) = h(1) = -4$ and $f(2) = h(k(2)) = h(8) = 6$.

Since f is a continuous function satisfying $f(-3) < b < f(2)$, the Intermediate Value Theorem guarantees that there is a value a, with $-3 < a < 2$, such that $f(a) = b$.

Notes: (1) The **Intermediate Value Theorem** says that if f is a continuous function on the interval $[j, k]$ and r is between $f(j)$ and $f(k)$, then there is a real number s with $j < s < k$ such that $f(s) = r$.

Note that "r is between $f(j)$ and $f(k)$" means either $f(j) < r < f(k)$ or $f(k) < r < f(j)$. It depends if $f(j) < f(k)$ or $f(k) < f(j)$.

(2) In this problem the interval is $[-3,2]$, $f(-3) = -4$, and $f(2) = 6$, $r = b$, and $s = a$. Here is a picture:

166

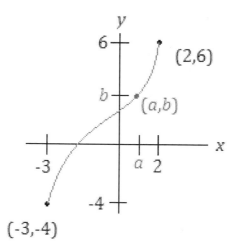

(-3,-4)

Let's just clarify the order of events that take place in this picture. First, b is given between $f(-3) = -4$ and $f(2) = 6$. Since f is continuous, the Intermediate Value theorem guarantees that the graph of f must pass through the point (a, b) for some a between -3 and 2. In other words, there is a real number a, with $-3 < a < 2$, such that $f(a) = b$.

150. Is there a value c for $-3 < c < 2$ such that $f'(c) = 2$. Justify your answer.

Solution: Since h and k are differentiable, so is f. In particular, f is continuous on $[-3,2]$ and differentiable on $(-3,2)$. So the Mean Value Theorem guarantees that there is a value c, with $-3 < c < 2$ such that
$$f'(c) = \frac{f(2)-f(-3)}{2-(-3)} = \frac{h(k(2))-h(k(-3))}{2+3} = \frac{h(8)-h(1)}{5} = \frac{6-(-4)}{5} = \frac{10}{5} = 2.$$

Note: See problem 46 for more information on the Mean Value Theorem.

151. Suppose that $h'(1) = k'(2)$ and $h'(8) = k'(-3)$. Explain why there must be a value d, with $-3 < d < 2$ such that $f''(d) = 0$.

Solution: $f'(x) = h'(k(x)) \cdot k'(x)$

$f'(-3) = h'(k(-3)) \cdot k'(-3) = h'(1) \cdot k'(-3)$

$f'(2) = h'(k(2)) \cdot k'(2) = h'(8) \cdot k'(2).$

Since $h'(1) = k'(2)$ and $h'(8) = k'(-3)$, we have $f'(-3) = f'(2)$.

Also, since h and k are twice-differentiable, so is f. So f' is differentiable. In particular, f' is continuous on $[-3,2]$ and differentiable on $(-3,2)$. So the Mean Value Theorem guarantees that there is a value d, with $-3 < d < 2$ such that $f''(d) = \frac{f'(2)-f'(-3)}{2-(-3)} = \frac{0}{2+3} = 0$.

Note: See problem 46 for more information on the Mean Value Theorem.

152. Suppose that $h''(x) = k''(x) = 0$ for all x. Find all points of inflection on the graph of f.

Solution 1: Since $h''(x) = k''(x) = 0$ for all x, it follows that h and k are linear functions. The composition of two linear functions is also linear. Therefore f is a linear function, and so the graph of f has no points of inflection.

Notes: (1) Since $h''(x) = 0$, it follows by integration that $h'(x) = C$ for some constant C. Integrating again gives $h(x) = Cx + D$ for another constant D. That is h is a linear function.

Similarly, k is a linear function, let's say $k(x) = Ax + B$.

(2) Let's compose h and k as defined in the first note.

$$f(x) = h\big(k(x)\big) = h(Ax + B) = C(Ax + B) + D = CAx + (CB + D).$$

So f is a linear function with slope $m = CA$ and y-intercept $(0, CB + D)$.

Solution 2: $f'(x) = h'\big(k(x)\big) \cdot k'(x)$

$$f''(x) = h'\big(k(x)\big) \cdot k''(x) + k'(x) \cdot h''\big(k(x)\big) \cdot k'(x).$$

Since $h''(x) = k''(x) = 0$ for all x, we have

$$f''(x) = h'\big(k(x)\big) \cdot 0 + k'(x) \cdot 0 \cdot k'(x) = 0.$$

Since $f''(x) = 0$ for all x, there are no x-values at which f'' changes sign. So the graph of f has no points of inflection.

153 – 160 * A particle moves along the x-axis so that its velocity v at time $t \geq 0$ is given by $v(t) = \cos(t^2)$. The position of the particle at time t is $s(t)$ and its position at time $t = 0$ is $s(0) = 2$.

153. * Find the acceleration of the particle at time $t = 4$. Is the speed of the particle increasing or decreasing at time $t = 4$? Justify your answer.

Solution: $a(t) = v'(t) = -2t\sin(t^2)$. So $a(4) = -8\sin 16 \approx \mathbf{2.303}$.

Also $v(4) = \cos 16 \approx -.958$.

Since $v(4) < 0$ and $a(4) > 0$, the speed of the particle is decreasing at $t = 4$.

Notes: (1) The acceleration function $a(t)$ is the derivative of the velocity function $v(t)$. That is, $a(t) = v'(t)$.

(2) Since $v(4) < 0$, the particle is moving to the left at time $t = 4$. Since $a(4) > 0$, the acceleration is acting in the opposite direction of the velocity. It follows that the particle is slowing down at time $t = 4$.

In general, if the velocity and acceleration have the same sign, then the particle is speeding up, and if the velocity and acceleration have opposite signs, then the particle is slowing down.

Important: Make sure that your calculator is in radian mode before beginning problems 153-160 (Press MODE and select Radian). Otherwise many of the answers will be incorrect!

154. * Find all values of t in the interval $0 \le t \le 2$ for which the speed of the particle is $\frac{1}{2}$. For each such value of t determine if the particle is moving to the right or to the left.

Solution: We solve the equation $|\cos(t^2)| = \frac{1}{2}$ and get the following two solutions in the interval $0 \le t \le 2$: $t \approx \mathbf{1.023}$ and $t \approx \mathbf{1.447}$.

Now, $\cos(1.023^2) \approx .501 > 0$ so that the particle is moving to the **right** at $t = 1.023$.

Also $\cos(1.447^2) \approx -.499 < 0$ so that the particle is moving to the **left** at $t = 1.447$.

Notes: (1) We can solve the equation $|\cos(t^2)| = \frac{1}{2}$ in our calculator as follows:

Press Y=, and next to Y_1 type abs(cos(X^2)) and next to Y_2 type 1/2. Note that to get "abs(", press MATH, scroll right to NUM, and press ENTER.

Next press WINDOW, set Xmin to 0, Xmax to 2, Ymin to 0, and Ymax to 1 (other windows will work, of course, but this window is not too big and contains all of the information we need). Next press GRAPH.

169

After the two graphs appear press CALC (2nd TRACE), followed by 5 (or scroll down and select 5:intersect). Press ENTER twice, then place the cursor close to the leftmost point of intersection and press ENTER again. The display will show that $x \approx 1.023$. Repeat the procedure again, but this time place the cursor close to the rightmost point of intersection before pressing ENTER the third time. This time the display will show that $x \approx 1.447$.

155. * Find the total distance traveled by the particle from time $t = 0$ to $t = 2$.

Solution: Total distance $= \int_0^2 |v(t)| \, dt \approx \mathbf{1.493}$.

Notes: (1) We can compute $\int_0^3 |v(t)| \, dt = \int_0^3 |\cos(t^2)| \, dt$ using our TI-84 calculator by first selecting fnInt((or pressing 9) under the MATH menu, and then going to the MATH menu again, moving right once to NUM and selecting abs((or pressing 1). The display will show the following:
fnInt(abs(

We then type the following: fnInt(abs(cos(X^2), X, 0, 2), and press ENTER.

The display will show 1.493441841. So we can answer 1.493.

(2) See problems 78, 92, and 126 for further explanation. Note that those problems required a lot more work because a calculator was not necessarily allowed.

156. * Find the position of the particle at time $t = 4$.

Solution: $s(4) = 2 + \int_0^4 v(t) \, dt = 2 + \int_0^4 \cos(t^2) \, dt \approx \mathbf{2.594}$.

Notes: (1) We do not need to worry about the particle changing direction in this problem since we only want the particle's position relative to its starting point.

(2) If we know the velocity function v of a particle, then we can find its position function s by integrating the velocity v. That is $s(t) = \int v(t) dt$.

(3) $\int_a^b v(t) dt = s(b) - s(a)$ gives the distance between the position of the particle at time a and the position of the particle at time b.

So $\int_0^4 v(t) \, dt$ is the distance between the position of the particle at time 0 and the position of the particle at time 4.

Since the particle started at position $s(0) = 2$, we must add 2 to $\int_0^4 v(t)\, dt$ to get the final position.

(4) Compare this to problem 155 where we were asked to find the *total distance* traveled by the particle. In that case we are concerned about where the particle changes direction (this is why we integrate the absolute value of the velocity instead of just the velocity), whereas here we are only looking for the final position and therefore do not care about changes in direction.

157. * Find all times t in the interval $0 \le t \le 3$ at which the particle changes direction. Justify your answer.

Solution: We first solve the equation $v(t) = 0$ (using our calculator), to get $t \approx 1.253$, $t \approx 2.171$, and $t \approx 2.802$.

Next we observe the following:

$v(t) > 0$ for $0 \le t < 1.253$ $v(t) < 0$ for $1.253 < t < 2.171$

$v(t) > 0$ for $2.171 < t < 2.802$ $v(t) < 0$ for $2.802 < t \le 3$

It follows that the particle changes direction at $t = \mathbf{1.253}$, $\mathbf{2.171}$, and $\mathbf{2.802}$.

Note: See problems 73 and 107 for more information about detecting changes in direction.

158. Determine all values $t \ge 0$ for which the acceleration is 0. Then determine all values of t, $0 \le t \le 3$, for which the particle is speeding up.

Solution: We first solve the equation $a(t) = v'(t) = -2t \sin(t^2) = 0$ (using our calculator), to get $t = \mathbf{0}$, $t \approx \mathbf{1.772}$, and $t \approx \mathbf{2.507}$.

Next we observe the following:

$a(t) < 0$ for $0 < t < 1.772$ $a(t) > 0$ for $1.772 < t < 2.507$

$a(t) < 0$ for $2.507 < t \le 3$

Let's put this information together with the information from problem 157 into one sign chart:

	0	1.253	1.772	2.171	2.507	2.802	3
$v(t)$	+	−	−	+	+	−	
$a(t)$	−	−	+	+	−	−	

So the particle is speeding up for $1.253 < t < 1.772$, $2.171 < t < 2.507$, and $2.802 < t \le 3$.

In interval notation, the particle is speeding up for t in

$$(1.253,1.772) \cup (2.171,2.507) \cup (2.802,3].$$

Notes: (1) The particle is speeding up when the velocity and acceleration have the same sign. The particle is slowing down when the velocity and acceleration have opposite signs.

(2) See problem 107 for more details.

159. * For $0 \le t \le 3$, find the time t at which the particle is farthest to the right. Explain your answer.

Solution: The particle changes from moving right to moving left at those times t for which $v(t) = 0$ with $v(t)$ changing from positive to negative. This happens at $t = 1.253$, and $t = 2.802$.

The particle's position at $t = 1.253$ is

$$2 + \int_0^{1.253} v(t)\, dt = 2 + \int_0^{1.253} \cos(t^2)\, dt \approx 2.977$$

The particle's position at $t = 2.802$ is

$$2 + \int_0^{2.802} v(t)\, dt = 2 + \int_0^{2.802} \cos(t^2)\, dt \approx 2.803$$

So the particle is farthest to the right at $t = 1.253$

Note: See problem 156 for more explanation on these integrals.

160. * Find the value of the constant B for which $v(t)$ satisfies $Ba(t)\cos(t^2) - 2tv(t)\sin(t^2) = 0$, where $a(t)$ is the acceleration of the particle at time t.

Solution: We solve $B[-2t\sin(t^2)][\cos(t^2)] - 2t\cos(t^2)\sin(t^2) = 0$.

$$-2t\sin(t^2)\cos(t^2)(B+1) = 0.$$

So $B + 1 = 0$, and $B = -1$.

SUPPLEMENTAL PROBLEMS
QUESTIONS

LEVEL 1: PRECALCULUS

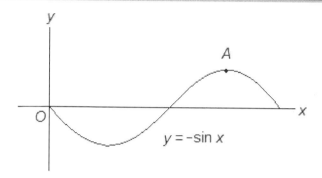

1. The figure above shows one cycle of the graph of the function $y = -\sin x$ for $0 \le x \le 2\pi$. If the maximum value of the function occurs at point A, then the coordinates of A are

    (A) $(\frac{\pi}{3}, 1)$

    (B) $(\frac{\pi}{3}, 0)$

    (C) $(\frac{\pi}{2}, \pi)$

    (D) $(\frac{3\pi}{2}, 1)$

2. If a and b are in the domain of a function g and $g(a) = g(b)$, which of the following must be true?

    (A) $a = b$
    (B) g fails the vertical line test.
    (C) there is a horizontal line that intersects the graph of g at least twice.
    (D) the graph of g is a horizontal line.

173

3. If $k(x) = \log_5 \sqrt[3]{2x + 1}$, what is $k^{-1}\left(\frac{2}{3}\right)$?

    (A) 8.7
    (B) 10.2
    (C) 11.5
    (D) 12.0

4. Which of the following lines is an asymptote of the graph of $g(x) = 5\ln(x + 2)$?

    (A) $y = -2$
    (B) $y = 0$
    (C) $x = -2$
    (D) $x = 0$

5. Which of the following is the graph of a function that is both even and odd?

(A)
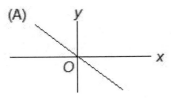

(B)

(C)
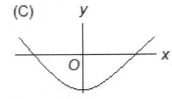

(D)
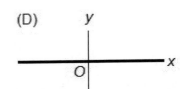

6. If $(x - 2)g(x) = x^3 - 5x^2 + 10x - 8$ where $g(x)$ is a polynomial in x, then $g(x) =$

    (A) $x + 4$
    (B) $x^2 + 4$
    (C) $x^2 + 4x$
    (D) $x^2 - 3x + 4$

7. How many roots does the function $f(x) = x^3 + x^2 - 2x$ have?

    (A) One
    (B) Two
    (C) Three
    (D) Four

8. If $k(x) = \frac{x^2-4}{x-2}$ and $h(x) = \frac{3\ln x^2}{8}$, then $h\big(k(e-2)\big) =$

   (A) .12
   (B) .5
   (C) .51
   (D) .75

9. If $f(x) = 5x^3 + 2 - \sec x$, then $f'(x) =$

   (A) $15x^2 - \sec x \tan x$
   (B) $15x^2 + \sec x \tan x$
   (C) $15x^2 + 2 - \sec x \tan x$
   (D) $\frac{5}{4}x^4 + 2x - \ln|\sec x + \tan x|$

10. If $g(x) = \left(\frac{x+2}{x-2}\right)^2$, then $g'(-2) =$

   (A) $-\frac{1}{4}$

   (B) $-\frac{1}{2}$

   (C) 0

   (D) $\frac{1}{4}$

11. If $h(x) = \frac{1}{6}x^6 - 2\ln(3x-2) + \frac{1}{\sqrt{x}}$, then $h'(x) =$

   (A) $x^5 - \frac{2}{3x-2} + \frac{1}{2\sqrt{x^3}}$

   (B) $x^5 - \frac{6}{3x-2} - \frac{1}{2\sqrt{x^3}}$

   (C) $\frac{1}{6}x^5 - \frac{2}{3x-2} + \sqrt{x}$

   (D) $\frac{1}{42}x^7 - \frac{2}{\ln(3x-2)} + 2\sqrt{x}$

175

12. The slope of the tangent line to the graph of $y = xe^{2x}$ at $x = \ln 3$ is

    (A) 9
    (B) 18
    (C) $18 \ln 3$
    (D) $18 \ln 3 + 9$

13. The instantaneous rate of change at $x = 1$ of the function $f(x) = \sqrt{x} \ln(2x^2 - 1)$ is

    (A) 4
    (B) 2
    (C) $\frac{5}{4}$
    (D) $\frac{1}{2}$

14. $\frac{d}{dx} \left[\frac{\pi^2}{7} + \frac{5}{\sqrt[3]{x^4}} + x^x \right] =$

15. If $y = x^{\cot x}$, then $y' =$

16. Differentiate $f(x) = \frac{(x-2) \log_3 x}{\sqrt[3]{x}}$ and express your answer as a simple fraction.

LEVEL 1: INTEGRATION

17. $\int (3x^2 - 6\sqrt{x} + e^x) \, dx =$

    (A) $6x - \frac{3}{\sqrt{x}} + e^x + C$
    (B) $x^3 - 4\sqrt{x^3} + e^x + C$
    (C) $x^3 - 3x + e^x + C$
    (D) $x^3 - 3x + xe^{x-1} + C$

18. $\int_0^\pi (3x^2 - 2 \cos x) \, dx =$

    (A) π^3
    (B) $\pi^3 - 2$
    (C) 6π
    (D) $6\pi - 2$

19. $\int e^{x^2 + \ln x} \, dx =$

    (A) $2x \ln x + C$

    (B) $\frac{1}{2} e^{x^2} + C$

    (C) $e^{x^2} + C$

    (D) $2e^{x^2} + C$

20. $\int \frac{x^5 + 2x}{\sqrt{x}} \, dx =$

21. $\int_0^1 \frac{x^2 + e^{3x}}{x^3 + e^{3x}} \, dx =$

22. $\int \left(\frac{3}{x^5} + \frac{5}{x} - 5\sqrt[3]{x} + \frac{3}{\sqrt[5]{x^4}} \right) dx =$

23. $\int \frac{x}{(3x^2+1) \ln(3x^2+1)} \, dx =$

24. $\int 3^{x \cos x} (x \sin x - \cos x) dx =$

LEVEL 1: LIMITS AND CONTINUITY

25. What value does $\frac{x^2 - 3x - 10}{5x + 10}$ approach as x approaches -2?

    (A) $-\frac{7}{5}$

    (B) -1

    (C) $-\frac{5}{7}$

    (D) 5

26. $\lim\limits_{x \to \infty} \frac{\sqrt{3x^2 - 1}}{2x - 5} =$

    (A) $\frac{1}{2}$

    (B) $\frac{\sqrt{3}}{2}$

    (C) ∞

    (D) The limit does not exist

27. The graph of the rational function r where $r(x) = \frac{x^2-2x-1}{x^2-4}$ has asymptotes $x = a$, $x = b$, and $y = c$. What is the value of $a + b + c$?

   (A) $-\frac{1}{4}$

   (B) $\frac{1}{4}$

   (C) 1

   (D) 3

28. If the function g is continuous for all real numbers and if $g(x) = \frac{x^3+2x^2-15x}{x-3}$ for all $x \neq 3$, then $g(3) =$

   (A) 12
   (B) 24
   (C) $+\infty$
   (D) $g(3)$ does not exist.

29. $\lim\limits_{x \to 0} \frac{\tan^4 2x}{x^4}$

30. $\lim\limits_{x \to 0} \frac{5 \sin x - 5 \sec^2 x \sin x}{x^3}$

31. Let f be a function such that $\lim\limits_{x \to c} f(x) = f(c)$ for all x in the interval $[a, b]$. Which of the following must be true?

   (A) f is continuous on (a, b)
   (B) f is differentiable on (a, b)
   (C) $f(c) = f(b) - f(a)$
   (D) $\frac{1}{b-a} \int_a^b f(x)\, dx = f(c)$

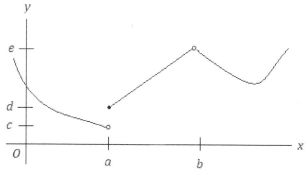

32. The graph of the function h is shown in the figure above. Which of the following statements about h is false?

(A) $\lim\limits_{x \to a^-} h(x) = c$

(B) $\lim\limits_{x \to a^+} h(x) = h(a)$

(C) $\lim\limits_{x \to b^-} h(x) = e$

(D) $\lim\limits_{x \to b} h(x)$ does not exist

LEVEL 2: PRECALCULUS

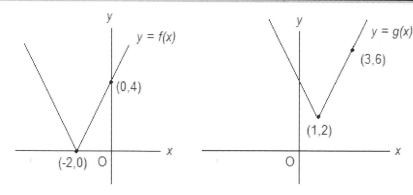

33. The figures above show the graphs of the functions f and g. The function f is defined by $f(x) = 2|x + 2|$ and the function g is defined by $g(x) = f(x + h) + k$, where h and k are constants. What is the value of $|h - k|$?

(A) 5

(B) 4

(C) 3

(D) 2

179

34. If $k(x) = (\sqrt{x} + 3)^3$, for all $x > 0$, then which of the following functions is equal to $f^{-1}(x)$ when restricted to $x > 27$?

(A) $\sqrt[3]{x}$

(B) $\sqrt[3]{x} - 3$

(C) $\left(\sqrt[3]{x} - 3\right)^2$

(D) $(x - 3)^2$

35. What is the range of the function defined by $\frac{1}{x^2} - 2$?

(A) All real numbers
(B) All real numbers except 0
(C) All real numbers except -2
(D) All real numbers greater than -2

36. If $a > 0$ and $b > 1$, and $\log_b a^2 = 4k$, then which of the following can be FALSE?

(A) $\log_b a = 2k$

(B) $\log_{b^2} a = k$

(C) $\log_{b^k} a = 2$

(D) $\log_{b^k} \frac{a}{2} = 1$

37. What is the range of the following function?

$$T(x) = -4\sin(2x + \pi) + 3$$

(A) $-7 \leq x \leq 1$
(B) $-1 \leq x \leq 7$
(C) $-1 \leq x \leq 4$
(D) $-4 \leq x \leq 7$

38. Consider the functions $f(x) = \sqrt{x - 1}$ and $g(x) = ax + b$. In the standard (x, y) coordinate plane, $y = f(g(x))$ passes through $(0, -1)$ and $(2,3)$. What is the value of $a + b$?

(A) 1
(B) 2
(C) 4
(D) 6

180

39. What is the period of the graph of $y = -4\sec(\frac{3}{7}\pi\theta - 1)$?

 (A) $\frac{\pi}{3}$

 (B) $\frac{14}{3}$

 (C) $\frac{14\pi}{3}$

 (D) $\frac{14\pi}{15}$

40. If $\arccos(\cos x) = \frac{\pi}{4}$ and $0 \le x \le 2\pi$, then x could equal

 (A) 0

 (B) $\frac{\pi}{6}$

 (C) $\frac{3\pi}{4}$

 (D) $\frac{7\pi}{4}$

LEVEL 2: DIFFERENTIATION

41. If $y = e^{\tan^2 x}$, then $\frac{dy}{dx} =$

42. If $A(x) = \cos^2(2 - x)\sin(3x - 6)$, then $A'(2)$ is equal to

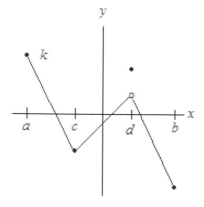

181

43. The function k, whose graph consists of three line segments, is shown above. Which of the following are false for k on the open interval (a, b) ?

    I. k has a nonremoval discontinuity at $x = d$.
    II. k is differentiable on the open interval (c, d).
    III. The derivative of k is negative on the interval $(c, 0)$.

    (A) I only
    (B) II only
    (C) III only
    (D) I and III only

44. If $f(x) = \dfrac{3x}{\sqrt{2x^2 + 5}}$, then $f'(x) =$

45. The slope of the tangent line to the curve $xe^{xy} + x = x^3y$ at the point $(-1, 0)$ is

46. Let $f(x) = x \ln x$. A value of c that satisfies the conclusion of the Mean Value Theorem for f on the interval $[e, e^2]$ is

47. If $h(x) = \dfrac{x^2 + \sqrt[3]{x}}{\sqrt[3]{x^2}}$, then $h'(8) =$

48. The *derivative* of $f(x) = xe^x$ attains its minimum value at $x =$

LEVEL 2: INTEGRATION

49. $\displaystyle\int_0^{\ln \sqrt{3}} \dfrac{e^x dx}{1 + e^{2x}} =$

50. $\displaystyle\int_0^{\frac{\pi}{4}} \sec x \,(\tan x - \sec x) dx$

51. $\displaystyle\int_0^2 \dfrac{x^3 + 2x^2 - x - 2}{x^2 - 1}\, dx =$

52. The solution to the differential equation $\dfrac{dy}{dx} = \dfrac{y^4}{x^2}$, where $y(1) = 1$, is

182

53. Each of the following is an antiderivative of $\cos x \sin x$ EXCEPT

    (A) $\dfrac{\cos^2 x}{2}$

    (B) $\dfrac{\sin^2 x}{2}$

    (C) $\dfrac{1+\sin^2 x}{2}$

    (D) $-\dfrac{\cos^2 x}{2}$

54. $\int \dfrac{5x}{\sqrt{3-x^2}} dx =$

55. The area of the region enclosed by the graph of $y = 2x^2 + 3$ and the line $y = 7$ is

56. A radioactive substance is decaying at a rate of $30e^{-\frac{3t}{5}}$ per year. At $t = 0$ years, there is 100 pounds of this substance. Find the amount present after 5 years.

LEVEL 2: LIMITS AND CONTINUITY

57. What is $\lim\limits_{h \to 0} \dfrac{\ln(e+h)-\ln e}{h}$?

58. $\lim\limits_{x \to \infty} (3 - e^{\frac{1}{2}-\frac{1}{x^2}}) =$

59. $\lim\limits_{h \to 0} \dfrac{1}{h} \log_3(\dfrac{5+h}{5})$ is equal to

60. Let the function f be defined by $f(x) = \begin{cases} \dfrac{\ln|x|}{\frac{1}{x}}, & \text{for } x \neq 0. \\ 0, & \text{for } x = 0. \end{cases}$

    Which of the following are true about f?

    I. $\lim\limits_{x \to 0} f(x)$ exists.
    II. $f(0)$ exists.
    III. f is continuous at $x = 0$.

    (A) I only
    (B) 1I only
    (C) I and II only
    (D) I, II, and III

61. Suppose that the differentiable function k satisfies $\lim\limits_{h\to 0}\frac{k'(3+h)-k'(3)}{h}=1$. Which of the following must be true ?

    I. k is continuous at $x=3$
    II. k' is continuous at $x=3$
    III. $k''(3)$ exists

        (A) I only
        (B) 1I only
        (C) I and II only
        (D) I, II, and III

62. $\lim\limits_{x\to -\infty}\dfrac{\sqrt{7x^6+3x^8}}{6-5x^2+2x^4}=$

63. $\lim\limits_{x\to 11^-}\dfrac{x+2}{(x-11)^3}=$

64. Let f be the function defined by

$$f(x)=\begin{cases}\dfrac{5\ln|x-3|+15}{1+\cos(x-2)}, & x\le 2 \\[3mm] \dfrac{15\sin(\frac{x\pi}{4})}{e^{x-2}}, & x>2\end{cases}$$

Is f continuous at $x=2$?

LEVEL 3: PRECALCULUS

65. If $\cot x = k$, then for all x in the interval $0 < x < \frac{\pi}{2}$, $\sin x =$

        (A) $\dfrac{1}{1+k}$

        (B) $\dfrac{k}{\sqrt{1+k^2}}$

        (C) $\dfrac{1}{\sqrt{1+k^2}}$

        (D) $\dfrac{1}{\sqrt{1-k^2}}$

66. Suppose the graph of $g(x) = -2x^3$ is translated 2 units down and 3 units left. If the resulting graph represents $G(x)$, what is the value of $G(-.5)$?

   (A) –33.25
   (B) –28.75
   (C) –17.25
   (D) –11.5

67. If $f(x) = \sqrt{3 - x}$ and $g(x) = \frac{1}{x^2-1}$, then the domain of $g \circ f$ is

   (A) all real numbers x
   (B) all x such that $x \geq 3$
   (C) all x such that $x \neq 2$
   (D) all x such that $x \neq 2$ and $x \leq 3$

68. If $0 < x < \frac{\pi}{2}$, then $\sec(\arctan x) =$

   (A) $\frac{1}{x}$

   (B) $\frac{1}{\sqrt{x^2+1}}$

   (C) $\sqrt{x^2 + 1}$

   (D) $\frac{1}{\sqrt{1-x^2}}$

LEVEL 3: DIFFERENTIATION

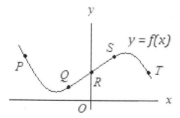

69. At which of the five points on the graph in the figure above are $\frac{dy}{dx}$ and $\frac{d^2y}{dx^2}$ both negative?

   (A) T
   (B) S
   (C) R
   (D) Q

185

70. Given the function defined by $f(x) = x^2 e^x$, find all values of x for which the graph of f is concave up.

71. If the line $2x - 3y = 3$ is tangent in the first quadrant to the curve $y = \ln(3x + 1)$, then c is

72. Find all relative extrema and points of inflection for the function f defined by $f(x) = \ln(x^2 + 1)$.

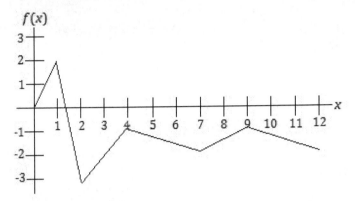

73. The graph of $f(x)$ is given above for $0 \le x \le 12$. On the same set of axes, sketch the graph of f'.

74. If $h(x) = \dfrac{x^{\frac{1}{3}}}{(x+3)^{\frac{1}{2}}}$ for all x, then the domain of h' is

75. $\dfrac{d}{dx}[\cot^{-1}(\frac{x^2}{4})] =$

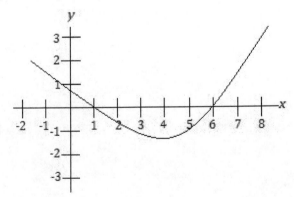

76. The **derivative** of f is graphed above. Give all x-values at which f has local extrema and points of inflection.

77. If $\sin(xy^3) = e^{xy}$, then $\frac{dy}{dx} =$

78. A point moves in a straight line so that its distance at time t from a fixed point of the line is $\frac{t^2-1}{e^t}$. The *total* distance that the point travels from $t = 0$ to $t = 3$ is

79. * Two particles start at the origin and move along the x-axis. For $0 \le t \le 2$, their position functions are given by $x = \tan^2 t$ and $y = te^{t^2+1}$. For how many values of t do the particles have the same velocity?

   (A) None
   (B) One
   (C) Two
   (D) Three

80. Consider the equation $x \ln(xy) = 1$. Find $\frac{d^2y}{dx^2}$ at $(1,1)$.

LEVEL 3: INTEGRATION

81. The area of the region in the first quadrant bounded by the graph of $y = \frac{\ln(2x+1)}{4x+2}$, the y-axis, and the line $x = 1$ is

82. A particle moves in a straight line with velocity $v(t) = \frac{t^2+2t+1-\sqrt{(t+1)^3}}{t+1}$ beginning at time $t = 0$. How far is the particle from its starting point at time $t = 3$?

83. The acceleration $a(t)$ of a body moving in a straight line, in ft/sec^2 is given in terms of time t by $a(t) = 5e^t - \cos\frac{t}{2}$. If at time $t = 0$ seconds, the body is moving to the right at a speed of 3 ft/sec, and if $s(t)$ is the distance of the body from the origin at time t, then $s(2\pi) - s(0) =$

84. The area of the region completely bounded by the curves $y = -x^2 + 3x - 2$ and $y = x^2 - 1$ is

85. Let f and g be continuous functions such that $f'(x) = g(x)$ for all x. It follows that $\int_a^b 2x \cdot g(x^2 + 1)dx =$

86. If $\frac{dy}{dx} = \frac{y \cdot e^x}{e^x+1}$ and if $y = 4$ when $x = 0$, then $y =$

187

87. The average value of $\tan x$ over the interval $\frac{\pi}{6} \leq x \leq \frac{\pi}{3}$ is

88. Evaluate $\int_{-\frac{1}{2}}^{1} g(x) dx$, where

$$g(x) = \begin{cases} \cos \pi x \sin^2 \pi x & \text{for } x < 0 \\ e^{\sin \pi x} \cos \pi x & \text{for } x \geq 0 \end{cases}$$

89. If $\int_{2j}^{2k} f(x) dx = st$, then $\int_{j}^{k} (5f(2x) - 3) dx =$

90. If $f(0) = 1$, $f(1) = e$, then $\int_{0}^{1} \frac{\ln[f(x)] \cdot f'(x)}{f(x)} dx =$

91. Calculate the approximate area under the curve $f(x) = \log_2 x$ and bounded by the lines $x = 1$ and $x = 4$ by the trapezoidal rule, using three equal subintervals.

92. A point moves in a straight line so that its velocity at time t is $\frac{x-1}{x^2 - 2x - 15}$. What is the *total* distance that the point travels from $t = 0$ to $t = 2$?

LEVEL 3: LIMITS AND CONTINUITY

93. If f is continuous for all c in the interval (a, b), which of the following *can* be false?

   (A) $f(c)$ is defined for all c in (a, b)

   (B) $\lim_{x \to c} f(x) = f(\lim_{x \to c} x)$ for all c in (a, b)

   (C) f is Riemann integrable on (a, b).

   (D) There is a c in (a, b) such that $f'(c) = \frac{f(b) - f(a)}{b - a}$.

94. Let g be defined by

$$g(x) = \begin{cases} e^x \cos x & \text{for } -2 \leq x \leq \pi \\ \frac{e^\pi}{\sin(x + \frac{\pi}{2})} & \text{for } \pi < x \leq 10 \end{cases} \cdot$$

   Is g continuous at $x = \pi$? Use the definition of continuity to explain your answer.

95. A 5000-gallon tank is filled to capacity with water. At time $t = 0$, water begins to leak out of the tank at a rate modeled by $R(t)$, measured in gallons per hour, where

$$R(t) = \begin{cases} \dfrac{300t}{t+1}, & 0 \le t \le 4 \\ 12e^{2-0.5t} + 228, & t > 4 \end{cases}$$

Is $\dfrac{dR}{dt}$ continuous at $t = 4$? Show the work that leads to your answer.

96. Let $g(x) = \dfrac{x^3 - 2x^2 - 3x}{2x^3 - 2x^2 - 4x}$. Find each x-value at which g is discontinuous, and classify each such discontinuity as removable or nonremovable. Define a function G such that G is continuous at each removable discontinuity of g and such that $G(x) = g(x)$ for all x in the domain of g.

LEVEL 4: DIFFERENTIATION

97. Suppose that f is an odd function (so that $f(-x) = -f(x)$ for all x), and that $f'(c)$ exists. Then $f'(-c)$ must be equal to

(A) $f'(c)$

(B) $-f'(c)$

(C) $\dfrac{1}{f'(c)}$

(D) $-\dfrac{1}{f'(c)}$

98. The function $f(x) = 2x^3 + x - 3$ has an inverse function g. Find $g'(15)$.

99. A container is in the form of a right circular cone with radius 4 inches, height 16 inches, vertex pointing downward. Water is being poured into the container at the constant rate of 16 inches^3 per second. How fast is the water level rising when the water is 8 inches deep?

100. If $y = \sin kx$, where k is a nonzero constant, then $\dfrac{d^{73}y}{dx^{73}} =$

189

101. The radius of a circle increases from 10 inches to 10.1 inches. Use a linear approximation to find the approximate increase in the circle's area.

x	4.2	4.3	4.4	4.5
$f(x)$	3	3.1	3.3	3.7

102. Let f be a function that is concave up for all x in the closed interval [4,5], with selected values shown in the above table. Which of the following inequalities must be true?

(A) $f'(4.3) > 3$
(B) $2 < f'(4.3) < 3$
(C) $1 < f'(4.3) < 2$
(D) $0 < f'(4.3) < 1$

103. Consider the differential equation $\frac{dy}{dx} = e^{y-x}$ Let $y = f(x)$ be the particular solution to the differential equation that passes through $(0,0)$. Write an equation for the line tangent to the graph of f at the point $(0,0)$, and use the tangent line to approximate $f(0.1)$.

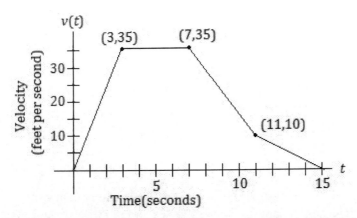

104. A bus is traveling on a straight road. For $0 \le t \le 15$ seconds, the bus's velocity $v(t)$, in feet per second, is modeled by the function defined by the graph above. Find the average rate of change of v over the interval $1 \le t \le 6$. Does the Mean Value Theorem guarantee a value of c for $1 < t < 6$, such that $v'(c)$ is equal to this average rate of change? Why or why not?

190

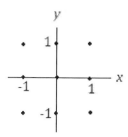

105. Consider the differential equation $\frac{dy}{dx} = (y + 1)^2 \sin\frac{\pi}{2}x$. On the axes provided above, sketch a slope field for the differential equation at the twelve points indicated. There is a horizontal line with equation $y = b$ that satisfies his differential equation. Find the value of b.

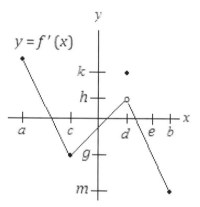

106. The graph of the *derivative* of a function f is shown above. For each of $f'(c)$, $f'(d)$, $f'(e)$, $f''(c)$, $f''(d)$, and $f''(e)$, find the value or explain why it does not exist.

107. Two particles are moving along the x-axis. For $0 \leq t \leq 5$, the position of particle A at time t is given by $a(t) = \cos t$, and the position of particle B at time t is given by $b(t) = t^3 - 6t^2 + 9t + 2$. For $0 \leq t \leq 5$, find all times t during which the two particles travel in the same direction.

x	0	$0 < x < 1$	1	$1 < x < 2$	2	$2 < x < 3$	3
$f(x)$	-4	$-$	-3	$-$	-1	$-$	-2
$f'(x)$	3	$+$	0	$+$	0	$-$	-5

108. The differentiable function f is defined for all real numbers x. Values of f and f' for various values of x are given in the table above. Find the x-coordinate of each relative minimum of f on the interval $[0,3]$. Justify your answers.

109. Consider a differentiable function g with domain $(-\infty, \infty)$, satisfying $g'(x) = \sqrt[3]{x}(x^2 - 7)$. Find the x-coordinates of all relative minima and maxima, find all intervals on which the graph of g is concave up, and find all intervals on which the graph of g is concave down. Justify your answers.

110. Let h be a function with derivative $h'(x) = \sqrt{x^2 + 7}$ such that $h(3) = -1$. Estimate $h(3.1)$ and determine if this estimate is too large or too small. Justify your answer.

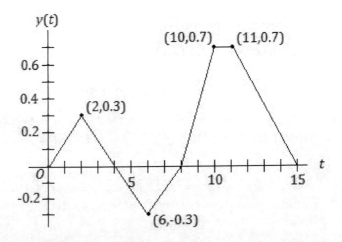

111. Joe is driving his car along a straight road. For $0 \le t \le 15$ seconds, his velocity $v(t)$, in miles per minute, is modeled by the function defined by the graph above. Let $a(t)$ be the car's acceleration at time t, in miles per minute. For $0 < t < 15$, write a piecewise-defined function for $a(t)$.

192

112. Does there exist a differentiable function g such that $g(-3) = 3$, $g(5) = 11$, and $g'(x) < 1$ for all x? Justify your answer.

LEVEL 4: INTEGRATION

113. The region in the xy-plane bounded by the graphs of $y = x^2$ and $x = y^2$ is rotated about the line $x = -1$. What is the volume of the solid generated?

114. * The rate, in tons per hour, at which bricks are arriving at a construction site is modeled by $K(t) = 5 + 32 \sin\left(\frac{t^3}{128}\right)$, where t is measured in hours and $0 \leq t \leq 5$. Approximately how many tons of bricks will arrive at the site during the 5 hours? Round your answer to the nearest ton.

115. Find the average value of $x^2 \cos x^3$ on the interval $[0,2]$.

116. * If $f'(x) = xe^{x^3 \cos x}$ and $f(1) = 3$, then $f(2) =$

117. Let D be the region in the first quadrant bounded by $y = 5\sqrt{x}$ and $y = 10x$. Write, but do not evaluate, an integral expression that gives the volume of the solid generated when D is revolved around the line $x = -2$.

118. * The function F defined by $F(x) = \int_0^x (u^5 - 3u^2 + 2)\, du$ on the closed interval $[0,5]$, has a local minimum at $x = a$ and a local maximum at $x = b$. Find a and b.

119. The expression $\frac{1}{75}\left(\sqrt[3]{0} + \sqrt[3]{\frac{1}{75}} + \sqrt[3]{\frac{2}{75}} + \cdots + \sqrt[3]{\frac{99}{75}} \right)$ is a Riemann sum approximation for $\int_0^1 g(x)\, dx$ for $g(x) =$

193

t (minutes)	0	2	4	6	8
$T(t)$ (degrees F)	110	100	92	86	84

120. As a cup of hot water cools, the temperature of the water is modeled by a continuous function T, where t is measured in minutes. Selected values of $T(t)$, measured in degrees Fahrenheit, are given in the table above. Use a trapezoidal sum with four subintervals indicated by the given data to approximate $\frac{1}{8}\int_0^8 T(t)\,dt$. Using correct units, explain the meaning of $\frac{1}{8}\int_0^8 T(t)\,dt$ in the context of the problem.

121. Consider the differential equation $\frac{dy}{dx} = 2xy^3$ Let $y = f(x)$ be the particular solution to the differential equation that passes through $(2,1)$. Find $y = f(x)$, and the domain of f.

x	0	1	2	3
$f(x)$	2	3	0	4
$f'(x)$	3	3	4	-1
$g(x)$	-1	-2	-3	4
$g'(x)$	2	1	-3	1

122. The differentiable functions f and g are defined for all real numbers x. Values of f, f', g, and g' for various values of x are given in the table above. Evaluate $\int_1^{\sqrt[3]{2}} x^2 g'\big(f(x^3)\big)f'(x^3)\,dx$.

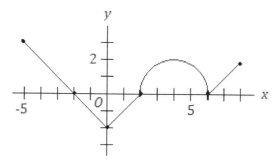

123. Let f be the continuous function defined on $[-5,8]$ whose graph, consisting of three line segments and a semicircle centered at $(4,0)$, is shown above. Compute $\int_{-5}^{8} f(t)\, dt$.

124. * The function h is defined for $x > 0$ by $h'(x) = \cos(\frac{1}{x} + x)$ and $h(3) = 1$. Write an equation for the line tangent to the graph of h at $x = 3.2$.

125. * Let $G(x) = \int_{0}^{x^2} \sin^3 t\, dt$. Find the average value of $G'(x)$ on the interval $[0,2]$.

126. * The rate, in tons per hour, at which bricks are arriving at a construction site is modeled by $K(t) = 5 + 32 \sin\left(\frac{t^3}{128}\right)$, where t is measured in hours and $0 \le t \le 5$. At time $t = 0$, there are already 10 tons of unused bricks at the site, and bricks are being used (for the construction) at a constant rate of 7 tons per hour. Write an expression for the amount of unused bricks at the construction site at any time t. Then find the maximum amount (in tons) of unused bricks at the site for $0 \le t \le 3$. Justify your answer.

x	1	5	6	8	11
$f(x)$	3	5	1	-3	4

127. Let f be a function that is continuous for all real numbers. The table above gives values of f for selected points in the closed interval $[1,11]$. Use a right Riemann Sum with subintervals indicated by the data in the table to approximate $\int_{1}^{11} f(x)\, dx$. Show the work that leads to your answer.

128. * Let R be the region in the first and second quadrants bounded above by the graph of $y = \frac{48}{2+x^4}$ and below by the horizontal line $y = 4$. The region R is the base of a solid whose cross sections perpendicular to the x-axis are rectangles with height twice the length of the base. Find the volume of this solid.

LEVEL 5: FREE RESPONSE QUESTIONS

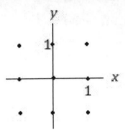

129 – 133 Consider the differential equation $\frac{dy}{dx} = y - 2x + 1$ and the figure above.

129. On the axes provided, sketch a slope field for the differential equation at the nine points indicated. Then describe all points in the xy-plane, $x \neq 0$, for which $\frac{dy}{dx} = 1$.

130. Write an equation for the line tangent to the solution curve at the point $(0,1)$. Use the equation to approximate $f(-0.5)$ where $y = f(x)$ is the particular solution of the differential equation with initial condition $f(0) = 1$.

131. Find $\frac{d^2y}{dx^2}$ in terms of x and y. Describe the region in the xy-plane in which all solution curves to the differential equation are concave down.

132. Let $y = f(x)$ be a particular solution to the differential equation with the initial condition $f(1) = 1$. Does f have a relative minimum, a relative maximum, or neither at $x = 1$? Justify your answer.

133. Find the values of the constants m and b, for which $y = mx + b$ is a solution to the differential equation.

134 – 137 * Machine A removes salt from a container at a rate modeled by the function M, given by $M(t) = 3 + 2 \cos \left(\frac{3\pi t}{20} \right)$. Simultaneously, machine B adds salt to the container at a rate modeled by the function N, given by $N(t) = \frac{e^t}{2+t}$. Both $M(t)$ and $N(t)$ have units of cubic feet per hour and t is measured in hours for $0 \le t \le 5$. At time $t = 0$, the container contains 20 cubic feet of salt.

134. * How much salt will machine A remove from the container during this 5 hour period, and how much salt will machine B add to the container during this 5 hour period? Indicate units of measure.

135. Write an expression for $K(t)$, the total number of cubic feet of salt in the container at time t.

136. * Find the rate at which the total amount of salt in the container is changing at time $t = 2$.

137. For $0 \le t \le 5$, at what time t is the amount of salt in the container a minimum? At what time t is the amount of the salt in the container a maximum? What are the maximum and minimum values? Justify your answers.

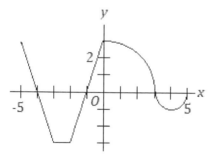

138 – 145 Let g be the continuous function defined on $[-5,5]$ whose graph, consisting of three line segments, a quarter circle centered at the origin, and a semicircle centered at $(4,0)$, is shown above. Let $G(x) = -3x + \int_0^x g(t)\, dt$.

138. Find the values of $G(-2)$ and $G(5)$.

139. Find $G'(x)$. Then evaluate $G'(-1)$ and $G''(-1)$.

140. Determine the x-coordinate of the point at which G has an absolute maximum on the interval $[-5,5]$. Justify your answer.

141. For $-5 < x < 5$, find all values of x for which the graph of G has a point of inflection. Explain your reasoning.

142. On what open intervals contained in $-5 < x < 5$ is the graph of G concave up? Justify your answer.

143. Find the average rate of change of g on the interval $[-5, -2]$. There is no point c with $-5 < c < -2$, for which $g'(c)$ is equal to that average rate of change. Explain why this statement does not contradict the Mean Value Theorem.

144. Suppose that g is defined for all real numbers x and is periodic with a period of length 10. The graph above shows one period of g. Find $G(10)$.

145. The function H is defined by $H(x) = g(\ln(x))$. Find an equation of the tangent line to the graph of H at the point where $x = \frac{1}{e}$.

146 – 151 * Let R be the region bounded by the graphs of $f(x) = \ln x$ and $g(x) = x - 3$.

146. * Write an equation for the tangent line to the graph of f at $x = 2$.

147. * Find the area of R.

148. * Find the volume of the solid generated when R is rotated about the horizontal line $y = -5$.

149. * Find the volume of the solid generated when R is rotated about the y-axis.

150. * The region R is the base of a solid. For this solid, each cross section perpendicular to the x-axis is a square. Find the volume of the solid.

151. The horizontal line $y = b$ divides R into two regions with equal areas. Write, but do not solve, an equation involving integral expressions whose solution gives the value b.

152 – 155 Let f be a twice-differentiable function that is defined for all real numbers and satisfies the following conditions:

$$f(1) = 3, f'(1) = 5, f''(1) = -2, f(3) = 2, f'(3) = 1, f''(3) = 0$$

152. Let b satisfy $2 < b < 3$ and let d satisfy $1 < d < 5$. Explain why there must be real numbers a and c with $1 < a, c < 3$ such that $f(a)f'(c) = bd$.

153. Is there a value c for $1 < c < 3$ such that $f''(c) = -2$? Justify your answer.

154. The function g is given by $g(x) = f(x) + xe^{kx}$ for all real x, with k a constant. Find $g''(1)$ in terms of k.

155. The function h is given by $h(x) = \sin(k\pi x) f(x)$ for all real x, with k an integer. Write an equation for the line tangent to the graph of h at $x = 3$.

156 – 160 A particle moves along the x-axis so that its acceleration at time $t > 0$ is given by $a(t) = \frac{\ln t}{t}$. At time $t = 1$, the velocity of the particle is $v(1) = -8$ and the position of the particle is $s(1) = 9$.

156. Write an expression for the velocity of the particle $v(t)$.

157. Find all values of $t > 0$ for which the speed of the particle is 6. For each such value of t determine if the particle is moving to the right or to the left.

158. Set up, but do not evaluate an expression involving an integral that gives the total distance traveled by the particle from time $t = 1$ to $t = 2$.

159. Find all times $t \geq 0$ at which the particle changes direction. Justify your answer.

160. Determine all values $t \geq 0$ for which the particle is speeding up, and all values $t \geq 0$ for which the particle is slowing down.

ANSWERS TO SUPPLEMENTAL PROBLEMS

LEVEL 1: PRECALCULUS

1. D
2. C
3. D
4. C
5. D
6. D
7. C
8. D

LEVEL 1: DIFFERENTIATION

9. A
10. C
11. B
12. D
13. A
14. $\frac{-20}{3\sqrt[3]{x^7}} + x^x(1 + \ln x)$

15. $x^{\cot x}\left(\frac{\sin x \cos x - x \ln x}{x \sin^2 x}\right)$

16. $\frac{3[(x-2)+x(\ln 3)\log_3 x]-(x-2)(\ln 3)\log_3 x}{3(\ln 3)\sqrt[3]{x^4}}$

LEVEL 1: INTEGRATION

17. B
18. A
19. B
20. $\frac{2\sqrt{x^{11}}}{11} + \frac{4}{3}\sqrt{x^3} + C$

21. $\frac{\ln(1+e^3)}{3} + C$

22. $-\frac{3}{4x^4} + 5\ln|x| - \frac{15\sqrt[3]{x^4}}{4} + 15\sqrt[5]{x} + C$

23. $\frac{\ln(\ln(3x^2+1))}{6} + C$

24. $= -\frac{3^x \cos x}{\ln 3} + C$

LEVEL 1: LIMITS AND CONTINUITY

25. A
26. B
27. C
28. B
29. 16
30. –5
31. A
32. D

LEVEL 2: PRECALCULUS

33. A
34. C
35. D
36. D
37. B
38. D
39. B
40. D

LEVEL 2: DIFFERENTIATION

41. $2e^{\tan^2 x} \tan x \sec^2 x$

42. 3
43. D
44. $\frac{15}{\sqrt{(2x^2+5)^3}}$

45. -1

46. $e^{\frac{e}{e-1}}$

47. $\frac{127}{48}$

48. −2

LEVEL 2: INTEGRATION

49. $\frac{\pi}{12}$

50. $\sqrt{2} - 2$

51. 6

52. $y = \sqrt[3]{\dfrac{x}{3-2x}}$

53. A

54. $-5\sqrt{3 - x^2} + C$

55. $\frac{16\sqrt{2}}{3}$

56. $50e^{-3} + 50$ pounds

LEVEL 2: LIMITS AND CONTINUITY

57. $\frac{1}{e}$

58. $3 - \sqrt{e}$

59. $\frac{1}{5\ln 3}$

60. D

61. D

62. $\frac{\sqrt{3}}{2}$

63. $-\infty$

64. No

LEVEL 3: PRECALCULUS

65. C

66. A

67. D

68. C

LEVEL 3: DIFFERENTIATION

69. A

70. $\left(-\infty, -2 - \sqrt{2}\right) \cup \left(-2 + \sqrt{2}, \infty\right)$

71. $\frac{7}{6}$

72. rel. max: $(0,0)$, points of inflection: $(\pm 1, \ln 2)$

73.

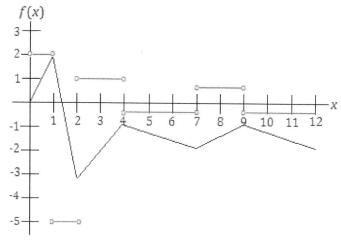

74. $\{x \mid x > -3 \text{ and } x \neq 0\}$

75. $-\frac{8x}{x^4 + 16}$

76. local max at $x = 1$, local min at $x = 6$, pt of inf at $x = 4$

77. $\frac{y^3 \cos(xy^3) - ye^{xy}}{xe^{xy} - 3xy^2 \cos(xy^3)}$

78. $\frac{e^3 + 8}{e^3}$

79. B

80. 2

LEVEL 3: INTEGRATION

81. $\frac{1}{8}(\ln 3)^2$

82. $\dfrac{17}{6}$

83. $5e^{2\pi} - 13 - 4\pi$ ft.

84. $\dfrac{1}{24}$

85. $f(b^2 + 1) - f(a^2 + 1)$

86. $2(e^x + 1)$

87. $\dfrac{3}{\pi} \ln 3$

88. $\dfrac{1}{3\pi}$

89. $\dfrac{5st}{2} + 3j - 3k$

90. $\dfrac{1}{2}$

91. $2 + \log_2 3$

92. $\ln \dfrac{16}{15}$

LEVEL 3: LIMITS AND CONTINUITY

93. D

94. Yes, $g(\pi) = \lim\limits_{x \to \pi^-} g(x) = \lim\limits_{x \to \pi^+} g(x) = -e^{\pi}$

95. Yes, , $R(4) = \lim\limits_{x \to 4^-} R(x) = \lim\limits_{x \to 4^+} R(x) = 240$

96. $x = -1$ (removable), $x = 0$ (removable), $x = 2$ (nonremovable)

$$G(x) = \begin{cases} \dfrac{x^3 - 2x^2 - 3x}{2x^3 - 2x^2 - 4x}, & x \neq -1, 0 \\ \dfrac{2}{3}, & x = -1 \\ \dfrac{3}{4}, & x = 0 \end{cases}$$

LEVEL 4: DIFFERENTIATION

97. A

98. $\dfrac{1}{25}$

99. $\dfrac{4}{\pi}$ in/sec

100. $k^{73} \cos kx$

101. 2π in^2
102. C
103. $y = x, f(0.1) \approx .1$
104. 5, no because v is not differentiable at $t = 3$
105. $b = -1$

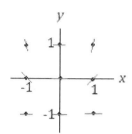

106. $f'(c) = g, f'(d) = k, f'(e) = g, f''(e) = \frac{m-h}{b-d}$

$f''(c)^+ > 0, f''(c)^- < 0$. So $f''(c)$ does not exist,

$f''(d)^+ < 0, f''(d)^- > 0$. So $f''(d)$ does not exist

107. $(0,1) \cup (3, \pi)$

108. There are no relative minima. The critical numbers of f are $x = 1$ and $x = 2$. At $x = 1$, f' does not change sign, and at $x = 2$, f' changes sign from positive to negative indicating a relative maximum.

109. rel max at $x = 0$, rel min at $x = -\sqrt{7}$ and $x = \sqrt{7}$, concave up on $(-\infty, -1), (1, \infty)$, concave down on $(-1,0), (0,1)$

110. $h(3.1) \approx -0.6$. The estimate is too small because $h''(x) > 0$ for $x > 0$.

111.

$$a(t) = \begin{cases} \dfrac{3}{20} & \text{if } 0 < t < 2 \\[2mm] -\dfrac{3}{20} & \text{if } 2 < t < 6 \\[2mm] \dfrac{3}{20} & \text{if } 6 < t < 8 \\[2mm] \dfrac{7}{20} & \text{if } 8 < t < 10 \\[2mm] 0 & \text{if } 10 < t < 11 \\[2mm] \dfrac{7}{40} & \text{if } 11 < t < 15 \end{cases}$$

205

112. No. By the Mean Value Theorem there must exist a c, $-3 <$ $c < 5$ such that $g'(c) = \frac{11-3}{5-(-3)} = 1$.

LEVEL 4: INTEGRATION

113. $\frac{29\pi}{30}$

114. 62

115. $\frac{1}{6}\sin 8$

116. 4.467

117. $\pi \int_0^{\frac{1}{4}}[\left(\frac{y}{10} + 2\right)^2 - \left(\frac{y^2}{25} + 2\right)^2] \, dy$

118. $a \approx 1.121$, $b = 1$

119. $\sqrt[3]{x}$

120. $\frac{1}{8}\int_0^8 T(t) \, dt \approx 93.75$

$\frac{1}{8}\int_0^8 T(t) \, dt$ is the average temperature of the water, in degrees Fahrenheit, over the 8 minutes.

121. $y = \frac{1}{\sqrt{9-2x^2}}$, $-\frac{3}{\sqrt{2}} < x < \frac{3}{\sqrt{2}}$

122. $-\frac{5}{3}$

123. $\frac{5}{2} + 2\pi$

124. $y - .808 = -.932(x - 3.2)$ or $y = -.932x + 3.79$

125. 0.614

126. $A(t) = 10 + \int_0^t (K(u) - 7) \, du$
$A'(t) = K(t) - 7 = 0$ when $t \approx 2$, $A(0) = 10$, $A(2) \approx 7$, $A(3) \approx 9$. So the maximum amount is 10 tons of bricks.

127. 27

128. 1447.428

129. $\frac{dy}{dx} = 1 \Leftrightarrow y = 2x$

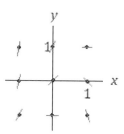

130. $y = 2x + 1, f(-.05) \approx 0$

131. $\frac{d^2y}{dx^2} = y - 2x - 1$, Solution curves will be concave down on the half-plane below the line $y = 2x + 1$.

132. f has a relative maximum at $x = 1$ because $\frac{dy}{dx}\big|_{(1,1)} = 0$ and $\frac{d^2y}{dx^2}\big|_{(1,1)} = -2 < 0$.

133. $m = 2, b = 1$

134. $\int_0^5 M(t)dt = 18.001$ ft^3, $\int_0^5 N(t)dt = 25.247$ ft^3

135. $K(t) = 20 + \int_0^t (N(u) - M(u))\, du$

136. decreasing at a rate of 2.328 ft^3/hr

137. $K'(t) = 0$ when $N(t) = M(t)$, ie. when $t \approx 2.82$, $K(0) = 20$, $K(2.82) = 11.514$, $K(5) = 27.246$. So the amount of salt is a minimum when $t \approx 2.82$ hours, and the amount of salt is a maximum when $t = 5$ hours. The minimum value is 11.514 ft^3 and the maximum value is 27.246 ft^3.

138. $G(-2) = 6, G(5) = \frac{7\pi - 60}{4}$

139. $G'(x) = -3 + g(x), G'(-1) = -3, G''(-1) = 3$

207

140. $G'(x) = 0$ when $g(x) = 3$. This occurs at $x = 0$. We also need to check the endpoints, $x = -5$ and $x = 5$. $G(-5) = 18$, $G(0) = 0$, $G(5) = \frac{7\pi - 60}{4}$. So G has an absolute maximum at $x = -5$.

141. The graph of G has a point of inflection at $x = 0$ and $x = 4$ because $G'' = g'$ changes sign at each of these values.

142. G is concave up when $G'' = g' > 0$, ie. when g is increasing. This occurs on the intervals $(-2,0)$ and $(4,5)$.

143. Average rate of change is -2. The statement does not contradict the Mean value Theorem because g is not differentiable at $x = -3$.

144. $\frac{7\pi - 132}{4}$

145. $y = 3ex - 3$

146. $y - .693 = 0.5(x - 2)$ or $y = 0.5x - .307$

147. 5.694

148. 163.542

149. 63.881

150. 8.945

151. $\int_{-2.948}^{b}(y + 3 - e^y)\,dy = \int_{b}^{1.505}(y + 3 - e^y)\,dy$

152. Since f is twice-differentiable, f and f' are continuous. Since f is a continuous function with $f(3) < b < f(1)$, the Intermediate Value Theorem guarantees that there is a value a, with $1 < a < 3$, such that $f(a) = b$. Since f' is a continuous function with $f'(3) < d < f'(1)$, the Intermediate Value Theorem guarantees that there is a value c, with $1 < c < 3$, such that $f'(c) = d$. Multiplying these two equations yields $f(a)f'(c) = bd$.

153. Yes. Since f is twice-differentiable, f' is differentiable. In particular, f' is continuous on $[1,3]$ and differentiable on $(1,3)$. The Mean Value Theorem guarantees that there is a value c, $1 < c < 3$ such that $f''(c) = \frac{f'(3) - f'(1)}{3 - 1} = -2$.

154. $-2 + k(k + 2)e^k$

155. $y = -2k\pi(x - 3)$

156. $v(t) = \frac{(\ln t)^2}{2} - 8$

157. The particle is moving to the left at $t = e^{-2}$ and $t = 2$, and moving to the right at $t = e^{-2\sqrt{7}}$ and $t = e^{2\sqrt{7}}$.

158. $9 + \int_1^2 \left| \frac{(\ln t)^2}{2} - 8 \right| dt$

159. $v(t) = 0$ when $t = e^{-4}$ and $t = e^4$.

$v(t) > 0$ for $0 < t < e^{-4}$ and $t > e^4$

$v(t) < 0$ for $e^{-4} < t < e^4$

It follows that the particle changes direction at $t = e^{-4}$ and $t = e^4$.

160. The particle is speeding up for $e^{-4} < t < 1$ and $t > e^4$. The particle is slowing down for $0 < t < e^{-4}$ and $1 < t < e^4$

209

ACTIONS TO COMPLETE AFTER YOU HAVE READ THIS BOOK

1. **Continue to practice AP Calculus problems for 20 to 30 minutes each day**

   Keep practicing problems of the appropriate levels until two days before the exam.

2. **Review this book**

   If this book helped you, please post your positive feedback on the site you purchased it from; e.g. Amazon, Barnes and Noble, etc.

3. **Sign up for free updates**

   If you have not done so yet, visit the following webpage and enter your email address to receive updates and supplementary materials for free when they become available.

   ## www.thesatmathprep.com/APcalcABtx.html

About the Author

Dr. Steve Warner, a New York native, earned his Ph.D. at Rutgers University in Pure Mathematics in May, 2001. While a graduate student, Dr. Warner won the TA Teaching Excellence Award.

After Rutgers, Dr. Warner joined the Penn State Mathematics Department as an Assistant Professor. In September, 2002, Dr. Warner returned to New York to accept an Assistant Professor position at Hofstra University. By September 2007, Dr. Warner had received tenure and was promoted to Associate Professor. He has taught undergraduate and graduate courses in Precalculus, Calculus, Linear Algebra, Differential Equations, Mathematical Logic, Set Theory and Abstract Algebra.

Over that time, Dr. Warner participated in a five year NSF grant, "The MSTP Project," to study and improve mathematics and science curriculum in poorly performing junior high schools. He also published several articles in scholarly journals, specifically on Mathematical Logic.

Dr. Warner has more than 15 years of experience in general math tutoring and tutoring for standardized tests such as the SAT, ACT and AP Calculus exams. He has tutored students both individually and in group settings.

In February, 2010 Dr. Warner released his first SAT prep book "The 32 Most Effective SAT Math Strategies," and in 2012 founded Get 800 Test Prep. Since then Dr. Warner has written books for the SAT, ACT, GRE, SAT Math Subject Tests and AP Calculus exams.

Dr. Steve Warner can be reached at

steve@SATPrepGet800.com

BOOKS BY DR. STEVE WARNER

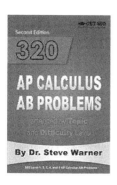

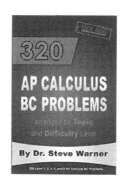

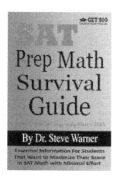

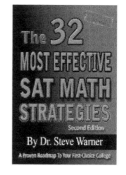

Made in the USA
Lexington, KY
13 June 2016